First World War
and Army of Occupation
War Diary
France, Belgium and Germany

48 DIVISION
Headquarters, Branches and Services
Adjutant and Quarter-Master General
30 March 1915 - 31 October 1917

WO95/2747/1

The Naval & Military Press Ltd
www.nmarchive.com
Published in association with The National Archives

Published by

The Naval & Military Press Ltd

Unit 10 Ridgewood Industrial Park,

Uckfield, East Sussex,

TN22 5QE England

Tel: +44 (0) 1825 749494

www.naval-military-press.com

www.nmarchive.com

This diary has been reprinted in facsimile from the original. Any imperfections are inevitably reproduced and the quality may fall short of modern type and cartographic standards.

© Crown Copyright
Images reproduced by permission of The National Archives, London, England, 2015.

Contents

Document type	Place/Title	Date From	Date To
Heading	WO95/2747-1 48 Div HQ-AQMG Apr 1915 Oct 1917		
Heading	48th Division 'A' & 'Q' Branch Apr 1915-Oct 1917		
Heading	Headquarters (A&Q) S. Midland Division Vol I		
Heading	War Diary Of "A" and "Q" Branch Headquarters 1/1st South Midland Division From 30.3.15. To 30.4.15 Volume I		
War Diary	Boulogne	30/03/1915	30/03/1915
War Diary	Oxelaere	31/03/1915	06/04/1915
War Diary	Merris	07/04/1915	15/04/1915
War Diary	Nieppe	16/04/1915	30/04/1915
Miscellaneous	South Midland Division Summary Of Casualties During April 1915		
Heading	Headquarters (A&Q) 48th Division Vol II 1-31.5.15		
Heading	War Diary Of "A" & "Q" Branch Headquarters 48th (South Midland) Division From 1.5.15 To 31.5.15 Volume II		
War Diary	Nieppe	01/05/1915	31/05/1915
Diagram etc	Casualty Chart		
Heading	48th Division Headquarters (A&Q) 48th Division Vol III 1-30.6.15.		
Heading	War Diary Of "A" & "Q" Branch Headquarters 48th (South Midland) Division From 1.6.15 To 30.6.15 Volume III		
War Diary	Nieppe	01/06/1915	27/06/1915
War Diary	Busnes	28/06/1915	29/06/1915
War Diary	Chateau Philomel	30/06/1915	30/06/1915
Diagram etc	Casualty Chart-June		
Miscellaneous	48th (S.M.) Division Summary Of Casualties.	30/06/1915	30/06/1915
Heading	48th Division Headquarters (A&Q) 48th Division Vol IV 1-31.7.15		
Heading	War Diary Of "A" & "Q" Branch Headquarters 48th (South Midland) Division From 1.7.15 To 31.7.15 Volume IV		
War Diary	Chateau Philomel	01/07/1915	01/07/1915
War Diary	Philomel	02/07/1915	17/07/1915
War Diary	Doullens	18/07/1915	18/07/1915
War Diary	Terramesnil	19/07/1915	20/07/1915
War Diary	Authie	21/07/1915	31/07/1915
Heading	48th Division Headquarters (A&Q) 48th Division Vol V August 15		
Heading	A & "Q" Branch-Headquarters 48th (South Midland) Division From 1-8-15 To 31-8-15 Volume V		
War Diary	Authie	01/08/1915	02/08/1915
War Diary	Bus-En-Artois	03/08/1915	03/08/1915
War Diary	Bus-Les-Artois	04/08/1915	31/08/1915
Heading	48th Division Headquarters (A&Q) 48th Division Vol VI Sept 15		
Heading	A & "Q" Branch-Headquarters 48th (South Midland) Division From 1-9-15 To 30-9-15 Volume VI		
War Diary	Bus Les Artois	01/09/1915	30/09/1915

Heading	48th Division Headquarters (A&Q) 48th Division Vol VII Oct 15		
Heading	A & "Q" Branch-Headquarters 48th (South Midland) Division From 1-10-15 To 31-10-15 Volume VII		
War Diary	Bus Les Artois	01/10/1915	31/10/1915
Heading	War Diary "A" & "Q" Branch-Headquarters 48th (South Midland) Division From 1-11-15 To 30-11-15 Vol VIII		
War Diary	Bus Les Artois	01/11/1915	30/11/1915
Heading	H.Q 48th Div (A&Q) Dec Vol IX		
War Diary	Bus Les Artois	01/12/1915	31/12/1915
Heading	48th Div (A&Q) Jan Vol X		
War Diary	Bus Les Artois	01/01/1916	31/01/1916
Heading	A&Q 48th Div Vol XI		
War Diary	Bus Les Artois	01/02/1916	29/02/1916
Heading	HQ A & Q 48 Div Vol XII		
War Diary	Bus Les Artois	01/03/1916	25/03/1916
War Diary	Couin	26/03/1916	31/03/1916
Heading	HQ A & Q 48 Div Vol XIII		
War Diary	Couin	01/04/1916	30/06/1916
Heading	War Diary A & Q 48th Division July 1916		
Heading	War Diary 48th (S.M) Division "A" & "Q" Period 1st To 31st July 1916 Volume XVI		
War Diary	Couin	01/07/1916	01/07/1916
War Diary	Mailly Mallet	02/07/1916	03/07/1916
War Diary	Couin	04/07/1916	15/07/1916
War Diary	Bouzincourt	16/07/1916	27/07/1916
War Diary	Le Plouy Domqueur	28/07/1916	31/07/1916
Heading	48th Division A & Q 48th Division August 1916		
War Diary	Le Plouy Domqueur	01/08/1916	08/08/1916
War Diary	Beauval	09/08/1916	12/08/1916
War Diary	Bouzincourt	13/08/1916	31/08/1916
Miscellaneous	1/Z		
Heading	48th Division A & Q 48th Division September 1916		
Heading	D.A.G., G.H.Q., 3rd Echelon	01/10/1916	01/10/1916
War Diary	Bertrancourt	01/09/1916	03/09/1916
War Diary	Beauval	04/09/1916	17/09/1916
War Diary	Bernaville	18/09/1916	29/09/1916
War Diary	Henu	30/09/1916	30/09/1916
Heading	War Diary "A" & "Q" Branch 48 Division October 1916 Volume XIX		
War Diary	Henu	01/10/1916	21/10/1916
War Diary	Doullens	22/10/1916	22/10/1916
War Diary	Baisieux	23/10/1916	31/10/1916
Heading	War Diary "A" & "Q" Branch 48th Divn November 1916 Volume XX		
War Diary	Millencourt	01/11/1916	02/11/1916
War Diary	Lozenge Wood	03/11/1916	30/11/1916
Heading	War Diary 48th (S.M) Division (A & Q) 1st To 31st December 1916 Volume 21		
War Diary	Lozenge Wood	01/12/1916	16/12/1916
War Diary	Albert	16/12/1916	31/12/1916
War Diary	Lozenge Wood	01/12/1916	16/12/1916
War Diary	Albert	16/12/1916	31/12/1916
Heading	War Diary "A" & "Q" Branch 48th Divn January 1917 Volume XXII		

War Diary	Albert Baizieux	01/01/1917	07/01/1917
War Diary	Baizieux Hallencourt	08/01/1917	27/01/1917
War Diary	Hallencourt Mericourt	28/01/1917	31/01/1917
Heading	War Diary "A" & "Q" Branch 48th Divn. February 1917 Volume XXIII		
War Diary	Mericourt Sur Somme	01/02/1917	02/02/1917
War Diary	Cappy	03/02/1917	28/02/1917
Heading	War Diary "A" & "Q" Branch 48th Divn March 1917 Volume XXIV		
War Diary	Cappy	01/03/1917	24/03/1917
War Diary	La Quinconce	25/03/1917	30/03/1917
War Diary	Tincourt	31/03/1917	31/03/1917
Heading	War Diary "A" & "Q" Branch 48th Division April 1917 Volume XXV		
War Diary	Tincourt	01/04/1917	21/04/1917
War Diary	K.11.a.79	22/04/1917	30/04/1917
Miscellaneous	48th Division List of "Honours and Rewards" awarded during April 1917 Appendix A		
Miscellaneous	Return Shewing Wastage In 48th Division From 31st March 1917 To 30th April 1917		
Heading	War Diary "A" & "Q" Branch 48th Divn May 1917 Volume XXVI		
War Diary	K 11 A 79	01/05/1917	02/05/1917
War Diary	Flamicourt	03/05/1917	14/05/1917
War Diary	Beaulencourt	15/05/1917	15/05/1917
War Diary	N 11 Central	15/05/1917	24/05/1917
War Diary	1.34.a.3.5	25/05/1917	30/05/1917
Miscellaneous	48th Division List Of Honours And Rewards Awarded During May 1917		
Miscellaneous	Return Showing Wastage In 48 Divn From 30 April To 31 May 1917		
Heading	War Diary 48th Division "A" & "Q" Branch June 1917		
War Diary	1.34.a.3.5	01/06/1917	30/06/1917
Miscellaneous	List Of Honours And Rewards Awarded To Officers, N.C.Os And Men Of 48th Division		
Heading	War Diary "A" & "Q" Branch 48th Divn July 1917 Volume XXVIII		
War Diary	I.34a.3.5	01/07/1917	03/07/1917
War Diary	Adinfer Wood X 26a (Sheet 51c)	04/07/1917	09/07/1917
War Diary	Adinfer Wood X 26a	10/07/1917	15/07/1917
War Diary	Adinfer Wood X 26a (Sheet 51c)	16/07/1917	22/07/1917
War Diary	Border Camp A.30b (Sheet 28)	22/07/1917	31/07/1917
Miscellaneous	Honours And Awards July 1917		
Heading	War Diary 48th Divn "A" & "Q" Branch 1st Aug To 31st Aug Vol XXXI		
War Diary	Border Camp A 30 Central Sheet 28 1/40,000	01/08/1917	03/08/1917
War Diary	Border Camp	04/08/1917	06/08/1917
War Diary	Brake Camp G6b.28 Sheet 28 1/40,000	07/08/1917	08/08/1917
War Diary	Brake Camp	08/08/1917	15/08/1917
War Diary	Brake Camp Canal Bank Ypres	15/08/1917	19/08/1917
War Diary	Brake Camp Canal Bank	19/08/1917	28/08/1917
War Diary	Wormhoudt	29/08/1917	31/08/1917
Miscellaneous	Casualties To Noon 16th August		
Miscellaneous	Casualties To Noon 17th August		
Miscellaneous	Casualties To Noon 18th August		
Miscellaneous	Casualties To Noon 22nd August		

Miscellaneous	Casualties To Noon 23rd August		
Miscellaneous	Casualties To Noon 24th August		
Miscellaneous	Casualties To Noon 25th August		
Miscellaneous	Casualties To Noon 26th August		
Miscellaneous	Casualties To Noon 27th August		
Miscellaneous	Casualties To Noon 28th August		
Miscellaneous	Casualties To Noon 29th August		
Miscellaneous	Casualties To Noon 30th August		
Miscellaneous	1/5th Royal Warwickshire Regiment		
Miscellaneous	1/4th Gloucester Regiment		
Miscellaneous	1/5th Gloucester Regiment		
Miscellaneous	1/4th Royal Berks Regiment		
Miscellaneous	48th Div. Signal Company, R.E		
Miscellaneous	5th R. Sussex Regiment		
Miscellaneous	240 Brigade S.M R.F.A.		
Miscellaneous	477 Field Company R.E		
Miscellaneous	48th Divisional Train		
Heading	War Diary 48th Division "A" & "Q" Branch 1st Septr To 30th Septr Vol XXXII		
War Diary	Wormhoudt	01/09/1917	17/09/1917
War Diary	Cocove Chateau Recques	17/09/1917	24/09/1917
War Diary	Brake Camp Poperinghe	28/09/1917	30/09/1917
Miscellaneous	Q Notes During Recent Operations	06/09/1917	06/09/1917
Miscellaneous	Appendix "A" Composition Of Pack Transport Column		
Operation(al) Order(s)	48th Division Order No. 217	14/09/1917	14/09/1917
Miscellaneous	Transport Movement Table To Accompany 48th Div Order No. 217		
Miscellaneous	48th Division Dispositions (Recques Area)	18/09/1917	18/09/1917
Miscellaneous	Casualties From 23rd To 30th Sept		
Operation(al) Order(s)	48th Division Order No. 218	24/09/1917	24/09/1917
Miscellaneous	Addendum No. 1 To 48th Div. Order 218	25/09/1917	25/09/1917
Miscellaneous	March Table To Accompany Addendum No. 1to 48th Division Order 218		
Miscellaneous	Addendum No.2 To 48th Division Order No. 218	26/09/1917	26/09/1917
Miscellaneous	48th Division No. S/303	25/09/1917	25/09/1917
Miscellaneous	Orders For Move Of Division In Connection With Addendum No. 1 To 48th Division Order No. 218	26/09/1917	26/09/1917
Miscellaneous	To Accompany War Diary For September 1917		
Miscellaneous	List Of Honours And Rewards Awarded To Officers, N.C.Os. And Men Of The 48th Division		
Heading	War Diary 48th Division "A" & "Q" Branch October 1917		
War Diary	Brake Camp (A.30.c) Sheet 28	01/10/1917	02/10/1917
War Diary	Canal Bank (C.28.c.2.3) Sheet 28	03/10/1917	10/10/1917
War Diary	X Camp (A.16.c.88) Sheet 28	11/10/1917	12/10/1917
War Diary	Pernes (Lens 11)	13/10/1917	17/10/1917
War Diary	Chateau D'Acq (Villers Au Bois) W.30.6.5.3 Sheet 36	18/10/1917	28/10/1917
War Diary	Chateau D'Acq (Villers Au Bois) W.30.6.5.3	29/10/1917	31/10/1917
Miscellaneous	Casualties To Noon 1st October		
Miscellaneous	Casualties To Noon 2.10.17		
Miscellaneous	Casualties To Noon 3.10.17		
Miscellaneous	Casualties To Noon 4th Oct.1917		
Miscellaneous	Casualties To Noon 5th Oct.1917		
Miscellaneous	Casualties To Noon 6th Oct.1917		
Miscellaneous	Casualties To Noon 7th Oct.1917		
Miscellaneous	Casualties To Noon 8 Th Oct.1917		

Miscellaneous	Casualties To Noon 9th Oct.1917
Miscellaneous	Casualties To Noon 10th Oct.1917
Miscellaneous	Casualties To Noon 12th Oct.1917
Miscellaneous	List Of Honours And Rewards Awarded To Officers, N.C.Os. And Men Of The 48th Division

WO95/2747 - 1

48 Div HQ — AQMG

Apr 1915 – Oct 1917

48TH DIVISION

'A' & 'Q' BRANCH.

APR 1915 - ~~MAR 1919~~
— Oct 1917

To ITALY

2747

121/5/106

48

Head Quarters (A & Q) S. Midland Division

Vol I   30.3 —— 30.4.15

Confidential.

War Diary

of

"A" and "Q" Branch - Headquarters, 11th South Midland Division.

From 30.3.'15.   To   30.4.'15.

(Volume I.)

Army Form C. 2118.

Head Quarters –
South Midland Division – "A" Branch

WAR DIARY
or
INTELLIGENCE SUMMARY.
(Erase heading not required.)

Place	Date	Hour	Summary of Events and Information	Remarks and references to Appendices
Boulogne	30.3.15	1.0 a.m.	G.O.C. and Staff with personnel of Divisional Head Quarters (less Transport and Railways with Horses and M.M.P.) Have disembarked.	
		11.0 a.m.	G.O.C., G.S.O.1, G.S.O.2, G.S.O.3, A.A.¬Q.M.G., D.A.Q. & Q.M.G., 1 A.D.C. and 2 supy. Dahilies, attached Divisional Head Quarters, left by motor car for G.H.Q. where G.O.C. interviewed C.I.G.S. Subsequently parties above referred to accompanied with the above received. Remainder of Head Quarters proceeded by trail from Boulogne to Cassel. Divisional Head Quarters established at Chateau du Jardin, Oxelaere.	
Oxelaere	31.3.15	11.0 a.m.	A.A. & Q.M.G. proceeded by motor to Head Quarters 2nd Army, to interview A.A.G. & D.A.Q.M.G. 2nd Army. Units of Division commenced to arrive. D.G.& T. & A.A.& Q.M.G. Billets arranged for Divisional Head Quarters personnel. Division allocated to 3rd Corps from midnight 31.1st Commenced embarked Warwick Infantry Brigade proceeded by march route to Armentières to attach units to 4th Division for purposes of instruction. D.A.A. & Q.M.G. visited Head Quarters 3rd Army for interview with D.A.A.G., D.A.Q.M.G., & D.D.S.& T.	
Oxelaere	2.4.15	3.0 p.m.	Visit by Brig. Genl. Campbell, D.A.& Q.M.G. 3rd Corps. Also discussed various points of detail. Divisional Supply Column arrived and detrained at Bavinchove pending orders from D.D.S.&T. 2nd Army	

Army Form C. 2118.

WAR DIARY
or
INTELLIGENCE SUMMARY.
(Erase heading not required.)

Instructions regarding War Diaries and Intelligence Summaries are contained in F. S. Regs., Part II. and the Staff Manual respectively. Title pages will be prepared in manuscript.

Place	Date	Hour	Summary of Events and Information	Remarks and references to Appendices
Oxelaere	3.4.15	3.30 a.m.	Concentration of Division completed with exception of Divisional Ammunition Park and (Cavalry) Nursing Station. Railway for whole Division at Hazebrouck when Supplies are forwarded by Auto Lorries direct to Units under arrangements made by D.S.D. of S. 17 2nd Army. D.A.A & Q.M.G. visited Head Quarters 3rd Corps to discuss points of detail with D.C.A. & D.A.Q.M.G. 3rd Corps. D.A.Q.M.G. proceeded to Morris area to arrange billets for Division to move into on departure from Oxelaere.	
Oxelaere	4.4.15	12.30 p.m.	O.C. Divisional Ammunition Park reported his arrival at Strazeele, having been sent there in the Order of I.G.C. to collect Ammunition left behind in England. He hitherto from 2nd Army, O.C. divided to house at Hazebrouck for orders as to billeting area. Reported to 2nd Army and 3rd Corps. Concentration of Division completed except Casualty Clearing Station. L.D.M.S. reported that Sanitary Section have not yet returned to 30th Lorry to which they are entitled by A.F.G. 1095. F.D. S. & T. 3rd Cavalry asked to supply. Telegram from 3rd Corps notifying that Ammunition Park took & was located at Fletre and with come under G.O.C. L.M.D. for all administration purposes.	
Oxelaere	5.4.15	10.25 a.m.	Telegram (Q.235.8) from 2nd Corps as follows: "All order as regards payment for Billets and hire of Army Boots 395 in connection with Billets are held in abeyance. English acting interpreter	

1577 Wt.W10791/1773 500,000 1/15 D. D. & L. A.D.S.S./Forms/C. 2118.

Army Form C. 2118.

WAR DIARY
or
INTELLIGENCE SUMMARY.
(Erase heading not required.)

Place	Date	Hour	Summary of Events and Information	Remarks and references to Appendices
			From to be taken as having not General Routine Orders to dates as Establishment for billets deply (Q.3365) received as follows:- "Keep records regarding billets but give no schedule of rent for the present. Fresh instructions being sent." Communicated this to all units. D.G.Q.R.G. proceeded to MERRIS to arrange billets &c. in anticipation of move of Divisional Head Quarters tomorrow. D.A. & Q.M.G. and A.A. & Q.M.G. 3rd Corps visited Divisional Head Quarters and discussed various matters connected with Supplies and Ordnance.	
Outtersteene	6.4.15	10 a.m.	Divisional Head Quarters moved to MERRIS. Head Quarter Office established at the Hospice. 2nd Lt. Sandford - A.S.C. 4th Divl. Supply Column, reported at 12 midnight, having been detailed to assist the O.C. Divl. Supply Column until the 15th inst. He is to remain at Head Quarters for the night and to proceed in the morning to the Je???ress to join the Divl. Supply Column at Railhead.	
MERRIS	7.4.15	8.15 a.m.	Telegram received from 3rd Corps Hd.Qrs. that 7th Field Co. R.E. is to be transferred to 5000 Rutland Division on 15th April (G.732/1.). Telegrams received from 3rd Corps (A-30) Hd. to A.D.S.T. Officer of Reference from the M.T. Park of 6th Divn. about M.T. to be attached to A.S Divl Amm Pk. Col 17th to left O.C. to organisation and administration	

1577 Wt. W10791/1773 500,000 1/15 D. D. & L. A.D.S.S./Forms/C. 2118.

Army Form C. 2118.

4.

WAR DIARY
or
INTELLIGENCE SUMMARY.
(Erase heading not required.)

Instructions regarding War Diaries and Intelligence Summaries are contained in F.S. Regs., Part II. and the Staff Manual respectively. Title pages will be prepared in manuscript.

Place	Date	Hour	Summary of Events and Information	Remarks and references to Appendices
MERRIS	8.4.15	10.40 a.m.	Telegram received from 3rd Corps notifying that 1/1st Field Coy R.E. lately taken over from 5th Divn. will be attached to 6th Divn. for work from 10th April. (G. 738/15). Notification received that 1 Squadron 9th King Edward's Horse to be sent from England as Divisional Mounted Troops for the Division.	
MERRIS	9.4.15	5.19 pm	Telegram received from 3rd Corps notifying that Glasgow Inf. 13th, 60 Divl. Mtd Troops, Horse Portion 9 Fd Amb. will be attached to 6th Divn. from 10th to 16th " not 13th to 18th ". Telegram received from 3rd Corps. Supply Railhead to move to CAESTRE. (AQ 919 of 9/4/15). DAA & QMG and G.S.O.3 proceed to 6th Division for attachment.	
MERRIS	10.4.15		Glasgow & Wore Inf. 13th proceed to ARMENTIERES for attachment to 6th Divn: 1/1 Field Company R.E., 60 Cyclist Company Divl. Troops, Horse Portion 1st Field Amb; 8th Section of Signal Coy proceed to 6th Divn for attachment. No. 3. Coy Divl. Train joins 6th Divl. Train —.	
		1.45 pm	Telegram received from 3rd Corps — Wore 13th to relieve 10th R.Scots of Argyll & Suth. High. on left section of 4th Division on night of 12th/13th April 15th. The 10th R.S. to take over Warwicks 13th billets in BAILLEUL. (G. 632/46 of 10th). D.A. QMG = A.A.QMG. III Corps visit Divl H.Q. A.C.QMG = DA. QMG = S.M Divn visit Amm. Park.	

1577 Wt. W10791/1773 500,000 1/15 D. D. & L. A.D.S.S./Forms/C. 2118.

Army Form C. 2118.

WAR DIARY
or
INTELLIGENCE SUMMARY.
(Erase heading not required.)

Instructions regarding War Diaries and Intelligence Summaries are contained in F. S. Regs., Part II. and the Staff Manual respectively. Title pages will be prepared in manuscript.

Place	Date	Hour	Summary of Events and Information	Remarks and references to Appendices
MERRIS	11.4.15	9.32am	Telegram received. - 1 Officer 8. R. War Regt. left Rouen 7.45 pm 10th (R.5422 J 10ᵇ).	
		3.4 pm	" 3ʳᵈ South Mid F. Amb: now attached to Div: to relieve 10th Field Amb: (G 744/2 J 11ᵗʰ).	
			" 2 " " F Amb now at Berissart to remain there & not accompany War Pᵈˢ ($\frac{377}{2}$) of 11ᵗʰ	
		5 pm	Orders re Transport. - 12ᵃ & 14ᵃ for units of Div: reserve".	
			Visit Q Office. 3ʳᵈ Corps - re Amᵐ Supply S.A.A. and Supply Services".	
			Visit Amᵐ Park at Flêtre order advanced echelon for S.A.A. 2 lorries - and SMall O.C. b⁰	
			Officer Vving Patrol Cartridges - Hand grenades + rifle grenades to be kept with advance J echelon.	
		6 pm	Phone from 3ʳᵈ Corps re Telephones - 38 allotted to S. M. Div.	
			Arrange for Div Amb⁰ (Wom + Heavy Battery to be moved to W. end of Area S.J Railway Morris.	
MERRIS	12.4.15		ADAMS to 6 Div: for attachment. - Heavy Battery + Amm Col: - Div Amm Col: move to W. of Area S.J MERRIS	
			CRE + Adj. return from attachment to 4 Div: - relieve at OUTTERSTEEN. - DAA 'QMG - SMD return from 6 DIV:-	
			DA-QMQ. visits NIEPPE. & arrange new quarters.	
MERRIS	13.4.15		D.A.Q.M.G. 69 am Visited Bakery ONE Brown NIEPPE. Erinially upon Ambulance	
			Buyces (Br. gen.s) Rolling I Officer (Major H.E. HAKE, 7ᵗʰ Warwick) from 4 A & arcl	
			One from Liberaricke. 2ⁿᵈ Lieut. Martineau, 2 Comdy 6ᵗʰ Berkshire, travnoded to Base for	
			Lonally Clearing Station Bailleul.	

6.

Army Form C. 2118.

WAR DIARY
or
INTELLIGENCE SUMMARY.
(Erase heading not required.)

Instructions regarding War Diaries and Intelligence Summaries are contained in F. S. Regs., Part II. and the Staff Manual respectively. Title pages will be prepared in manuscript.

Place	Date	Hour	Summary of Events and Information	Remarks and references to Appendices
MERRIS	14.4.15	7.15 p.m.	Telegram (A.G. 510) received from 3rd Corps notifying that an officer with Colonial badges Maitland Rose and Metayer were on 2nd Div. Staff had been asking questions of Lan. of 3rd Potash. when on the 13th. He had been seen at 1.5 p.m. that day near Bethune and again at 7.30 p.m. Zer Zeventie stating he had been questioning the Tom as to what battalions had been firing. On receipt of the telegram Officers were at once dispatched to Headquarters of all formations and instructions issued to arrest the Man if seen. The O.C. Div. Cyclist Co. was also ordered to put round a Guard (double sentry by night and one by day) at the cross roads in Outtersteene with order to NOT all Cround them at light and to send them all round to Officers by day. This Guard to be continued until 6 a.m. 16th inst.	
MERRIS	15.4.15	11.30 a.m.	Telegram (C. 880) received from 3rd Corps notifying that 4.7 inch Battery G.M. Division, to come under the orders of M.G. Div. Group from Midnight 17/18th. South and land Infantry Brigade Headquarters established at 7.29 d. (Telegram BM/103.)	
NIEPPE	16.4.15	1.30 p.m.	Divisional Headquarters moved to NIEPPE. Head Quarter Office opened at the Mairie at 11- a.m. Some congestion and difficulty experienced in billeting owing to crowded NIEPPE being to presence of M. Division.	will be issued
NIEPPE	17.4.15	2.45 p.m.	Telegram (A.G. 918) received from 3rd Corps notifying that 10,000 sandbags to the distribution	

Army Form C. 2118.

WAR DIARY
or
INTELLIGENCE SUMMARY.
(Erase heading not required.)

Place	Date	Hour	Summary of Events and Information	Remarks and references to Appendices
(contd.)			On the 18th Arranged with "G" that there should be drawn by C.R.E. and issued weekly to his division, R.E. Stores. A letter to this effect to him C.R.E. 48th Division gets the following issues at once:- Warwick Brigade 4000, South Midland Brigade 3000, Gloucester & Worcester Brigade 3000. Application received from Warwick Inf. Bde. for 2936 Detonators and Hand Grenades, C.A.F.D. 2.9.48 36.05 arranged to issue 30 and sent instructions accordingly to Warwick Bde. Glossos & Worcester Brigade informed from attachment to 6th Divn. Brigade Head Quarters now MILLER at Estaminet on Pacant DR1 (Musemore) (B.11.6. Sheet 36.B.)	
NIEPPE	18/3/15		Instructions received from 3rd Corps to report that the Rest Stores and Ammunition are drawn from R.E. Park and from Administrative Railhead. Communicated A.E.R.R., I.W.M., Notificata received that M.M. Sinnott, C.R.E. is to proceed to Rouen for duty, and that he will be succeeded as C.R.E. of the Division by Lt. Col. Marshall, R.E. 16 Josephs M.T. Driver to Ruminghem Park transferred to Rouen being in accordance with instructions from 3rd Corps.	
NIEPPE	19/3/15		Notification received that B. Gardiner King Edward's Horse will join the Division in two days as Divisional Orderly. D.A.Q.M.G. arranged to billet them at 1 Pan, S.E. of NIEPPE.	

1577 Wt. W10791/1773 500,000 1/15 D. D. & L. A.D.S.S./Forms/C. 2118.

Army Form C. 2118.

WAR DIARY
or
INTELLIGENCE SUMMARY.
(Erase heading not required.)

Instructions regarding War Diaries and Intelligence Summaries are contained in F.S. Regs., Part II. and the Staff Manual respectively. Title pages will be prepared in manuscript.

Place	Date	Hour	Summary of Events and Information	Remarks and references to Appendices
(Continued)			S.&Q.M.G. 3rd Corps British Head Quarters Cob arranged that C.R.E. should draw 13,000 sandbags on alternate days from Steenwerck for issue to Division Sunday. Lt Col Hackett left to take his appointment as L.R.E. II M Pirkill left for Rouen Bombed and reported upon to Line to 3rd Corps.	
NIEPPE	20/4/15		A.A. & Q.M.G. & D.A.A.T.Q.M.G. visited Supply Refilling Point at RABOT. Supplies were dumped at sides of road and by 7.30 a.m. all the lorries had cleared. For 1 Brigade and Divisional Troops Supplies were dumped by formation. In the case of the 3rd Brigade (Nourish) each unit was allotted a fixed place on the road, independently of Brigade or Battalion the different items of supply had been previously collected in various items being taken from the various lorries as they passed slowly down the line. This system proved the quickest Repartition of the two, and to A.A.T.Q.M.G. gave instructions that this system should be tried for the other two Brigades for the next half a hour to ascertain which is the best method to adopt. Refilling was completed about 8-40 a.m. Lieut. C.F.R. BARNETT 5th Gloucesters, reported killed – the First Officer of the Division to fall. Lt Col Shipley-Baillie A.S.O.I of pressure to England today to upper to Military Secretary	
NIEPPE	21/4/15			

1577 Wt. W10791/1773 500,000 1/15 D. D. & L.   A.D.S.S./Forms/C. 2118.

WAR DIARY
or
INTELLIGENCE SUMMARY.
(Erase heading not required.)

Army Form C. 2118.

Place	Date	Hour	Summary of Events and Information	Remarks and references to Appendices
(Yorkshire?)			Box Offices on selection for duty took to the Mediterranean Expeditionary Force. Lt.Col. J.C. Bown - Gordon reported his arrival at 5.30 p.m. in succession to Lt.Col. Simpson-Baikie. Telegram received from 3rd Corps Advancing issue of 10,000 handbags to be sent to the 9th, 28th & 26th Div. (A.Q/193.) A.P.D.M.G. & A.A.T.Q.M.G. & O.C. Sanitary Section visited Huts occupied by 46th (1st Staffordshire) Regt. (T.26 A) in order to see system adopted therein. Latrine, Refuse, Urinals, and Sanitary arrangements generally to operate the best system to establish for the Huts held in the 5th Lancashire Brigade for the Bathing unit. The Arrangements inspected had been very temporary. Planned and first proposed a temp. fixed system.	
NIEPPE	22/7/15		Telegram received from Comdt. Havre Army arrived from England of "B" section King Edward's Horse Sturgitt 6 Officers, 140 O.R., 150 Horses, 3 four Wheeled G.S. Wheeled Vehicles, 6 Bicycles. A.A.T Q.M.G. visited Ordnance Store opened at the Lie Creche also Ordnance Shop which has been started for the repair of Rifles and Bicycles. Bn. Armourer Staff-Sgt. per Brigade is being detailed to the Staff of the Shop.	
NIEPPE	23/7/15		A.Q. & A.D.L.G. & D.A.A.&Q.M.G. visited all Brigade Head Quarters & 1st & 2nd Field Ambulances	

A.D.S.S./Forms/C. 2118.

10.

Army Form C. 2118.

WAR DIARY
or
INTELLIGENCE SUMMARY.
(Erase heading not required.)

Place	Date	Hour	Summary of Events and Information	Remarks and references to Appendices
(continued)			Notification received from G.H.Q. (Q.1230) that Divisional Railhead from 24th instant to be HAZEBROUCK. R.A. Officer attached to Ammunition Park ordered (under arrangement with G.O.C. R.A.) to have up to the advanced section of the Park as being at once convenient place from which to discharge his duties.	
NIEPPE.	24/4/15.		Telegram (A.2800) received from 3rd Corps, 12.15 p.m., notifying appointment of Lt.Col. Schofield L.E. Ox. & Bucks L.I. as O.C. No: 8 Sup: Base Depôt, Havre. B. Squadron King Edward's Horse detained at STEENWERK this evening and proceeded by March into NIEPPE. Met by D.A.Q.M.G. at detraining station and conducted to billets S.W. of NIEPPE. Telegram from 3rd Corps 7.55 A.M. (A.Q.995) notifying change of Supply Railhead on 25th inst. to STEENWERCK. Hours of loading as follows:- 4th Div: 7.0 a.m. to 8.0 a.m.; 6th Div: 8.0 a.m. to 10.30 a.m.; Lahore Div: 10.30 a.m. to 12.30 p.m.; 4th Div: 2.0 p.m. to 3.0 p.m. O.C. Supply Column to O.C. Train notified.	Vide.
NIEPPE.	25/4/15.		A.A.& Q.M.G. & D.A.A.& Q.M.G. visited Railhead at 11.30 a.m. Loading proceeding Smoothly. Lorries clear of station by 12.20 p.m. Instructions given by D.A.Q.M.G. 3rd Corps that in future loading will commence at 8.30 a.m. each day. Notification received that 9th Reinforcements for Division left Dieppe at 2.21 p.m., due 7.15 a.m. 26th. O.C. Train instructed to arrange for them to be met.	Vide.

1577 Wt.W10791/1773 500,000 1/15 D.D.&L. A.D.S.S./Forms/C. 2118.

WAR DIARY or INTELLIGENCE SUMMARY

Army Form C. 2118.

Place	Date	Hour	Summary of Events and Information	Remarks and references to Appendices
NIEPPE.	26/4/15.		The Remounts arrived STEENWERCK Station this morning and were removed under orders of O.C. Train to LA CRECHE where issue was made to units in the afternoon. Divisional Supply Column has now moved from CAESTRE to East of the Turn to NEUVE EGLISE on the BAILLEUL – ARMENTIERES road. In accordance with instructions from 3rd Corps D. Section item 1.31 Field Ambulances proceeded to BAILLEUL today to assist O.C. No. 2 Casualty Clearing Station in dealing with wounded, taking all its Equipment with it and as many spare blankets as possible.	
NIEPPE	27/4/15.	Midnight	Telegram received from 3rd Corps to effect that Medical Authorities consider best flannel the best preventative for Asphyxiating Gases and that G.H.Q. is providing 5000 yards for Division. This provision has been rendered necessary by the use of Asphyxiating Gases by the Germans in the recent fighting round YPRES. At first it was intended to purchase gauge for use as respirators in this connection, but it has found impossible to obtain this locally. A.A. & Q.M.G. & D.A.A. & Q.M.G. visited Papilling Point and Railhead this morning. All arrangements satisfactory.	
NIEPPE	28/4/15			
NIEPPE	29/4/15		Baths at PONT de NIEPPE taken over from Dist and placed under control of A.D.M.S. D.A.D.O.S. completed arrangements for starting Dist Shoemaker's Shop in La Crèche	

Army Form C. 2118.

WAR DIARY
or
INTELLIGENCE SUMMARY.
(Erase heading not required.)

Place	Date	Hour	Summary of Events and Information	Remarks and references to Appendices
NIEPPE	30/7/15	11.0 a.m.	Telegram received from 3rd Wops notifying that 1/1st Field Co. & 1/2nd Field Co. & 1/7th Field Co. R.E. has allotted to S.M. Div. Field of 7th Field Co. arranged to be done by S.M. Div. on C.O. from 2nd Army. Telegram (A.Q.25.) received from 3rd Corps notifying that Infantry and Administration of Section No. 1 Bridging Train & No. 14 Ambulance section are to be transferred to S. Mid. Div. as early as possible. C.R.E. & A.D.M.S. & A.D.V.S. to be notified. Div. Supply Column, Div. Train, 2/1 Field Ambulance, Lettr Ambulance Workshop and Div. Ammunition Park. Report received from G.O.C. R.A. that units under his command are not receiving their proper share of daily Newspapers. O.C.A.S.C. instructed to take a Census for one week of Numbers received from the Base, and to report daily at the 6.0 p.m. conference as to distribution.	

D.A.A. & Q.M.G. South Midland Division.

SOUTH MIDLAND DIVISION.

SUMMARY OF CASUALTIES DURING APRIL, 1915 :-

UNIT	Officers			O. R.		
	K	W	M	K	W	M
5th R. Warwickshire R.	-	-	-	7	13	-
6th - do -	-	-	-	2	11	-
7th - do -	-	1	-	1	23	-
8th - do -	-	1	-	5	20	1
4th Gloucestershire R.	-	-	-	3	23	-
6th - do -	-	-	-	3	7	-
7th Worcestershire R.	-	1	-	2	10	-
8th - do -	-	-	-	-	4	-
5th Gloucestershire R.	1	-	-	1	12	-
4th Oxf. & Bucks L. I.	-	-	-	2	3	-
Bucks Bn. Ox. & Bucks L.I.	-	1	-	4	4	-
4th R. Berkshire R.	-	-	-	2	4	-
1/2nd S. M. Fd. Coy., R.E.	-	1	-	-	-	-
	1	5	-	32	134	1

Headquarters (A&Q) 48th Division

Vol II 1 — 31. 5. 15

CONFIDENTIAL.

WAR DIARY.

OF

"A" & "Q" BRANCH - HEADQUARTERS, 48th (SOUTH MIDLAND) DIVISION.

FROM 1.5.15. TO 31.5.15.

(VOLUME II)

Army Form C. 2118.

WAR DIARY
INTELLIGENCE SUMMARY.
(Erase heading not required.)

Instructions regarding War Diaries and Intelligence Summaries are contained in F. S. Regs., Part II. and the Staff Manual respectively. Title pages will be prepared in manuscript.

Place	Date	Hour	Summary of Events and Information	Remarks and references to Appendices
MEPPE.	1 5/15.		Notification received from 3rd Corps (A.398g) that Captain R. DUGMORE, D.S.O. has been selected for temporary command of 4th Oxford & Bucks L.I. with temporary rank of Lieut. Colonel, vice Lt. Col. SCHOFIELD. Arrangements made with A. & Q. Staff for H.Q. No: 2 Mountain Bn. Coy. to be attached to 5th Div. under Lt. Dir: Harris. C.R.E. reported (7.45 p.m.) that transfer of 1/1st S.L. Field Co., 1/2nd Field Co. R.E. and 7th Field Co. R.E. to the Division completed.	
MEPPE.	2 5/15.		Telegram received from No: 7 Stationary Hospital that Lt. Col. ELTON, 7th Berwicks, is to be invalided to England almost immediately. On receipt of the Telegram G.O.C. forwarded to 3rd Corps application for a Regular C.O. to be appointed to the Battalion.	
		2.45 p.m.	(A.Q.33.) received from 3rd Corps directly immediate steps to be taken to obtain lime bottles, or seals of same for sector, to be issued to all firing and support trenches. The bottles or lock solution of bicarbonate of soda for use to counteract effects of asphyxiating gases. 800 bottles have at once secured in MEPPE and arrangements made for conveying them to the Trenches tonight. 5000 Respirators have been issued to the Troops through Bde. Hd. Qrs. and arrangements made to convert 5000 caps comforters into Respirators. For this purpose female labour has been engaged & a start is being made forthwith.	

WAR DIARY
or
INTELLIGENCE SUMMARY.
(Erase heading not required.)

Army Form C. 2118.

Place	Date	Hour	Summary of Events and Information	Remarks and references to Appendices
NIEPPE	3/5/15	5.45 p.m.	Telegram received from 3rd Corps (A.Q.414) notifying that pending of 32nd Bde. R.F.A. is to be taken over by S.A.A. Div. Supply Column from 32nd Dist. from 4th Div. Supply Column. For the purpose the requisite number of lorries will be transferred from 4th Div. Supply Column, and the Supply Wagons will join the S.A.A. Train. Hd. Qrs. 4th Div. Artillery will also be fed by S.A.A.	
NIEPPE	4/5/15		Head Quarters 4th Div. left NIEPPE today; Head Quarters Canadian Div. arrived. Times for loading Supply Columns at Railhead fixed as follows: Canadians 7.0 a.m. to 9.0 a.m. York Midland 8.30 a.m., 6th Div. 9.0 a.m.	
NIEPPE	5/5/15		Divisional Head Quarters moved from La Lourie to No. 7 Rue d'Armentières. Telegram received from 3rd Corps (A.Q.55) directing that loading of Supply Columns at STEENWERCK Station from tomorrow henceforth will be as follows: Canadian Div. N. side of Railway 7.0 a.m. to be clear of Station by 8.45 a.m.; 6th Div. S. side of Station 9.0 a.m. to be clear of Station by 10.30 a.m.; S. Mid. Div. S. side of Station 10.30 a.m.	
NIEPPE	6/5/15		Telegram from 3rd Corps (A.Q.59) notifying that loading for S.A.A. & Supply Columns at STEENWERCK will be at 7.0 a.m. and not in notified yesterday. 2 Batteries 32nd Bde. R.F.A. under orders to move. Orders issued to Div. Train to send Baggage & Supply Wagons accordingly. Lorries	

Army Form C. 2118.

WAR DIARY
or
INTELLIGENCE SUMMARY.
(Erase heading not required.)

Place	Date	Hour	Summary of Events and Information	Remarks and references to Appendices
(continued)			On return from 4th Divl Supply Column also ordered to report than Lothian. Orders received for 3rd Corps for Colonel Rayward, A.D.M.S. to proceed to England. Colonel Thompson D.S.O. succeeds him. Report received from G.O.C. Schr. Infy. Bde. at 6.30 p.m. of an accident during grenade instruction. 2/-Lt. H.G.C. GUISE and one had killed, six wounded	
NIEPPE.	7/5/15		Major Genl. Heath having been placed on the sick list, Brig. Genl. M°CLINTOCK assumed temporary command of the Division at 11.0 p.m. Lt. Col. O.P. SEROCOLD, 4th Berks Regt. assumed temporary command of South Midland Brigade; Major R.J. CLARKE assumed temporary command of 4th Berks Regt. Rum arrangements reported by wire to 3rd Corps & 2nd Army. Laying ahead of Chaplain, Rev. F.N. WHEELER, arrived from Rouen & is attached to 1st Field Ambulance (A.G. 76). Instructions received from 3rd Corps that 40 sprayers & 3 cwt. Chemicals are being sent from Boulogne for use in Trenches — to be divided equally between 6th & F.S.A. Divs.	
NIEPPE.	8/5/15		Instruction (A.Q.79) received from 3rd Corps that 16 of the 40 sprayers are allotted to F.S.A. Div & 24 to 6th Div. A new pattern of Respirator was received today from 3rd Corps, and a Supply of material for their manufacture. The workwomen who have been employed to make them were immediately started on the work.	
NIEPPE.	8/5/15		Instructions received from 3rd Corps (G.1137) that on the relief of the 4th Divn artillery on the North	

WAR DIARY
or
INTELLIGENCE SUMMARY.
(Erase heading not required.)

Army Form C. 2118.

Place	Date	Hour	Summary of Events and Information	Remarks and references to Appendices
(Continued)			of 107-115 the Canadian behalf of 29th Bde R.F.A. and the single battery of the 22nd Bde R.F.A. not come under the G.O.C. 1st Lowland Bde for tactical purposes but will be administered by Canadian Divisional Artillery Commander. Colonel RAYWOOD, A.D.M.S. left for England today on relief by Colonel THOMPSON, D.S.O.	
NIEPPE.	10/5/15.		Confidential instructions issued from 3rd Corps (A.C. 293) that Colonel ROSS-JOHNSON, D.S.O. D.S.O. has been relieved of command of the Artillery of the Division, vice Brig. Gen'l BUTLER, and is to proceed to England. Colonel ROSS-JOHNSON reported his arrival at 3.0 p.m.	
		12.10 p.m	Telegram received 3rd Corps (A.Q. 99) asking whether all Troops to the number/character of which or was distributed, pack and Artillery transport, lists, Replies (Q. 72) that all will be in possession of the Range and Cotton lists & last & October by tomorrow.	
NIEPPE.	11/5/15.		Brig. Gen'l ROSS JOHNSON assumed command of the Divisional Artillery today: Brig. Gen'l BUTLER left for England. Lieut-Col. DUGMORE, D.S.O., relieved in command and assumed command of the 143 Ox. & Bucks L.I. vice Lt. Col. SCHOFIELD appointed to command No. 7 Infy. Base Depot, HAVRE. Major Gen'l HEATH proceeded on sick leave to TREPORT today. 29th Bde R.F.A. left and was relieved by the Canadian Artillery. Shortage of supply at Railhead, of which the has been many previous complaints, show considerable improvement.	

WAR DIARY / INTELLIGENCE SUMMARY

Army Form C. 2118.

Place	Date	Hour	Summary of Events and Information	Remarks and references to Appendices
NIEPPE	12/5/15		Arrangements continued for moving Div: Head Quarters to LA CRECHE at an early date. Field Post Office and all Brigade Post Offices moved in to the Mairie, NIEPPE in the afternoon. No. 2 Train moved to LAMPERNISSE FARM (B.3.c.). 3rd Corps General Routine Orders received. Brigade Artillery and Infantry Divisions will be attacked 143rd, 144rd, 145th Infy. Bdes. Artillery, R.E. and No. 3 Infy. Bdes. will be Quartered 143rd, 144th, 145th Infy. Bdes. Artillery, R.E. (Signal Co.) & Indirect Shells (Field Veterinary Section) before the Div: is assembled.	
NIEPPE	13/5/15		Move of Div: Head Quarters to LA CRECHE postponed. Instructions for the movement of 143rd Bde. Ray be repeated shortly as Pontoon wagons & temporary bridges for the movement of 143rd Bde. Ray be repeated shortly as Pontoon wagons & Pontoons were under strength. Reply (DAQX.293) received that temporary arrangements for entire Division have been or detained for short term & work and will be dispatched as soon as demands are complied with by War Office.	
NIEPPE	14/5/15		Canadian Div: received Orders to move Today, which they continued to do in the afternoon. Telegram (AQ.141) received from 3rd Corps that no more laterals are to be furnished for Artillery Officers, and a return formed on final which it was in process of being made up be completed, the return further beforehand is to be stopped. Telegram (AQ.145) received from 3rd Corps Artillery that Canadian Artillery attached	
NIEPPE	15/5/15			

Army Form C. 2118.

WAR DIARY
or
INTELLIGENCE SUMMARY

(Erase heading not required.)

Place	Date	Hour	Summary of Events and Information	Remarks and references to Appendices
(Continued)			Division will be relieved and forged by Ln. 5th Canadian Infantry Brigade. R.A.K. to finish supply officer. Escorts & Forage and Horses to R.K. finish supply officer at HILLERS on 18th and from Billets in Relief at STEENWERCK.	
NIEPPE	16 5/15		Information received that Headquarters 9th K.O.S. (New Army) are to be located at NIEPPE and Billets on District, taken over in Billets Rd., occupied by the Canadians. 9th K.O.S. Billets will relieve Canadian Billeting on night 18th/19th. Details Report of Reconnaissance in Portion of District (all Echelons) called for by 3rd Corps and forwarded at 6.0 p.m.	
NIEPPE	17 5/15		Headquarters 9th Division arrived this afternoon. Lieut. Col. G. F. B. E. C. & L. E. Divide Infantry Brigade Headquarters to arrange to take over the Respective Sector of Command and 13 officers and 19 N.C.O.s arranged each Unit. Would make a Reck. before their casualties seemed the best spot at which to approach and issue a Clearing station, I have had offers of Ambulances, and also to determine which. Hay. Stores can be taken to forward parties, as Stretcher Party, trained number of horses in Powell 4st. Pt. As regards arrangements of Wounded it was suggested that there is a lesson of injury, wounds and N.C.'s officers should be loved there due to Carnwall, to open should be dealt with for ambulances of others from 21.	

Army Form C. 2118.

WAR DIARY
or
INTELLIGENCE SUMMARY.
(Erase heading not required.)

Place	Date	Hour	Summary of Events and Information	Remarks and references to Appendices
NIEPPE.	18/5/15		Telegram received from 3rd Corps (A.Q. 163) notifying that Battery of H.Q. 9th Div. tactically subject under 6th & 48th Division will continue to be administered by 9th Div. Ammunition will be replenished from Advanced Section of 9th Div. Park at PONT de NIEPPE and detachment from 9th Div left wing point. Advance Engineers is to be supplied thro' D.O.O. 9th Div.	
NIEPPE.	19/5/15		Telegram received from 3rd Corps (Q. 3356) authorizing that issue of following ammunition from Railhead from causes for the present; 4.5", 6 Lel., 13 pr., 15 pr., 4.7 cigarette & 12 cwr. ponsh., 3300 Lebel proof Rugs received today from 3rd Corps to carry the Anti-Aero-Suppression Ammunition have been handed over to the F.O.A.S. for issue – Authorised to Nieppe Rest Camp.	
NIEPPE.	20/5/15			
NIEPPE.	21/5/15	3 p.m.	Telegram from 3rd Corps (G.1263) stating that for purpose of administration No. 14 A.A. Aircraft Section is attached to 48th Div. Reporter of the limit for tactical purposes will continue to be related to the instructions issued from time to time by Corps H.Q. to O.C. Anti-Aircraft Section. Letter received that 2/Lieut HANBURY and 2/Lieut WETHERED are have left HAVRE to join 7th & 6th Berwicks respectively. Order received (Telegram A.4/4589) from 3rd Corps to have Situation & Obstacle Plans known to Forma kilometre North of FOURTE CROIX Landmark (W.13.B.) sent up to G.H.Q.	

Army Form C. 2118.

WAR DIARY
or
INTELLIGENCE SUMMARY.
(Erase heading not required.)

Instructions regarding War Diaries and Intelligence Summaries are contained in F. S. Regs., Part II. and the Staff Manual respectively. Title pages will be prepared in manuscript.

Place	Date	Hour	Summary of Events and Information	Remarks and references to Appendices
NIEPPE	22 5/15		Colonel HANBURY and Lt. Colonel WETHERED reported their arrival from England today & assumed Command of the 7th and 6th Bn. R. Warwickshire Regt. respectively. Lieutenant Coldham-Fussell reported arrival at about 9 P.M. and last billeted. W. O. Letter No: 100/Gen: No:/2340 (S.D.2.) of 17.5.15 received authorizing that in future the Brigade Machine Gun officer will be seconded to vacancy counted one Infantry Brigade.	
NIEPPE	23 5/15		Telegram received at 10.0 a.m. announcing that the Italian Gov't. has ordered a General Mobilization the first day of mobilization being the 23rd. Report sent to 3rd Corps on the subject of selection of hospitals for T.F. Battalions to replace Casualty G.O.C. recommended that four Staff Officers of suitable qualifications should be selected & attached to Regular Battalions for training purposes. This forming a reserve of potential Captains to the Ter. Ter. Division.	
NIEPPE	24 5/15		Italy declared war against Austria. Telegram (A.36455) received from 3rd Corps directly that, in badius of asphyxiating gases attack in autumn conditions & steps of 2 to 4 a.m. it is imperative that all Troops should at all times have in their personal position by day and by night an Effective respirator. Compresses & pads complete were being issued in the Division. G.O.C. & N/G. had interviews with D.A. & F.D.S. of 5 Troops at which he was informed that, according to present arrangements, his Brigade will be lent & that of 2nd Division to Division	

1577 Wt. W10791/1773 500,000 1/15 D. D. & L. A.D.S.S./Forms/C. 2118.

WAR DIARY
INTELLIGENCE SUMMARY
(Erase heading not required.)

Army Form C. 2118.

Instructions regarding War Diaries and Intelligence Summaries are contained in F.S. Regs., Part II. and the Staff Manual respectively. Title pages will be prepared in manuscript.

Place	Date	Hour	Summary of Events and Information	Remarks and references to Appendices
NIEPPE	25/5/15		Instructions received from 3rd Corps that before all arrangements carried by Engineers from 8th Div. on failure of Engineering Relief Scheme must be hurriedly reported by wire (A.4508).	
NIEPPE	26/5/15		G.O.C. A.H.Q. had a reconnaissance for purpose of finding all suitable billets to house the Divisional Area for the Divisional Ammunition Column, it having been decided not to proceed position (near FLEURBAIX) to be used for the further discharge of its duties. Notification received that Major BOWLES, Staff Captain R.E. 6th Div., has been appointed Brigade Major R.E. 8th Division vice Major MURRAY-SMITH posted to 3rd Divisional Column. Colonel YOUNG A.M.S. ordered to relieve Colonel H.W. THOMPSON D.S.O. appointed D.D.M.S. 6th Corps. One Company	
NIEPPE	27/5/15		Brigade of 9th Division landed at Billet Post at NIEPPE-ARMENTIÈRES.	
NIEPPE	28/5/15		Letter received (3rd Corps A/735/11) asking for the names of any Officers (Colonels, Lt. Cols. or Majors) considered suitable for the command of Infantry Brigades. G.O.C. recommended Lt. Col. BAUMGARTNER G.S.O.1, Major MONK D.S.O. Bde. Major M.S. Bde., Major HIGGINSON Bde. Major 143rd Bde.	
NIEPPE	29/5/15		Copy of Divisional Ammunition Column to S.29-S.30 (Map 40.040) sanctioned by 3rd Corps & arranged for upon the issue of Units. Telegram (A.4586) received from 3rd Corps notifying appointment of Brig.-Genl. R. FANSHAWE to command Division & to be temporary Major-General. Telegram from 3rd Corps (A0125)	

WAR DIARY
INTELLIGENCE SUMMARY.
(Erase heading not required.)

Army Form C. 2118.

Place	Date	Hour	Summary of Events and Information	Remarks and references to Appendices
(contd.)			Lieut. Colonel SYMONS D.A.C. & O.C. No 2 Coy C.R.E. asked it should take over Ravensburg Supply and Ammunition section of the road. Very heavy shelling this aft. shrapnel before N.E. of estaminet.	
MEPPE	30/5/15		Two kinds & different capacities being used for this. S.A.A's previously sent have given place to heavier 4.5 in shells fired by Germans at Pontatier It is being reported to a higher authority. 50th Bde R.F.A. (G/Bty) relieved by 2nd S. Bde Howitzer Battery lying further east 2 artillery mountain. Field Artillery not have 6 rounds & could hear 14 rounds of rifle firing to Ration & Ration firing from Kasperkine. Both Coast moved to F/A.D.C. moved to by him. Report 4th reported Farwell F/A.D.C. moved to by him.	
MEPPE	31/5/15		Major General FANSHAWE assumed Command of the Division Brig-Gen McCLINTOCK having handed over. 145th Inf. Bde. Butter, Hill, Ag with North the Reinforced Bn. at 2-30 A.M. and reported the arrangements for billets. During this ??y. Bn. 75. G.O.C. 137 Bde took command of all Units in the area previously occupied by 6th Div. at 10 a.m. H.Q. N. of St. CROIX au BAC. Total Casualties in the Division for the period 1-5-15 to 31-5-15 are as follows :-	
			Officers Killed 4. Wounded 25. Other Ranks Killed 93. Wounded 235.	
			Total Casualties H.Q. & A.S.C. Officers Killed 5. Wounded 30. O.R. Killed 125. Wounded 569	

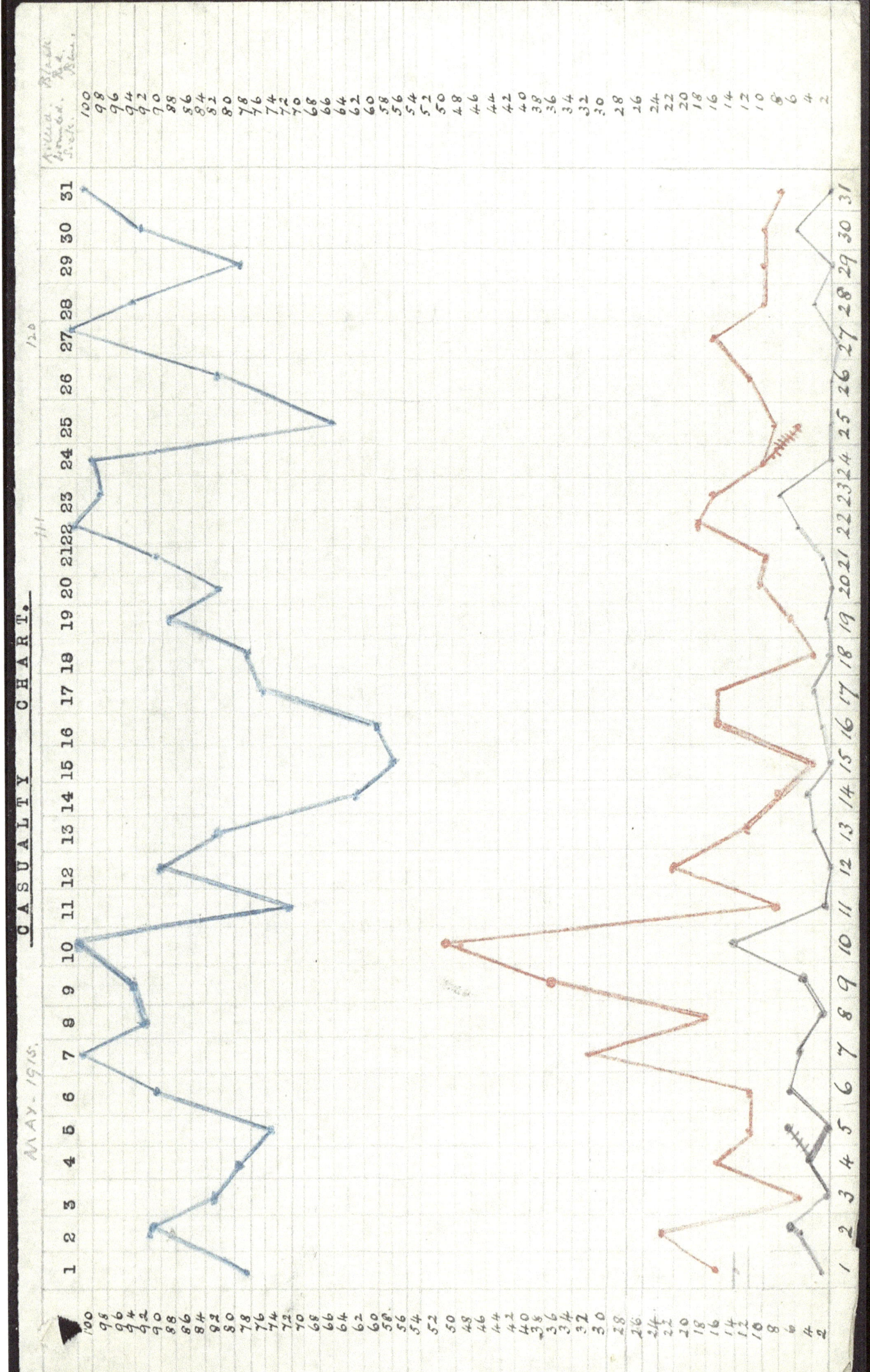

10/594

48th. Division

Headquarters (A & Q) 48th Division

Vol. III — 1 — 30.6.15

CONFIDENTIAL.

WAR DIARY.

OF

"A" & "Q" BRANCH - HEADQUARTERS, 48th (SOUTH MIDLAND) DIVISION.

FROM 1.6.15.   TO 30.6.15.

VOLUME III.

Army Form C. 2118.

WAR DIARY
INTELLIGENCE SUMMARY.
(Erase heading not required.)

Place	Date	Hour	Summary of Events and Information	Remarks and references to Appendices
NIEPPE	1/6/15		Wrote letter sent to Brigadier Calling for a report on his station in recent has been done by F.O.C.M. for his/her D.O. Post. An officer was detailed to the first review of the Slaughter Lines. The G.O.C. inspected the incinerator wire netting & draft a general outline for Subject. The total number of cows in the last few weeks is 10.	
NIEPPE	2/6/15		The Question of the present position of Zone Veterinary N.C.O.'s who, in accordance with previous B.a. Office instructions, had been handed billeting Book Orders, having been referred to 3rd Corps, a reply was received from 3rd Corps stating that Zone N.C.O.'s are now to be absorbed to Regional Establishment, the name further Regular N.C.O.'s and that hereafter they should never be confused with Zone Book & duty with the Reserve Army to ascertain whether he is attached for Quarts. for Rat. & for light supplies. Rules, Regulations, Duties &c. which have been satisfactory.	
NIEPPE	3/6/15		Telegram (A.H.73) from 3rd Corps notifying appointment of Lieut. HIGGINSON, Reserve Regt. as 2nd V.O., 2nd Rate, Reserve Cav. Bde., vice Capt. MARSHALL FORD, Reserve Cavalry. Dispatch in Services of Vet. Officers and & showed Lieut. HIGGINSON to Rat. Regt. C.O.C. inspected horses of 4th C.S.Fortn and a series of Supply Column the afternoon. Later received property issued to van of Charges for Officers of Vet. F. Regt. Hosp. F. Call for Remarks. A.O.C. light & Forage Depart. A.O.C. in charge to forward Establishment.	

1577   Wt. W10791/1773   500,000   1/15   D.D. & L.   A.D.S.S./Forms/C. 2118.

2.

Army Form C. 2118.

WAR DIARY
INTELLIGENCE SUMMARY.
(Erase heading not required.)

Instructions regarding War Diaries and Intelligence Summaries are contained in F.S. Regs., Part II. and the Staff Manual respectively. Title pages will be prepared in manuscript.

Place	Date	Hour	Summary of Events and Information	Remarks and references to Appendices
NIEPPE.	4/6/15		G.O.C. presided at a Conference of Brigadiers, Staff & Heads of Departments at 12 noon at which he announced his intention of carrying out certain changes in the disposition of the troops lately, & first had a General readjustment of Sectors. As a result of this, one Brigade (less one Batt:) at a time will be withdrawn from the Firing Line & brought slightly back for four days' rest, each Brigade with Brigade & each Section of the Trenches in turn, and Brigade Headquarters and Divn Accordingly. These changes are to be carried into effect as early as possible. G.s.O.I.N.S. today carried out a personal experiment with Chlorine & Bromine fumes. He forced a Brother believed not let in a room filled with gas for ½ hour without any unpleasant consequence. I./0/1 Hospital, R.A.M.C. who are also present have a Respirator & Goggles, but L.t.L.S. case from pocket of the throat, that have been frequently. The conclusion is to that in attack our troops will be better used to combat the Gas.	
NIEPPE.	5/6/15		Head Quarters 9th Division have a from NIEPPE this afternoon. Telegram (A.Q. 267) received from 3rd Corps Battery that from tomorrow inclusive, G.Q. Motor Battery will be fed by the Div: Train, Lorry and Train vehicles to be transferred to A & S Supply Column & Div: Train respectively.	
NIEPPE.	6/6/15		Head Quarters 12th Division arrived today. Reinforcements received from the base Corps (2 Offs) NZRNZLR 33 NCOs, BOR ; 13 Field Ambulance have had killed at NIEPPE. ARMENTIERES. ROCHE...	

1577 Wt. W10791/1773 500,000 1/15 D.D.&L. A.D.S.S./Forms/C. 2118.

WAR DIARY

INTELLIGENCE SUMMARY

Army Form C. 2118.

Place	Date	Hour	Summary of Events and Information	Remarks and references to Appendices
(Kemmel)			Also received (C.1420) that on 18th Bn. Battery Brigade from 127 Bde will be placed at disposal of G.O.C. from 8 A.M. 5th 7th to relieve Brigade of 5th Bde. withdrawn. S.A.A. & T. provided to England today, on 8 days leave. 3rd Troop (a. Expert R. Barley) between 4 Squadrons to be at disposal of R.E.	
NIEPPE	7/6/15		Captain MINSHULL FORD rejoined and resumed his position as staff of Bde. Major 4th Inf. Bde. Major HIGGINSON appointed to command 2nd Royal Scottish Fusiliers. Resumed command of disposition took place today. 1st Bde. (less 1 Battn.) bivouacked Section held by 4 Battn at Jonesville Huts (in Back), ROMARIN (in Back) & PONT de NIEPPE (in Back). 2nd Br. stationed at LAMPERNISSE. Rest. Riflemen from 3rd Tps. (M.H.B.L.) and Batty held at Bde Divn in place at disposal of G.O.C. from town at Achicourt. G.S.O. Battling Bde. will leave for NIEPPE shortly in early morning of the 8th inst. B.A.A.	
NIEPPE	8/6/15		2nd Lt. BARLEY listed to Lt. Rankin, 5th Gloucesters & Lt. Oxford on respirators. C.H.R. demonstration the use of Respirators Blk. prepared. These instruction will be the Officers of all Junior Subalterns. R.E. to be in touch were respirators will be provided with a smoke helmet. Instructions received R.E. E.E. 12 Divn with instructions for instructions from M.L.B. 205 L.H. N. H.Q of 1 Bde. M.H. P.O.A.	

4.

Army Form C. 2118.

WAR DIARY
of
INTELLIGENCE SUMMARY.
(Erase heading not required.)

Instructions regarding War Diaries and Intelligence Summaries are contained in F. S. Regs., Part II. and the Staff Manual respectively. Title pages will be prepared in manuscript.

Place	Date	Hour	Summary of Events and Information	Remarks and references to Appendices
NIEPPE.	9/6/15.		Notification received from G.H.Q. that the Field Marshal C in C., had authorised H.M. The King, has awarded R.E.C.M. to 3 N.C.O.'s & men of the Division, to accordance with the attached List. Letter from G.O.C. 9/12 S.h. Field Co. R.E. London Today (Strength 4 Officers, 211 O.R., 79 horses, 5 4 wheel Vehicles, 19 2 wheel, 33 Bicycles). Billeted in vicinity of ROMARIN.	
NIEPPE.	10/6/15.		1 Officer & 6 men from each Battalion, R.G., R.E., & R.A.M.C., proceeded to BAILLEUL Today for a demonstration of asphyxiating gas. G.S.O.2. & G.S.O.3 & O.R.S. attended. Details of their methods of asphyxiating gases demonstrated. This and next duplicate are now to be issued to every Officer & man.	
NIEPPE.	11/6/15		Colonel McEwen. D.S.O. of Gurantis Regt. being here temporarily. Joined on sick list, G.O.C. approved of Captain & Adjutant Nicholson of placed in temporary command of the Battalion.	
NIEPPE.	12/6/15.		Lieut. BARLEY returned to 3rd Barracks on ax of Respirators today. Instructions. (Q.3914/15.) received from 3rd Corps that in future Army Artillery will be getting 3rd Corps Supply Column the necessary Lorries. Remembrance for Barracks Heavy Battery, 114 Heavy Battery Siege, Heavy Battery, 1st Sub. Heavy Battery will be attached to 3rd Corps Troops Supply Column for the next 4 days Vehicles will return with their rations from Osnabruck.	
NIEPPE.	13/6/15.		Lieut BARLEY returned on ax of Respirators to 7th Barracks.	

1577 Wt. W10791/1773 500,000 1/15 D. D. & L. A.D.S.S./Forms/C. 2118.

WAR DIARY
or
INTELLIGENCE SUMMARY.
(Erase heading not required.)

Army Form C. 2118.

Place	Date	Hour	Summary of Events and Information	Remarks and references to Appendices
NIEPPE.	14/6/15		Following card of 13⁵ Div⁵ are attached to the Div⁵ for instructional purposes from 14⁵ to 20⁵ June:- Hd.Qrs. 37ᵗʰ Inf. Bde., One Sqdn. Bde., 1 Field Co. R.E., 1 section A.V. Corps, 1 Coy. Div⁵ Train. G.O.C.'s instruction to Officers of the Brigade in their duties. Brigade Head Quarters daily. D.A.C. & A.A.& S. meet served today.	
NIEPPE.	15/6/15		2ⁿᵈ Lieutenant received that Trench Howitzer Battery (1 Officer, 22 men - 4 Trench Howitzers) and Section Armrn. Column (1 Officer, 11 men - 17 wagons) also received from 3ʳᵈ Inf. Bde. 72 Pte. & Cooks to be transferred at our from date to 2. 50ᵗʰ Division.	
NIEPPE.	16/6/15		93ʳᵈ French Howitzer Battery joined Division today & broke into billets at Bailleul. 25 Officers & men. Messages that all gas cylinders for enemy shell of the Division are carefully being watched. BAILEY Lorry transport posted to C.H.Q. for duty. Orders received from 3ʳᵈ Corps (G.1500), to march at 7.00 a.m. tomorrow on VLAMERTINGHE.	
NIEPPE.	17/6/15		9ᵗʰ Field Co. R.E. at 7.00 a.m. for John 50ᵗʰ Division. At 1st Stewart, 63 horses & wagons 6 Hospital ran hangers to No.2 Casualty Clearing Station today.	
NIEPPE.	18/6/15		A.C.V.D.L.S. returned from leave today.	
NIEPPE.	19/6/15		G.O.C. issued instructions for one days return of Biscuit, Jam & Milk to be stored in Rear Travs. Much of Trenches for Infantry & R.E. for use in cases of attack. D.A.D.C.S. & senior instructors in Bridge on trip to R.	

Army Form C. 2118.

WAR DIARY
INTELLIGENCE SUMMARY.
(Erase heading not required.)

Instructions regarding War Diaries and Intelligence Summaries are contained in F. S. Regs., Part II. and the Staff Manual respectively. Title pages will be prepared in manuscript.

Place	Date	Hour	Summary of Events and Information	Remarks and references to Appendices
NIEPPE.	20/6/15.		Letter received from 3rd Corps (C.1601) His Battery of 4 Sect. Bde R.F.A. (How) allotted to 27th Div. and to be withdrawn from that unit and rejoin Divisional Telegram (A.3018) received informing 3rd Corps asking if Lieut. Col. J.S.J. BAUMGARTNER, C.S.O.1., will accept command of a Battalion of the Indian Reserves Supply (A.238.) sent to the C/of the above.	
NIEPPE.	21/6/15.		No 21 A.R. Convoys not to joined 16th A.A. Section Etaples for instruction and is attached to the Division for administration. [3rd Corps War G.1609.] G.O.C. Inspected Baker of 4/Linc BROWN, R. Inisk. Bde, 1 CATHORNE-HARDY, 1st Brig. for whole hundred Parade for just broke down. Major Lumsden rejoined Red. Division will shortly leave sent to 1st or 2nd Corps.	
NIEPPE.	22/6/15.		Orders for move of the Division received.	
NIEPPE.	23/6/15.		1.1. To. Div. Train move to BAILLEUL. Right of 24/7/25: 143rd Bde. with 1 Field Co., 1 Fd. Co. Eng., 1 Field Ambulance, Batt. of 144 Bde. move night of 25/26: Remainder of 144 Bde. information from Light of 26/27: Div. H.Q. and Remainder of Div. Troops 2nd body day on 27. Div. arrival at VIEUX BERQUIN Division comes under orders of 1st Army.	
NIEPPE.	24/6/15.		Wheelers received that destination of Division is BUSNES. D.A.A.Q.M.S. visited Head Quarters 1st Corps to ascertain billet area, and he and I reconnoitred to billets at VIEUX BERQUIN.	
NIEPPE.	25/6/15.		Telegram (AQ.350) from 3rd Corps notifying that Supply Railhead will be at LILLERS on 27 inst.	

WAR DIARY
INTELLIGENCE SUMMARY

Army Form C. 2118.

Place	Date	Hour	Summary of Events and Information	Remarks and references to Appendices
(continued)			to proceed to 26? and 25 clear of it's present billets by 12 noon. Arranged that Supply drawn at STEENWERCK on 26" (for 28") should be issued to them tomorrow at their respective billeting areas. In morning of the 28", two existing Supply Columns to proceed to H.Q. 1st Can: Railhead empty. Orders received by wire (A.Q. 351) from 3rd Corps for Siviv Ammunition Park & have GIVENCHY on 28", to arrive there by 12 noon. O.C. Ammunition Park instructed to move at 9.30 a.m. for the Orders (AQ. 355) received at 3-5 p.m. that Park Ind proceed to BUSNES arriving there at 1-0 p.m. and take over billets of Canadian Ammunition Park. O.C. Ammunition Park instructed accordingly. H.Q.s Bde. Group arrived at billets in BAILLEUL. Ous about 1-0 a.m. Arrive R.Q.G. Field Bde, Head Quarters & Ammunition train about 7-30 a.m. but found all correct. Q.A. & A. & C. Bde & BUSNES to arrange billets for Siv? Head Quarters Group.	
NIEPPE	26/6/15		No. 2 Group arrived during the night at BAILLEUL. B.G.R.A., B.Q.M.S., Brit: Bryd: Head Quarters. and both at 9 a.m. and found all comfortably settled. No. 1 Group moved to VIEUX BERQUIN from BAILLEUL during night. Supply arrangements were as follows:- 1 Section of Supply Column proceed from STEENWERCK to VIEUX BERQUIN, issued to No. 1 B/ G. 2's Train : 1 Section of Supply Column issued No. 2 Co. Train at BAILLEUL: 1 Section issued to H.Q. 2? C. Tn. No. 3 Co. at LA CRÈCHE. On completion Supply Column proceeded empty to LILLERS.	

Army Form C. 2118.

WAR DIARY
INTELLIGENCE SUMMARY.
(Erase heading not required.)

Place	Date	Hour	Summary of Events and Information	Remarks and references to Appendices
NIEPPE	27/6/15		No: 3 Coys moved during night 26/27 to BAILLEUL: No: 1 Coys to GONNEHEM: No: 2 Coys to VIEUX BERQUIN. Div. Head Quarters Coys moved at 6.0 a.m. from NIEPPE to VIEUX BERQUIN, where it halted for the day and continued it's march to BUSNES at night, arriving at 11-30 p.m. Div. Head Quarters closed at NIEPPE at 6.0 a.m. and opened at BUSNES at same hour. Following moves of Coys took place during night 27/28:- No:1 from GONNEHEM to ALLOUAGNE. No:2 from VIEUX BERQUIN to HAM-en-ARTOIS; No: 3 from BAILLEUL to VIEUX BERQUIN.	
BUSNES	28/6/15		Moves during night 28/29 as follows: No: 2 Coys from HAM-en-ARTOIS to BOZINGHEM: No: 3 Coys from VIEUX BERQUIN to ROBECQ.	
BUSNES	29/6/15		Div: Head Quarters closed at BUSNES at 9.0 a.m. and opened at CHATEAU PHILOMEL at LILLERS at same hour. (our trains of Sup: (exept for certain Head Quarts Coys.) completed today. No: 3 Coys arrived in it's billeting area at BURBURE. A.A. 3 m.G. D.A.A.& Q.M.G. billeted 4½ top: Head Quarters at HINGES for evening.	
Chateau PHILO-MEL	30/6/15		No: 8 Trench Mortar Battery attached to the Div: reported 9 3/4 inst, and is billeted with M.O. of 1st S. Inf. Bde. Two 3 P.a.f. Naval Armoured cars - B. Section, No: 18 Squadron - reported from Oriel and are taken on strength of the Division. 4½ top: Head Quarters closed at HINGES at same hour. Div: closed today and opened at LA BUISSIÈRE at same hour.	

L.G.F. [signature]
D.A.A. & Q.M.G. 48th (S.M.) Division.

June
~~May~~ - 1915.

CASUALTY CHART. - JUNE.

Killed. --------- Black.

Wounded. -------- Red.

Sick. --------- Blue.

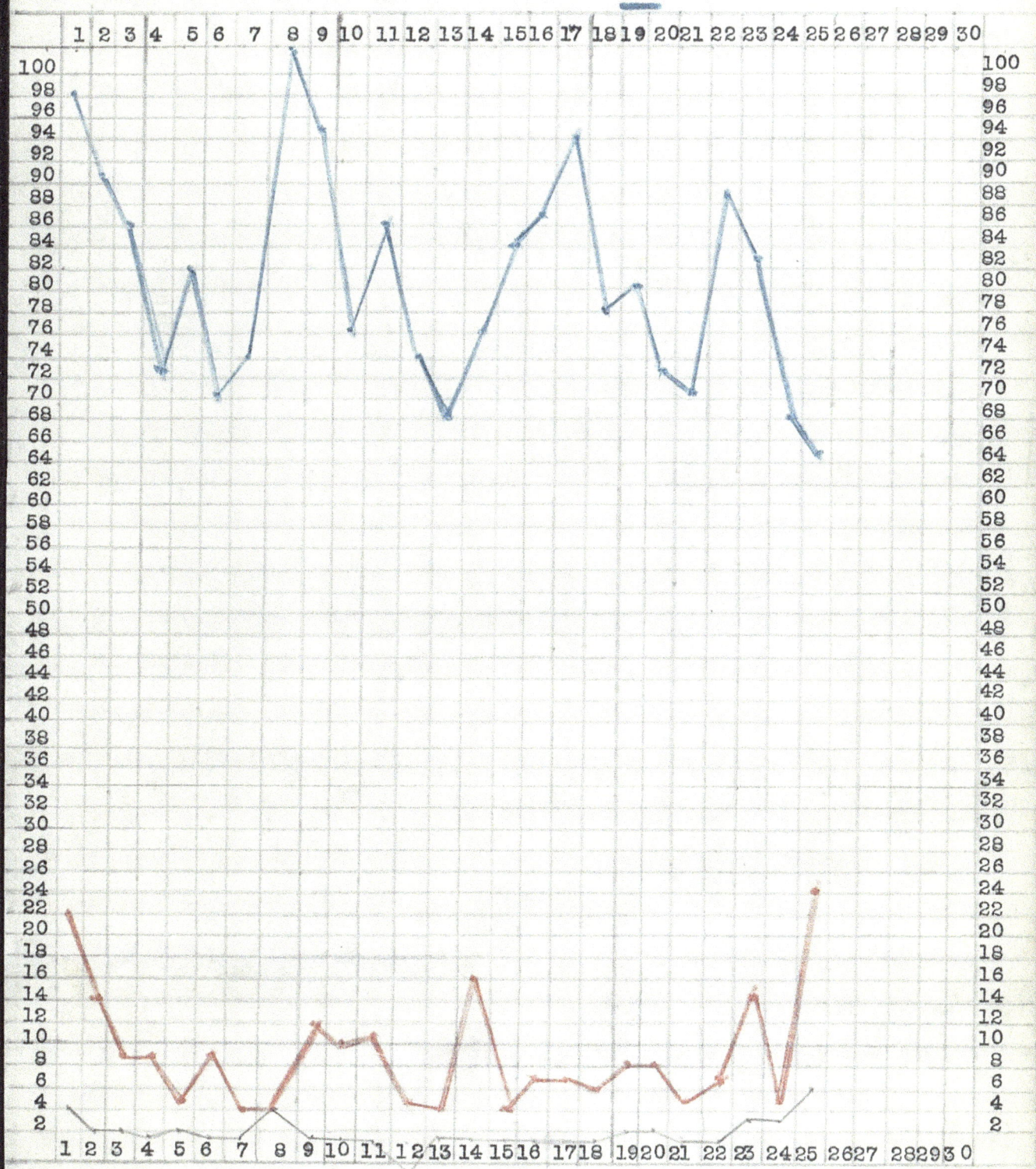

48th (S. M.) DIVISION.

SUMMARY OF CASUALTIES.   To 30th JUNE, 1915.

UNITS	OFFICERS						OTHER RANKS					
	Prior to June		During June		Total		Prior to June		During June		Total	
	K	W	K	W	K	W	K	W	K	W	K	W
5 R. Warwick Regt.	-	2	2	-	2	2	16	58	2	16	18	74
6 R. Warwick Regt.	-	2	-	1	-	3	14	41	6	19	20	60
7 R. Warwick Regt.	-	1	-	-	-	1	9	80	6	15	15	95
8 R. Warwicks Regt	-	2	-	3	-	5	16	48	4	12	20	60
4 Gloucester Regt.	-	-	1	4	1	4	6	72	3	36	9	108
6 Gloucester Regt	-	2	-	1	-	3	15	42	4	17	19	59
7 Worcester Regt.	-	4	-	-	-	4	9	37	2	14	11	51
8 Worcester Regt.	-	2	1	3	-	5	4	38	4	33	8	71
5 Gloucester Regt	2	1	-	-	2	1	10	32	3	9	13	41
4 Ox.& Bucks L.I.	2	3	-	-	2	3	7	25	2	14	b9	39
Bucks Bn.	-	4	-	2	-	6	10	36	1	4	11	40
4 R. Berks Regt.	1	-	-	1	1	1	2	18	-	6	2	24
1/2nd.Fd.Co.R.E.	-	1	-	-	-	1	2	9	1	-	3	9
7th Fd.Co.,R.E.	-	-	-	-	-	-	-	6	-	3	-	9
1/1st Fd.Co.R.E.	-	-	-	-	-	-	4	15	-	-	4	15
B Squadron K.E.H.	-	1	-	-	-	1	-	3	-	-	-	3
3 S.M.Bde.R.F.A.	-	3	-	-	-	3	-	2	-	2	-	4
2 Mtn.Batt.R.G.A.	-	-	-	-	-	-	-	3	-	1	-	4
Signal Co., R.E.	-	-	-	-	-	-	-	-	-	1	-	1
Sanitary Section	-	-	-	-	-	-	1	-	-	-	1	-
Cyclist Company	-	-	-	-	-	-	-	3	-	-	-	3
2 S. M. Bde.R.F.A.	-	-	-	-	-	-	-	2	-	-	-	2
4 S.M. Bde. R.F.A.	-	-	-	-	-	-	1	-	-	-	1	-
2/1st Fd. Co.,R.E.	-	-	-	-	-	-	-	-	-	3	-	3
	5	28	4	15	9	43	126	570	38	205	164	775

48th Division

Headquarters (A & Q) 48th Division

Vol IV 1 — 31.7.15.

187/6231

S/73/A.

CONFIDENTIAL.

WAR DIARY

OF

"A" & "Q" BRANCH - HEADQUARTERS, 48th (SOUTH MIDLAND) DIVISION.

FROM 1.7.15.   TO 31.7.15.

VOLUME IV.

WAR DIARY or INTELLIGENCE SUMMARY

Army Form C. 2118.

(Erase heading not required.)

Instructions regarding War Diaries and Intelligence Summaries are contained in F. S. Regs, Part II. and the Staff Manual respectively. Title pages will be prepared in manuscript.

Place	Date	Hour	Summary of Events and Information	Remarks and references to Appendices
CHATEAU PHILOMEL	1.7.15		Telegram received from D.A.G.-Base (B.A.G.E.36) notifying that large numbers of reinforcements for the Division are at HAVRE and asking for Officers to be sent to take them over. Brigades informed and Officers despatched to bring down. D.A.G. & Q.M.G. and A.P.M. visited MARLES & MINES to inspect Baths found by 143rd Inf. Bde. 2 & C.15 Coy visited billets Q's to discuss Straight Returns and Casualty Reports.	
PHILOMEL	2.7.15		G.O.C. presided at Conference of Brigadiers and Staffs at G.S.O. when arrangements for future Billets, lines of march, and Staff duties generally	
PHILOMEL	3.7.15		Instructions (Q.1476) issued by wire to all Brigades to exchange damageable Rawhide Valises immediately. Instruction (A.340) issued by wire to 143rd Bn. to find Guards at MARLES les MINES from G.O.C. 5n areas to whilst of 143rd Bde. Ratification received for Helopis	
PHILOMEL	4.7.15		that 18 Officers & men for these were to be sent down to Sketch Orders from the Division. Ordering the 143rd S.A. Field A. D.S. attend to proceed to LABOURSE for work upon Improvements R.E.	
PHILOMEL	5.7.15		Draft orders line of Defences and works to be expected to be established by 1st Div. Telegram received giving Arrangements for Special Train from Base & Bank & and new Billets	
PHILOMEL	6.7.15		A.A.G. & Q.M.G. visited 143rd Bde Hrs. 1st Bilot (VAUDRICOURT) to Study Area from C.A.G. 1st Army Cavalry, the key to succeeding instructions from C.A.G. 1st Army	

Army Form C. 2118.

WAR DIARY
or
INTELLIGENCE SUMMARY.
(Erase heading not required.)

Instructions regarding War Diaries and Intelligence Summaries are contained in F. S. Regs., Part II. and the Staff Manual respectively. Title pages will be prepared in manuscript.

Place	Date	Hour	Summary of Events and Information	Remarks and references to Appendices
PHILOMEL.	7/7/15.		Notification received the afternoon that Lord Kitchener will pass through Divisional Area tomorrow 2 o'clock. D.A.A. & Q.M.G. proceeded to Corps Headquarters to obtain full instructions at 6.30 a.m. G.C. and returned with orders. G.O.C. held a Staff Parade in the afternoon which A.A.& Q.M.G., G.S.O., A.D.M.S., D.C.A., D.A.D.S. spent the day at NOEUX-les-MINES arranging billets for Divisional Hd. Qrs. in anticipation of the Division being ordered to take over the line held by the 47th Div.	
PHILOMEL.	8/7/15.		G.O.C. accompanied by Staff met Lord Kitchener at 10.30 a.m. at the Cross Roads, LILLERS-Infantry Brigades lined road from LILLERS to CHOCQUES.	
PHILOMEL.	9/7/15.		Telegram (A.940) from 4th Corps ordering 1st and 2nd Field Co. R.E. to move Southward of 11th R.E. Wells to be arranged with C.R.E. 4 R.E. Telegram (G.4923) from 4th Corps stating that No. 5 Trench Mortar Battery will be temporarily transferred to 47th Div. and supported by A.H. CATHORPE HARDE of Rm 21st Div. CATHORPE HARDE of Rm Received orders R.E. to Note.	
PHILOMEL.	10/7/15.		Telegram (A.5150) received from 3rd Corps notifying that 8.A. & A.G. kickd by G.H.Q. French Mortar Battery left to join 47th Div. at 6.40 p.m. Corps Hd. wanted to discuss Artillery Relief in case it is decided to take over this front.	
PHILOMEL.	11/7/15.		Telegram (A.5563) received from 4th Corps notifying that Orders are being prepared for a Subsequent Combined Divisional Relief and a readjustment of Artillery areas on the lines discussed yesterday. Hd. Qrs. to Sub: D.A.D.S. & 1/1st 1/25 Field Ym moved at 9.0 a.m. Head Quarters to NOEUX-les-MINES, 1/1st to BRUAY.	

WAR DIARY or INTELLIGENCE SUMMARY.

Army Form C. 2118.

(Erase heading not required.)

Place	Date	Hour	Summary of Events and Information	Remarks and references to Appendices
(continued)			(General instructions only for 147th Bde.) 1/125th Fd. to LABOURSE (attached to 1/1st Div. for act. transport) and Barracks for attached to 1/4th Div.	
PHILOSOF	12/7/15		Orders received that Division is to relieve 47th Div. in the trenches on the night 13/14 – 9 Royals to the line and one in reserve. 147th Bde Quarters will be divided into 2 Sections as under, Section A NOEUX-LES-MINES and remainder at GOSNAY, Infantry Brigades Support & Reserve Bde Ey. lines tonight. At 10.45 p.m. Orders were received cancelling the above.	
PHILOSOF	13/7/15		Infantry Brigades took part in Manoeuvres based today as follows: 143rd at HOUCHIN, 144th at HESDIGNEUL, 145th at NOEUX-LES-MINES. In the afternoon Orders were received for 146th Bde. to proceed to LES BREBIS & MAROCO for work on Reserve Trenches. B.G.R.A. & L.G. proceeded to RUITZ & co-op. with Bde/s. to recce areas at 6.0 p.m.	
PHILOSOF	14/7/15		Special Instructions received. H.Q. of the 14th British Division will be transferred to PHILOSOF. 73 Coy. of the 3rd Cavalry orders (Q.139) received from 1st Army for G. of 19 21 Supply & S. Transport Squadrons to the M.L.F. to be transferred to LAHORE and MEERUT Divisional Squadrons R.Tr. when (1) complete, but failure to be detached to 21st Div's from after landing area. reserve that Revd. BURROWS and MORGAN C. of E. Chaplains — are on leave today & form to MEERUT discard to attach him temporarily to 15th Field ambulance as senior.	

Army Form C. 2118.

WAR DIARY
or
INTELLIGENCE SUMMARY.
(Erase heading not required.)

Place	Date	Hour	Summary of Events and Information	Remarks and references to Appendices
THILOMEL	15/7/15		A.A. & Q.M.G. proceeded to G.H.Q. in accordance with instructions and received full information as to the impending move of the Division to the vicinity of DOULLENS. The two Companies of the 17/15th R. Welsh Fus. from Infantry Brigade and R.E. ordered to come to the assistance of the area selected yesterday and to place Units and forwards right.	
THILOMEL	16/7/15		A.A. & Q.M.G. and D.A.A. & Q.M.G. visited orders from 7th Corps to proceed to DOULLENS to meet Corps Commander and his staff with a view to selection of Divisional area. Tour was made throughout area, but found Troops had found to be in possession of all available billets. Consequently Staff Captains could not be brought forward for billeting reconnaissance. Corps Commander returned to ST OMER on conclusion of Tour to place before Enemy Commander with a view to getting an area altered. A.A. & Q.M.G. & D.A.A. & Q.M.G. returned to THILOMEL. Telegram (G.H.) received from 7th Corps at 7.30 p.m. that no Officers are to be sent to reconnoitre new area. Further hills instructions on receipt of telegram (C.5.) received from 7th Corps at 2nd Army that following villages are available for Concentration of Division on 18th :- "THIÈVRES, VAUCHELLES, SARTON, LOUVENCOURT, BEAUQUESNE, and G/16 G.O.C. & R.G., A.A. & Q.M.G. & G.S.O.2, 3 Staff Captains, 1 R.C. Officer and 1 Officer R.A.M.C. for courses & to the Later at ACHEUX. On receipt of there orders D.A.A. & Q.M.G., G.S.O.2, 3 Staff Captains, 1 R.A.C. Officer and 1 Officer Vet. proceeded.	
THILOMEL	17/7/15			

Army Form C. 2118.

WAR DIARY
INTELLIGENCE SUMMARY
(Erase heading not required.)

Instructions regarding War Diaries and Intelligence Summaries are contained in F. S. Regs., Part II. and the Staff Manual respectively. Title pages will be prepared in manuscript.

Place	Date	Hour	Summary of Events and Information	Remarks and references to Appendices
(Continued)			by Motor to DOULLENS, arriving there at 4.30 p.m. Billets were then allotted, and detailed reconnaissance books constructed. A Sketch Plan of the entire billeting area was prepared at once accommodation into each Sub-division shown. Each Infantry Brigade was had responsible for a Field Ambulance, 1 R.E. & Co., 1 Field Co. R.E. L'te Scove, and the R.C. for the Mounted Troops. It was not found possible to accommodate the Divisional Troops in the allotted villages and Packer Wood obtained for the use of TERRAMESNIL, which was found to be void of French Troops. Detailed reconnaissance of billeting areas was completed early. Itinerary of Division commenced at 11.33. Detachment was divided between DOULLENS and MONDICOURT, being divided between LUCHEUX & MONDICOURT, two roads, alternately to each, thus from LILLERS to MONDICOURT, thus from BERGUETTE to DOULLENS. DOULLENS being the billeting Station. Itinerary and detraining Staff Officers were as follows :– D.A.Q.M.G. at LILLERS, G.S.O. 3 at BERGUETTE ; D.A.A.I.Q.M.G. at DOULLENS, G.S.O. 2 at MONDICOURT. Trains arrived at approximate intervals of 2 hours, and detrainment proceeded smoothly & was expeditiously throughout the day. Div. Hd. Qrs. established at TERRAMESNIL. Orders received from Div. Hd. Qrs. for D.A.C. & D.A.L.S. & G.S.O. 1 to return as soon as possible after handing over to 2 Officers from 145th Infy. Bde., the trans. precessory being to sleep at work at Hd. Qrs. Handing over took place at 1.30 p.m. & Staff Officers proceeded forthwith to TERRAMESNIL.	
DOULLENS.	18/7/15.			
TERRAMESNIL. BONNERS	19/7/15.			

1577 Wt. W10791/1773 500,000 1/15 D. D. & L. A.D.S.S./Forms/C. 2118.

Army Form C. 2118.

Instructions regarding War Diaries and Intelligence Summaries are contained in F.S. Regs., Part II. and the Staff Manual respectively. Title pages will be prepared in manuscript.

WAR DIARY
or
INTELLIGENCE SUMMARY.
(Erase heading not required.)

Place	Date	Hour	Summary of Events and Information	Remarks and references to Appendices
TERRAMESNIL	20/7/15.		G.O.C. decided to move Div. HdQrs. to AUTHIE, and move both places at 4 o.p.m. to order to provide accommodation area for the 4th Div., 7th Corps issued instructions for following places to be occupied by units of the Div., by 4.0 p.m. 21st: THIÈVRES, SARTON (except Field Ambulances) TERRAMESNIL, MARIEUX, BUS and VAUCHELLES by 4.o.p.m. 22nd. LOUVENCOURT (except Field Ambulances) Arrangements made for clearing units left behind and available billets for Sub. Stores.	
AUTHIE.	21/7/15.		Light 20/21. 2 Batt 143rd Bde. moved into the Trenches & came under command of French Formations. D.A.G./Q.L.Q. visited BUS les ARTOIS to arrange for advanced Headquarters for G.O.C. from 23rd. Plans to COIGNEUX, SAILLY (to arrange billets arrangements for 143rd & 145th Bdes) COURCELLES (to ascertain suitable position for 1st line Transport of Bde in light rear of the Trenches) and BEAUQUESNE. During night 21/22 2 Battalions of 143rd Bde. moved into Trenches and came under command of French Formations.	
AUTHIE.	22/7/15.		Evacuation of area beginning by 4th Div. for concentration purpose was completed to-day by all Batteries of H.Q. received 18/pdrs & Ammunition Wagons and instructions were received for 10 of 15/pdrs/hows to be sent to Ordnance Workshops at BEAUVAL, and for remainder to be returned to Base.	
AUTHIE.	23/7/15.		G.O.C. and G.S.O.1 proceeded to advanced HeadQuarters at BUS-les-ARTOIS today for preparation.	

1577 Wt. W10791/1773 500,000 1/15 D. D. & L. A.D.S.S./Forms/C. 2118.

Army Form C. 2118.

Instructions regarding War Diaries and Intelligence Summaries are contained in F. S. Regs., Part II. and the Staff Manual respectively. Title pages will be prepared in manuscript.

WAR DIARY
~~OF~~
INTELLIGENCE SUMMARY.
(Erase heading not required.)

Place	Date	Hour	Summary of Events and Information	Remarks and references to Appendices
(Continued)			The G.O.C. Artillery returned by bus from General DAWON. She is T.O.C. & proceeded to COIGNEUX to reconnoitre ground on which to put Brigade Transport & Artillery Ammunition Column.	
AUTHIE	24/7/15		G.O.C. attached establishment of same at 6.0 a.m. Telegram received from 7th Corps (Q. 92) that 25th Anti-Aircraft Section from 7th Corps today and will be attached to 46th Div. for administration and feeding. Notification also received that 183 Siege Battery R.G.A. is on its way and will be administered by Division. 25th Anti-Aircraft Section arrived.	
AUTHIE	25/7/15		11.0 p.m., O.C. Captain W. H. LEWIS. 183 Siege Battery R.G.A. reported arrival today, O.C. being E.C. L. PELLEY. Orders issued for 1st line Transport of 143rd and 143rd Bdes. to go to bivouac at COIGNEUX so as to leave them respective baths. Telegram (Q.139) from 7th Corps notifying arrival from tomorrow happen [onwards] to refill at Railhead at G.O.C. daily. Telegram (Q.133) from 7th Corps directing that in event of an Artillery unit being transferred from one Corps to another the G.O.C. to [send] in [detail] with 7th Corps, Corps or Div. from which transferred, also details of unit to which it is [transferred] & also details of [how and where] transferred to, also date at it is to [leave] & the [nature] of the [movement] must continue to stand [in] its daily [report] & the [from and to] which it is transferred.	

1577 Wt. W10791/1773 500,000 1/15 D. D. & L.   A.D.S.S./Forms/C. 2118.

Army Form C. 2118.

WAR DIARY
INTELLIGENCE SUMMARY.
(Erase heading not required.)

Instructions regarding War Diaries and Intelligence Summaries are contained in F. S. Regs., Part II and the Staff Manual respectively. Title pages will be prepared in manuscript.

Place	Date	Hour	Summary of Events and Information	Remarks and references to Appendices
AUTHIE.	26/7/15.		First line Transport of 143rd & 145th Bdes. moved to bivouacs at COIGNEUX Rotary Place selected will be permanent for the Brigades in the first line.	
AUTHIE	27/7/15.		Telegram (Q.191) from 7th Corps notifying that Supply Column will be administered from the Office and that all returns etc. will be rendered through 3rd Div. Q.	
AUTHIE.	28/7/15.		Telegram (Q.109) from 7th Corps that one of the R.F.A. Brigades of the Div. will be placed at the disposal of the 10th Corps, further details being furnished later. Letter informing (Q.178) received that 2 Vickers guns are allotted to Bde. Bn. will be distributed as follows: 6th Berwicks 4; 7th Berwicks 3.	
AUTHIE	29/7/15.		Notification received that the Division will extend its front on night 30/31, taking over Trenches from left Batt. of 4th Div. consequent on this rearrangement of Infantry Brigades front as follows:– Bde. Hd. Qrs. & 3 Batts. at HABUTERNE, 1 Batt. at SAILLY. Left Brigade — Right Brigade — 4 Batts in Trenches less 1 Co. from each in billets at COLINCAMPS; Bde. Hd. Qrs. at COLINCAMPS. Bde's in Div. Reserve. Hd. Qrs. 1 Bn. SAILLY, 1 Bn. COURCELLES, 1 Bn. BAYENCOURT, 1 Bn. COIGNEUX. First Line Transport of Brigades in front line remain at COIGNEUX; Half of remaining Batt. at ST. LEGER. Remainder of Brigade Transport for 1st Line [?] 1st Line Transport of Reserve Brigade at COIGNEUX (2 Bns.) and	
AUTHIE	30/7/15.			

Army Form C. 2118.

WAR DIARY
INTELLIGENCE SUMMARY.
(Erase heading not required.)

Instructions regarding War Diaries and Intelligence Summaries are contained in F. S. Regs., Part II. and the Staff Manual respectively. Title pages will be prepared in manuscript.

Place	Date	Hour	Summary of Events and Information	Remarks and references to Appendices
(Unlocated) AUTHIE	31/7/15		ST. LÉGER (2 R2). G.O.C. directed that 13th Bn. Transport of Reserve Brigade should now be dealt with Battalion. Orders issued accordingly.	

D.A.A & Q.M.G. AGS (S.M.L) Division

121/6737

48th Division

Headquarters (A&Q) 48th Division

Vol V

August 15

S/102/A
48 Div

"A" & "Q" BRANCH - HEADQUARTERS 48th (SOUTH MIDLAND) DIVISION.

FROM - 1-8-15.

TO - 31-8-15.

VOLUME V

WAR DIARY or INTELLIGENCE SUMMARY

Army Form C. 2118.

Place	Date	Hour	Summary of Events and Information	Remarks and references to Appendices
AUTHIE	1/8/15	1 pm	Major LAW to report for duty D of S. ABBEVILLE on 2/8/15 - A.552.	
		8.5 A.M.	Reinforcements - 20 Drivers for Div Ammn Col. - 1 Officer - 11 Buchers B?? -	
		7.45 PM	Supply wagons of DIV TRAIN left with units for meat from LILLERS. Instructions issued re service of Venereal Sporozoans and Scabies at Hq/ao. Road Control posts established by A.P.M. S.O.C. 143" Inf Bde detailed to provide party - 1 Officer 1 NCO 25 men for harvesting at SAILLY cause of Advance for DIV: - VII Corps Instruction A/100 - 19 Officers + men -	
AUTHIE	2/8/15		Investilling Fair to remain at LOUVENCOURT & VAUCHELLES - Q.951. 4 DIV. 7 Corps require to see scheme in Subply dump by army before put into operation Q 325" M.G. school party from WISQUES allowed to return 3/8/15. GHQ.T.1871. 7 Corps ack to 7.773 from S.S.O. Q.321. Reply to Q.295 VII Corps - No 1½" or 2" Very Pistols in charge - Reply to Q.322 VII Corps - 7. Victrero Guns received - . Major LAW. deposits at A.D.Q.S. ABBEVILLE - Major DANIELSEN - 16 R War R. acts DAA.QMG, G.O.C. held conference of Staff, Bde Commanders at BUS-LES-ARTOIS.	VII Corps / GAH?

1577 Wt.W10791/1773 500,000 1/15 D. D. & L. A.D.S.S./Forms/C. 2118.

Army Form C. 2118.

WAR DIARY
or
INTELLIGENCE SUMMARY.
(Erase heading not required.)

Instructions regarding War Diaries and Intelligence Summaries are contained in F. S. Regs., Part II. and the Staff Manual respectively. Title pages will be prepared in manuscript.

Place	Date	Hour	Summary of Events and Information	Remarks and references to Appendices
BUS-EN-ARTOIS	3-8-15	.	Application from 7th Corps to accommodate some 2000 horses & 4th Divn South of AUTHIE. Shown towards SARTON 7th Corps at 353 — Reply accommodation not available. A.S.6.8. Notice received of return of 4 convalescents out of rest. Reinstation A.H.6.1. D.389. Units notified. 7th Corps A.370(A) of July re Turkish and Greek interpreters. Reply A.544. 4.8.4. Div. N.I. Instructions received 7th Corps (N°. A.58) Rations to be demanded by units daily on Army Form S.5. etc. Reply 61374 system to be adopted forthwith. Advice reissue 11 corks carts C.T. being sent from H.Q.O. 61337. 7th Corps. (one per battery). Report to 7th Corps all blanket waggons returned. 7th Corps A.323. Divisional Ammn Col. moved to AUTHIE. A+L Branch Divl H.Q. also moved AUTHIE to BUS-LES-ARTOIS. O.C. Divl Train proceeds on leave of absence to England for 6 days. No 3rd Whipper in ship from his duties during absence.	
BUS-LES-ARTOIS	4-8-15		AA+QMG accompanied Senior Chaplain + Liaison Officer so instructed by Third Army selected site for graves adjacent men are at HEBUTERNE and at LOUVENCOURT one which makes use of the existing French cemetery. DA+Q.M.G. and A.Q.M.G. 7th Corps visited Divisional H.Q. Also in reference to accommodation for 4th Div horses (2000) near SARTON. DA+QMG and S.O. of Division visited Corps H.Q. Also in reference to new rating of empty meat and bread from Railhead. H.Q. the Divl R.E. moved AUTHIE to BUS-LES-ARTOIS. Machine gun party from WISQUES returned 2nd Lieut ARENO 5th R. War R, 2nd Lieut DURRANT 5th Glos Regt and 5 O.R.	

1577 Wt. W10791/1773 500,000 1/15 D. D. & L. A.D.S.S./Forms/C. 2118.

Army Form C. 2118.

WAR DIARY
or
INTELLIGENCE SUMMARY.
(Erase heading not required.)

Instructions regarding War Diaries and Intelligence Summaries are contained in F. S. Regs., Part II. and the Staff Manual respectively. Title pages will be prepared in manuscript.

Place	Date	Hour	Summary of Events and Information	Remarks and references to Appendices
BUS-LES ARTOIS	4-8-15		Private HAYCOCK 6115 2nd S. Staffs and Driver HOUNSON "A" Battery R.H.A Groom Driver H.A.C.M returned to duty.	
BUS-LES ARTOIS	5-8-15		Divnl. Cyclist Coy moved BUS-LES-ARTOIS to HEBUTERNE.	
			LIEUT. TROUTBECK. BUCKS. BN. proceeded to BEAUQUESNE as Supply Officer Railhead Sh 389. 7th Corps. 4/8/15.	
		3.10	7th Corps. M 400 re-return of Troops Soldiers PANZANI 137th Regt. Prote Turenne HEBUTERNE to HENENCOURT proceed to	
			14th Inf Bdy for immediate action.	
			36 Steel Helmets received for trial and report.	
			Meat received at Railhead issued to troops for consumption tomorrow. System now visited double issue now 2 hours delay. Authority received for issuance of Divnl. one-ne filling points bt at LOUVENCOURT commencing 9th inst.	
BUS-LES ARTOIS	6-8-15	11.A.M	D.D.O.S. Third Army called. Report received from A.D.V.S. that supplies of officers chargers on reduction to new establishment has been received by Mobile Veterinary Section. 7th Corps ame Sh 422 directing 19th Supply Column to return to surplus lorries to Troops Supply Column 3rd Army. Forwarded brigade surplus to establishment of Field Ambulances returned to BASE 7th Corps. A126 of 23/7/15. 7th Corps Sh 419 Armourd Trench Mortar Battery to join Division 8th August. R.A directed to draw ammunition for Trench Mortar Battery from Sub-park.	
BUS-LES ARTOIS	7-8-15		1st S. In Field Ambulances moved SARTON to ARQUEVES. 7th Corps Sh 438 advise parliamentary commission without location in 3rd Army area 7th & 8th inst. 7th Corps Sh 44 have convalescence 1st Lieut PRAGER TINER. Consequence of 1H33AX Forwarded. Half-Battalion entraining & arriving at VAUCHELLES twenty to fifteen	

WAR DIARY or INTELLIGENCE SUMMARY

Army Form C. 2118.

Instructions regarding War Diaries and Intelligence Summaries are contained in F. S. Regs., Part II, and the Staff Manual respectively. Title pages will be prepared in manuscript.

(Erase heading not required.)

Place	Date	Hour	Summary of Events and Information	Remarks and references to Appendices
BUS-LES-ARTUS	8.6.15		Arrangements made at Louvencourt cancelled. Reported 3rd Army informed. Trunk number 143 Ry. 80th 2 O/R 3 Civilians 20 men from VAUX-VRAUCOURT are attached to 144th S. Eng. Pry. French artillery pushed up to 7th Corps ad. Larry off SAILLY. July 31 mt trench by railway envied road on western extension. 7th Brigade A HQ to 444 443. In night 3.7 Corps 64 480 ground pt occupied to Seltie road Louvie C016ve UX 11 am 19th inst from Mesopotamia Grenade 1/6. 19th Sup Party an ambusiness 5. Lines (?) illus) F A 3rd Army troop Supply Column BEAUVERGNES	
BUS-LES-ARTUS	9.6.15		Traffic control post established at ST LEGER, at cross roads South of COUIN, at CO16VEUX, at cross roads, South West of BAYENCOURT & the cross roads at the two exists south of Authil, the except instead A along roads leading to BUS between 5 AM and 7.30 PM. Notes as to what supped up. Civilian BURROWS from 2nd S M Field Ambulance hospital N. 20 hrs clearing Station ST. O M E R. F.C. A.H.E. of D428, 232, 7th TAYLOR E 5 2 vice R rejoins from BASE. 3 officers reinforcements joined 7th R. WAR R. from BASE.	
BUS-LES-ARTUS	10.6.15		Div Salv Co formed to date 11 August. 10 Munitions of Reserve 4th Oct, 1 Sept 3 Corps Co 1 Pt. man, 36 Privates. 2 Officer. 16 O/Rs transferred. 7th pts control posts established 9th mid-noon. Reinforcements arrived 2/10th 8 G. R. E. Som av. 11st S. A. G. R. E. 25 1/2 4th G. R. E. 33 men. Report on works accommodation requested for units at 7th Corps as of 7th Corps A 2274 45 Sm 1367KV. Accommodation arranged in LOUVENCOURT for 141st and 143 Companies Fortress R.E. due 12th inst 7th Corps 64.507 and 64 524.	

WAR DIARY or INTELLIGENCE SUMMARY

Army Form C. 2118.

(Erase heading not required.)

Instructions regarding War Diaries and Intelligence Summaries are contained in F. S. Regs., Part II. and the Staff Manual respectively. Title pages will be prepared in manuscript.

Place	Date	Hour	Summary of Events and Information	Remarks and references to Appendices
BUS-LES ARTOIS	10.8.15		N° 3552 Pte Graham J. 5th R. War. R. sent to Hd Qrs 3rd Army for duty as clerk to D.A. & QMG.	
BUS-LES ARTOIS	11.8.15		N° 2826 Pte HARTLAND H. 6th Bn Glos. Regt sent to H'Qrs 3rd Army for duty as mapping clerk. 140 Remounts received and distributed. Captain Wilson of the Survey Coy Reinforcements visited the sites selected for graves at HEBUTERNE and LOUVENCOURT yesterday. 7th Corps G581 advising that N° 2 Wells Flame Grenades are not to be issued until further orders. All units informed & instructors acknowledged. Bomb Salvage Coy arrived at HEBUTERNE. Col. Roberts O.C. Divnl Train return from leave & takes over command of Divisional Train. Major Norton Griffiths inspects condrs to Tunnelling companies R.E. Application made for authority to employ chosen numbers to enable chosen personnel in Trenches. Bomb Sanitary Section moved yesterday from AUTHIE to BUS-LES-ARTOIS.	
BUS-LES ARTOIS	12.8.15		Refilling point moves to LOUVENCOURT, copy RAMC GHQ G/5/10/1 of 31.7.15. re machine guns twenty/six/circums for protection of mind of points pro forwarded to 3 Inf Bde. Conference by Maj. Gen Commdg Divn attended by Sh/1 Officer G and A, Liaison Officers attending. Subjects discussed arrangements for storing empties, dealing with manure. Circular with ref to concealment forward to all units G.X.1587. 52 other ranks 1/6 High Battln left for Base 11th Aug not executed in of establishment. Major Norton Griffiths interviewed 2nd Lt R.F. IRVING 4th Glosters and A/t Pinbald Alex.Cowie 4th S.M. Huntley Roy being candidates for Commission in Tunnelling Coys R.E. Lieut Baumgartner G.S.O.I forwarded to England on leave. Returned 7th Corps Machine gun section K.E.H. with 12th Divn.	

1577 Wt. W10791/1773 500,000 1/15 D. D. & L. A.D.S.S./Forms/C. 2118.

Army Form C. 2118.

WAR DIARY
or
INTELLIGENCE SUMMARY.
(Erase heading not required.)

Instructions regarding War Diaries and Intelligence Summaries are contained in F. S. Regs., Part II. and the Staff Manual respectively. Title pages will be prepared in manuscript.

Place	Date	Hour	Summary of Events and Information	Remarks and references to Appendices
BUS-LES ARTOIS	12.8.15		Lord Mayor of Birmingham and Lord Bishop of Birmingham visited Divn HdQrs. 5th, 6th & 8th Bns R.War.R. and 3rd S.M. Bty R.F.A.	
BUS-LES ARTOIS	13.8.15		141st and 143rd Forage Corps R.E. arrived at LOUVENCOURT. Three recruits by G.O.C. 3rd Army at MARIEUX viz 2366 Pte R. JEFFS 8th Bn R.War.R. 2286 L.Cpl WHEELDON H.P. 8th Bn R.War R. and 1677 Pte SHEIL B.R. 8th Bn R War R. Pte. 7th Corps A587 ref to on LATTEY LEWIS sights authority telegram A6745. 7th Corps A551 No.5 J (illegible) Hand Grenades to be used until further orders. 7th Corps A611 No.5 J (illegible) Hand Grenades to be returned to Railhead. A503	
BUS-LES ARTOIS	14.8.15		A.D.A.M.S. reconnoitre area ref. purr to harvesting and removal of manure. 7th Corps A631 confirm quantity of charcoal needed for week up to 15.57 & Xmas Bray. 11th inst. R.W. 12 trucks per week A754 (754). 7th Corps A629 Officers and men proceeding on leave or otherwise bound to say on by was either VAUCHELLES or ACHEUX stations where R.T.O. will furnish necessary movement orders. Report received that at pool near Foley men drank from AUTHIE ADMS takes action. One soldier mistaken of water and was 2 miles above AUTHIE	
BUS-LES ARTOIS	15.8.15		Polluting river AUTHIE has been traced to be due to the presence in the river at ST.LEGER of a dying horse, flesh thereby being known in pieces unknown. Investigation continues. Report as to hutting for units accommodation of men and horses wanted. 14th (illegible) and supplemented to Army 7th Corps A55 48th Div. 1367 A.X. No. 56 Trench Mortar Battery. Sd. R.M. Richmond 2/Lt C.G. HYDE and 23 others who having 13 in armed counter-attacks in attached 1st Grenadier Guards. Telegram 7th Corps A680 Third Army direct all 18 pr H.E. ammunition in exhibit to be	

1577 Wt. W10791/1773 500,000 1/15 D.D. & L. A.D.S.S./Forms/C. 2118.

Army Form C. 2118.

WAR DIARY
or
INTELLIGENCE SUMMARY.
(Erase heading not required.)

Instructions regarding War Diaries and Intelligence Summaries are contained in F. S. Regs., Part II. and the Staff Manual respectively. Title pages will be prepared in manuscript.

Place	Date	Hour	Summary of Events and Information	Remarks and references to Appendices
BUS-LES ARTOIS	16.8.15		Return ex arrival of ammunition with Mark II shells. Brigadier Genl 7th Corps AH 39 re ammunition supply returned. See note to 7th Corps C/35 received directing no 1 for H E Ammunition to be carried. Bird Amm Col and only 5% of the 18pr ammunition carried in the field in front of Bird Amm Col and in Ammun Subs Parks shall be H.E. ammunition. The H E ammunition in excess will continue to railheads & replace by shipment. Forwarded to C.R.A. for action today. Notification received that Lt.Col. PEAKE, G.R. 1/8 B'n were Regt has been invalided to England and will 1/9 shrapnel shells from from 11/8/15. 7th Corps 550/30 octr 16/8/15.	
BUS-LES ARTOIS	17.8.15		MAJOR WALSH, G.H.Q. appointed D.A.A. & Q.M.G. 48th Div to take up duties on arrival. 7th Corps C/36 stating 1/5th Royal Sussex Regt & 1/8 B'n as Pioneer Battalion received. DD S & T 3rd Army notified was that transport of the battalion can be received by own Train at once. Returned 7th Corps 61032 g/16th and to telegram Q770 g/16th and all ammunition munitions has been sent to Railhead for examination. Q 778. 48th Div. The mission AUTHIE	
BUS-LES ARTOIS	18.8.15		A sally prohibited for all carts and by transport. 5th B'n R. Sussex Regt ordered by 7rd/M.3rd Army AR 3 58 due DOULLENS 20th inst 20'53 hrs. Arrangements made for billeting night of 20th inst at SARTON. Q'Rona escorting for the march of the Regtl Section on it & emergency rations allotted to 1/5th N.N.E. coming LA SIGNY FARM.	
BUS-LES ARTOIS	20.8.15		5th B'n R. Sussex Regt 25 officers 740. O. R. arrived DOULLENS and billetted at SARTON.	

1577 Wt.W10791/1773 500,000 1/15 D. D. & L. A.D.S.S./Forms/C. 2118.

WAR DIARY
or
INTELLIGENCE SUMMARY.
(Erase heading not required.)

Army Form C. 2118.

Place	Date	Hour	Summary of Events and Information	Remarks and references to Appendices
BUS-LES ARTOIS	21/8/15		5th Bn R. Sussex Regt moved HdQrs and 2 coys to LOUVENCOURT and 2 coys to COLINCAMPS. Commenced returning Mark B. S.A.A. to Railhead. All Mills N.5 grenades returned to Railhead telegram Q.S.02 to 7th Corps in reply to 7th Corps Q.757. Major WALSH Worcestershire Regt assumes the duties of D.A.A. & Q.M.G. on arrival from G.H.Qs in relief of Major DANIELSEN temporarily performing the duties.	
BUS-LES ARTOIS	22/8/15		Instructions received from 7th Corps that the 48th (S. Midland) Bombing pt. tte & that No. 12 Store of Advance was to be given till 30th mmly instructions were received. All leave/Absence half Remittes was consequent cancelled till further notice. Orders received from 7th Corps that – 141st Army Troops Co. R.E. would be transferred from the Divn to the 4th Division from 24th inst. inclusive. Instructions received from 7th Corps that 3rd Army had decided that until further orders no 18 Smith H.E. Ammunition was to be used except in a case of emergency, and in no circumstances by Anti Aircraft guns. Notification received that the extra transport for the 5/Royal Sussex, Pioneer Battn of the Division was being sent to join the Battalion tomorrow.	
Rue de ARTOIS	23/8/15		Lt. Col. H. A. Boyce R.F.A. arrived from England to take over the appointment of A.A. & Q.M.G. of the Division.	

Army Form C. 2118.

WAR DIARY
or
INTELLIGENCE SUMMARY.
(Erase heading not required)

Instructions regarding War Diaries and Intelligence Summaries are contained in F.S. Regs., Part II. and the Staff Manual respectively. Title pages will be prepared in manuscript.

Place	Date	Hour	Summary of Events and Information	Remarks and references to Appendices
BUS-LES ARTOIS	24/8/15		Leave of absence (closed since 22nd inst.) re-opened.	
"	25/8/15		Board assembled to schedule billeting accommodation in divisional area. Consequently in landing over 8 nights line to 4th Division, the following allotments in billets took place in 25th & night 25/26 August :— 2 Bns 143rd Inf. Bde to hivouac in BOIS du WARNIMONT, 2 Cos 144th Bn from SAILLY to COIGNEUX. 2 Co. R. Sussex Regt. from COLINCAMPS to SAILLY (incl. 2 sections from LA SIGNY FARM). HQ 143 Bde & 1 or S.M. Bde RFA remained in COLINCAMPS.	
	26/8/15		8th R. War. Regt. from the trenches to AUTHIE.	
	27.8.15		11 (France) Fd. Rly works 6.27th Division arrived, attached for training, & billetted at HEBUTERNE. Orders received (7th Corps. Tel. Line A 901) for Lt Reilly to proceed to England and report in writing to War Office on arrival.	
	28.8.15		3rd London Battalion arrived DOULLENS station evening of 28th, & reached BUS Area morning of 29th. Camped in BOIS du WARNIMONT. Colonel Reilly (late AA & QMG) left for England.	
	29.8.15		Great distribution of leave days numbers raised, to include Sussex Regt.	

Army Form C. 2118.

WAR DIARY
or
INTELLIGENCE SUMMARY.
(Erase heading not required.)

Instructions regarding War Diaries and Intelligence Summaries are contained in F. S. Regs., Part II. and the Staff Manual respectively. Title pages will be prepared in manuscript.

Place	Date	Hour	Summary of Events and Information	Remarks and references to Appendices
Bus les ARTOIS	30/8/15		5th Warwicks moved into billets at Bus. 6th Warwicks at SAETON (early ? 6 p.m.) HD & 2 Cos. 8th Worcs joined remaining 2 Coys being 9 gone point at SAILLIE. HQ & 2 Co 6/gloucs from SAILLIE to LOUVENCOURT. 2 Co 8 Worcs sent from COIGNEUX to LOUVENCOURT. Lieut De Denlier took over Divl Haison Officer duties vice Mahony	
	31/8/15		—	

1577 Wt. W10791/1773 500,000 1/15 D. D. & L. A.D.S.S./Forms/C. 2118.

48th Division

121/7082

Headquarters (A & Q) 48th Division
Vol VI
Sept 15

"A" & "Q" BRANCH - HEADQUARTERS 48th (SOUTH MIDLAND) DIVISION.

- VOLUME Vl. -

- FROM - 1 - 9 - 15.

TO 30 - 9 - 15.

Army Form C. 2118

WAR DIARY
or
INTELLIGENCE SUMMARY.
(Erase heading not required.)

Instructions regarding War Diaries and Intelligence Summaries are contained in F.S. Regs., Part II. and the Staff Manual respectively. Title pages will be prepared in manuscript.

Place	Date	Hour	Summary of Events and Information	Remarks and references to Appendices
BUS le ARTOIS	1.9.15		Casualties. Nil.	
	2.9.15		Casualties - Nil.	
	3.9.15		5k Warwicks moved from Bus to Trenches; 7th Warwicks SAILLY to Trenches; 6 Warwicks SARTON to Ferme de la HAIE. Casualties OR wounded 1.	
	4.9.15		2/m 1/6" Warwicks Ferme de la HAIE to FONQUEVILLERS; 2nd Fd Co COURCELLES to FONQUEVILLERS & SAILLY. 3 m Fd Co AUTHIE & ROSSIGNOL. Draft of 30 men arrived to 1/5 Warwicks. Casualties - Nil. 7 Corps asked temporarily motor lorries with troops & supply into & FONQUEVILLERS, where interior reported unfit for billeting. Temporary arrangements made meanwhile with a type CA lorries & on 1.43 Wale assumed command of FONQUEVILLERS sector, taken over from the French at 10 a.m.	
	5.9.15		Reliefs:- 144 k Bde from Divl. reserve to trenches at HEBUTERNE. 145 k Inf Bde from HEBUTERNE:- 4/R Berks to AUTHIE, Bucks Bn to BUS, 4 Ox/ds to COURCELLES, 5th Gloucester to SAILLY. Casualties OR. 1 killed, 1 wounded.	
	6.9.15		Casualties - Nil.	
	7.9.15		Moves:- Bucks Bn (Oxf. Bucks) from BUS to COUIN & Casualties OR wounded 2. (2 wounded on 6/9/15 not entered)	10/9/15
	8.9.15		Moves:- 5/ Gloucesters from SAILLY to BUS. 2 Co "R E COURCELLES to FONQUEVILLERS v SAILLY. Casualties OR. 1 wounded	

1577 Wt. W10791/1773 500,000 1/15 D. D. & L. A.D.S.S./Forms/C. 2118.

WAR DIARY or INTELLIGENCE SUMMARY

Army Form C. 2118

Place	Date	Hour	Summary of Events and Information	Remarks and references to Appendices
BUS-LES-ARTOIS	9.9.15		3 Cas R.E. Auth to ROSSIGNOL. Casualties OR wounded 4.	
	10.9.15		Glanders horse not in 3(Warwick) Bde R.F.A. Shore destroyed. 66 horses mallienied. Area pu not ground of precautions taken. Casualties OR killed 1, wounded 1	
	11.9.15		6 mules horses of 3rd Bde R.F.A destroyed. Remaining 18 falling in obtained. D.V.S. Expedit Force (Blay-Genel. J. Moore D.S.O.) & D.V.S. 3rd Army (Col. H J Arc.) visited Lines. 13 R Manchester & E Shropshire (66 & Inf Bde) arrived. Attachment 15/4" & 16 Bde Camp	
			16 August 14/12 Left in Bois de WARNIMONT.	
			Orders received from 7 Corp Bus Pois lt mont (incl) have only be farmed by Corp: & only then exceptional circs. the transfer. Casualties Nil.	
	12.9.15		13 Manchester & 8" Shropshire moved into the trenches at HEBUTERNE for instruction. Casualties OR wounded 2.	Vimy
	13.9.15		7 pm Hon. kn of 3 Warwickshire, helpd in impact of 11 Rt Reg't destroyed. (One whole 18 destroyed)	
			20 horses of 1st Warwick R.F.A tested weight of 12/13 Sept. Remainder of the Batteries weight 13/14 to 8 pm. of 3 Killed & 3 injured (Type 23). 67 horses of 1 Wily Bde destroyed. 5 miles south of 3 Warwick Bde Antwerp	
	14.9.15		4 Officers arrived higher 14/15 Sept. Klockerstadt:- Lieut Co. Gasker, 16 Rn Debeck Res. Rgpt. Read Field Hosp. 115 higher Hosp, Major Ross D.S.O Sec hop't, 4 Carr King of Auge 19 (Reserve) Im Walt Rgt. Mary have been absorbed ADS/DR1, waren added to 143 Inj Res.	

WAR DIARY
or
INTELLIGENCE SUMMARY.
(Erase heading not required.)

Army Form C. 2118.

Instructions regarding War Diaries and Intelligence Summaries are contained in F. S. Regs, Part II. and the Staff Manual respectively. Title pages will be prepared in manuscript.

Place	Date	Hour	Summary of Events and Information	Remarks and references to Appendices
BUS-les-ARTOIS	14.9.15 (cont)		Orders issued for taking into his new entrenchments (trenches) at COUIN from 15th Kings	
			COIGNEUX complete the transport closed from 16.15pm	
	15.9.15		1 horse 3rd Warwick Bde destroyed (TM/24) his "reaction" w/ 1st Warwick Bde 84 hours 7/2 Warwick. Bty tested night 14/15 Sept No "reaction" Casualties Nil.	
	16.9.15		Capt T.J. Leahy, 2/R Dublin Fus arrived as G.S.O.3 vice Major A.C. Girdwood D.S.O. 63 hours 2nd Warwick Bty tested night 15/16 Sept; no reaction Casualties OR wounded 4.	
	17.9.15		145th Bde relieved 144 in trenches at HEBUTERNE. 8th Worcesters to BUS; 4th Gloucesters to AUTHIE; 6th Gloucesters to COUIN; 7th Worcesters to COURCELLES. The 4 attached officers of 5th New Army & Major Girdwood proceeded to BOULOGNE for embarkation. 7 S hours 9 Am Cu 3 S.M. Bde tested night 16/17. Casualties OR killed 1, wounded 1.	
	18.9.15		6 S 11mes 9 Am Cu 3 S.M. Bde tested night 17/18 Sept to distribute areas. 13th Manchesters and 8th Yorkshires Left trenches & camped night 18/18/15 Sept in Bois du WARNIMONT on his way back to his Division. Casualties OR killed 1, wounded 5. (La 3 Capt Profeit 8/ Yorkshires + 3 OR wounded)	
	19.9.15		4 hours destroyed. Casualties. OR killed 1, wounded 3.	
	20.9.15		Testing 9/ 3 S.M. Bde N.T.R. now complete for the present. Orders received to be prepared to move if necessary (III Army Conference). Casualties OR killed 1.	hours

Army Form C. 2118

WAR DIARY
or
INTELLIGENCE SUMMARY.
(Erase heading not required.)

Instructions regarding War Diaries and Intelligence Summaries are contained in F. S. Regs., Part II and the Staff Manual respectively. Title pages will be prepared in manuscript.

Place	Date	Hour	Summary of Events and Information	Remarks and references to Appendices
BUS-les-ARTOIS	21.9.15		Casualties. Lt. Finn S/Lne, accidentally wounded	
	22.9.15		Railhead changed from DOULLENS to AUTHIEULES from 23rd. Casualties O.R. wounded 4.	
	23.9.15		1/1st Warwicks to COURCELLES & SOUASTRE. Casualties O.R. wounded 2.	
	24.9.15		Traffic of Limbers east of BAYENCOURT & SAILLY stopped during daylight. Enemy taking rapes to form walls, poles & wicket suspended to each interval by wire in emergency in case of an advance. 1st Warwicks. Casualties included to Greame & Warwicks, to Walker & Warwicks O.R. wounded 1. 1st Warwicks (9 S.O.I.) to hospital. 1st Daventrye O.R. wounded. Double line of wire & entered posts just out, just new line from quest wood of FONQUEVILLERS to huts	
	25.9.15		of SAILLY; 2nd line BUS-ST. LEGER-TOUIN. Casualties O.R. killed 1, wounded 1.	
	26.9.15		Casualties – wounded 2 O.R.	
	27.9.15		Lt W. Roberts (Eng. Train) to hospital. Casualties Holcroft heid TH Moore S/Lne, ctr wounds killed 1, wounded 4, missing 1	
	28.9.15		Casualties. Other ranks wounded 3.	
	29.9.15		Casualties – Nil. 1/4th huf Bde relieved 145th huf Bde in trenches at HEBUTERNE 145th huf Bde moved: – S'Glouzestre to BUS; 4/OXF & Bucks to COURCELLES; Bucks Bn to COUIN; & 4/7 Berks to SOUASTRE.	6mis

Army Form C. 2118

WAR DIARY
or
INTELLIGENCE SUMMARY.

(Erase heading not required.)

Instructions regarding War Diaries and Intelligence Summaries are contained in F. S. Regs., Part II. and the Staff Manual respectively. Title pages will be prepared in manuscript.

Place	Date	Hour	Summary of Events and Information	Remarks and references to Appendices
BUS-LES-ARTOIS	30.9.15		Casualties – NIL.	Apps

1577 Wt.W10791/1773 500,000 1/15 D. D. & L. A.D.S.S./Forms/C. 2118.

48th Known

121/3844

Head Quarters (A×Q) 48th Division

Oct 15

"A" & "Q" BRANCH - HEADQUARTERS 48th (SOUTH MIDLAND) DIVISION
—o—o—o—o—o—o—o—o—o—o—o—o—o—o—o—o—o—o—o—o—o—o—o—o—o—o—o—o—o—o—o—o—o—o—o—

FROM 1 - 10 - 15.   TO 31 - 10 - 15.

VOLUME Vll.

Army Form C. 2118.

WAR DIARY
or
INTELLIGENCE SUMMARY.
(Erase heading not required.)

Instructions regarding War Diaries and Intelligence Summaries are contained in F. S. Regs., Part II. and the Staff Manual respectively. Title pages will be prepared in manuscript.

Place	Date	Hour	Summary of Events and Information	Remarks and references to Appendices
Bus-les-ARTOIS	1.10.15		Casualties OR wounded 6	
	2.10.15		Casualties OR wounded 1.	
	3.10.15		Casualties OR wounded 2.	
	4.10.15		Casualties; wounded Temp/Lieut E.C. Sladen 5th Warwicks; OR 5.	
	5.10.15		Conference at Bri'Hq	
			4/Berks from SOUASTRE to AUTHIE	
	6.10.15		Casualties OR wounded 1	
			Casualties OR wounded 1.	
	7.10.15		Casualties Killed 1 OR. Wounded Lieut T.C.M. Badgeley 6/9 Gloster & 15 OR. Capt A.L. Chandler, 6th	
			Gloster 48th Division commenced attachment to A+QMS Branch Hqs. for instruction in Staff duties.	
	8.10.15		Casualties OR wounded 3	
	9.10.15		Casualties OR Killed 4 wounded 5	
			2/2 Ldn F.A. Bde (36th Division) arrived for attachment; camped at THIEVRES.	
	10.10.15		Casualties OR Killed 1 wounded 5.	
			10th R. Irish Rifles & 15th Bn R. Irish Rifles (36th Division) arrived for attachment; encamped at COUIN.	
	11.10.15		Casualties OR wounded 2.	
			10 & 15 R. Irish Rifles moved to Trenches for instruction	

Army Form C. 2118

WAR DIARY
or
INTELLIGENCE SUMMARY.
(Erase heading not required.)

Instructions regarding War Diaries and Intelligence Summaries are contained in F. S. Regs., Part II. and the Staff Manual respectively. Title pages will be prepared in manuscript.

Place	Date	Hour	Summary of Events and Information	Remarks and references to Appendices
BUS-LES ARTOIS	12.10.15		Casualties, OR 3 wounded.	
	13.10.15		121st & 150th Field Co. R.E. (36th Division) arrived for training under 7th Corps. 1 killed & 1 wounded at ARROUSES. 122nd	
	14.10.15		Casualties OR wounded 8 (incl. 6 in 15th R. Irish Rifles, attached). One section of 50th Siege Battery arrived at BUS (2-6" guns)	
	15.10.15		Casualties NIL.	
	16.10.15		Casualties NIL. Railhead changed from DOULLENS to MONDICOURT.	
	17.10.15		Casualties: OR 1 killed 3 wounded (incl. 2 of 15th R Ir Rifles attached.) Casualties NIL.	
	18.10.15		10th & 15th R.I. Rifles from trenches to camp at COUIN. Casualties wounded Lt Winterbottom 11th S.Glo.R.gt.; OR. wounded 7. Attached (22nd Bde R.F.A) wounded OR. 3.	
	19.10.15		10th & 15th R.I. Rifles from COUIN returned to 36th Division. 9th R.I.F. arrived at COUIN, to attachment; also 108th Fd. Ho. (Brig. Gen'l. Hackett-Payne). 9th R.I.F. and 13 R.I. Rifles arrived 12th Fd. Co. RE from ARQUEUES to VAUCHELLES. Casualties Capt J N Trethe 4/Oxfords killed. OR 1 killed 2 wounded. 144th Inf Bde. relieved 145th in HEBUTERNE sector. 9th R.I.F. & 13th R.I.R. to trenches to instruction. 2nd Lieut. F. A. Isle taft.	

Army Form C. 2118.

WAR DIARY
or
INTELLIGENCE SUMMARY.
(Erase heading not required.)

Place	Date	Hour	Summary of Events and Information	Remarks and references to Appendices
BUS-les-ARTOIS	20.10.15		Casualties OR. Killed 1 Wounded 2	
	21.10.15		1/4th London Bde R.F.A. (36th Divn) arrived; billeted at THIEVRES. Casualties. Killed 1 Sergeant 8/standards. OR. killed (accidental) 1, wounded 2.	
	22.10.15		Casualties NIL. wounded OR. wounded one	
	23.10.15		Casualties OR. Wounded 2 (incl. 1 R.I. Fus attached).	
	24.10.15		Casualties NIL.	
	25.10.15		9th R.I.Fus & 13th R.I.Rifles from Trenches & Camp at COUIN. Casualties – NIL.	
	26.10.15		Ammunition Railhead moved from FLESSELLES to AUTHIEULE, and Sub-Park Wells from TALMAS to ORVILLE. 10th R.I.Fus & 14th R.I.Rifles reached Dist Area (Corps) to night 9.26/27 at COUIN. 9th R.I.F. & 13th R.I.R., & HQr. 108th Inf. Bde left the area, marching to BEAUVAL. Casualties – OR. 1 wounded.	
	27.10.15		10th R.I.Fus & 14th R.I.R. & Trenches at HEBUTERNE & FONQUEVILLERS respectively for attachment & training. 145th Inf. Bde relieved 146th in Trenches. Casualties – OR. wounded 1.	

Army Form C. 2118.

WAR DIARY
or
INTELLIGENCE SUMMARY.
(Erase heading not required.)

Place	Date	Hour	Summary of Events and Information	Remarks and references to Appendices
BUS-les-ARTOIS	28.10.15		Casualties OR wounded 3.	
	29.10.15		46th Bde RGA arrived at AUTHIE. Casualties - OR wounded 3 (incl. 1 R.I.R & 10"R.I.Fus).	
	30.10.15		Casualties OR killed 1 (1"S.M.R.T.A,R.A) wounded 1.	
	31.10.15		17"(H) Bde RGA Headquarters arrived, camped between BUS & AUTHIE. 46"(H) Bde RGA arrived, camped between BUS & AUTHIE. 3"Lnd.Bde.R.F.A left Div"area. Casualties wounded 2Lt E.L Chadwick (accidentally), 1. OR (attached -14"R.I.Rifles)	hm²

M Pompe
Lieut-Col.
A.A. & Q.M.G. 48th (S.M.) Division.

48th Division

WAR DIARY.
o-o-o-o-o-o-o-o-o

"A" & "Q" BRANCH - HEADQUARTERS 48th (SOUTH MIDLAND) DIVISION.

FROM 1 - 11 - 15.   TO 30 - 11 - 15.

Vol VIII

Army Form C. 2118.

WAR DIARY
or
INTELLIGENCE SUMMARY.
(Erase heading not required.)

Instructions regarding War Diaries and Intelligence Summaries are contained in F. S. Regs., Part II. and the Staff Manual respectively. Title pages will be prepared in manuscript.

Place	Date	Hour	Summary of Events and Information	Remarks and references to Appendices
BUS-les-ARTOIS	1915 1 Nov.		Casualties - O.R. Killed 1, wounded 2 (not rep. inspected) - all accidental.	
	2 "		10" R. Irish Fus. & 14 R. Ir. Rifles left trenches & camped at COUIN. Casualties - NIL.	
	3 "		10" R. Irish Fus. & 14 R. Ir. Rifles left Div" area - marched to BEAUVAL. Casualties - NIL.	
	4 "		144th Bde relieved 145th in HEBUTERNE sector. Casualties; wounded Lieut R.C. Lowe 6" Warwicks, O.R. 1.	
	5 "		Casualties O.R. 5 wounded.	
	6 "		Casualties O.R. wounded 1.	
	7 "		Casualties - Accidentally wounded Capt P.S. Tomkinson 5 Otr. 7/Worc.kyr. Casualties. wounded O.R. 2.	
	8 "		121st Co R.E. arrived VAUCHELLES & AR QUEVES. 17 (H) Fd. Amb. R.A.M.C. began hire from BUS-AUTHIE and camp at ST. LEGER. 15" (H) M.G. Lfs 14" Div" area. Casualties - NIL.	
	9 "		Casualties - O.R. wounded 2.	
	10 "		Railhead changed from MONDICOURT to DOULLENS.	
	11 "		Casualties. O.R. wounded 1.	

WAR DIARY or INTELLIGENCE SUMMARY.

Army Form C. 2118.

Place	Date	Hour	Summary of Events and Information	Remarks and references to Appendices
BUS-les- ARTOIS	1915 12 Nov		Casualties - O.R. wounded 4.	
	13.		14:15 hrs. Bde relieved 14th in trenches, HEBUTERNE Sector. Casualties wounded OR 1.(accidentally) injured (tree felling) OR 3.	
	14.		Casualties OR wounded 1.	
	15.		13th R.I. Rifles arrived in Div lines. to attachment, encamped at COUIN night 15/11/15. 12 R.I.Rifles moved for attachment - marched direct to FONQUEVILLERS, encamped in tents (four companies in tents at BAYENCOURT) { Capt Fairclough attached 7th D.G., Capt Petters 10th Lancers, 2 Lt Gregson 20th Hrs., all from Indian Cavalry Corps, attached for instruction, for 1 month. Casualties - NIL.	
	16.		13' R.I.R. from COUIN to HEBUTERNE Sector, for attachment to 145th Inf Bde. Casualties - NIL.	
	17.		Casualties O.R. 3 wounded (incl. 1 accidentally, & 1 R.I. Rifles attached). One case of Trench Feet	
	18.		Casualties O.R. wounded 1 (attached - accidentally wounded).	
	19.		Four Officers of 16th Div joined for instruction, attached as follows: - To 143 Inf Bde Lt Col Williams & R Munster Fus & Capt J.C. Brown 8 R. Irish Fus. To 145 Inf Bde. Lt Col Downing 8 R. Munster Fus & Lt Col Corkett 11th Hampshire Pioneers. Casualties. OR. wounded (13 R.I. Rifles) 1.	

Army Form C. 2118.

WAR DIARY
or
INTELLIGENCE SUMMARY.
(Erase heading not required.)

Instructions regarding War Diaries and Intelligence Summaries are contained in F. S. Regs., Part II. and the Staff Manual respectively. Title pages will be prepared in manuscript.

Place	Date	Hour	Summary of Events and Information	Remarks and references to Appendices
BUS-LES-ARTOIS	1915. 20 Nov.		144th Bde relieved 145th in trenches, HEBUTERNE sector.	
	21 "		Casualties. NIL.	
	22 "		Casualties. NIL.	
	23 "		Casualties. Wounded Capt Wilson-Sharpe & 2 OR. Also 1 OR. accidentally.	
			Casualties. Killed Temp/Lieut C.E. Schurhsu 1/6 Glouc Rgt. Wounded and 1 OR. Wounded 7 Other ranks (incl 2 attached) 1 Rfleld 1 accidentally).	
	24 "		Casualties - Killed one - wounded 2. attached 12th RB Riflemen wounded 1. 2/Lt BOYCE MANNING left	
	25 "		Casualties - NIL. 12th & 13th R B Rifles on extension of attachment for training joined 3 6 ORs from B3 13 & R74.	
	26 "		Casualties. Killed Capt. P.G. IRVINE. 6/Glouc Wounded 2/Lt J.M.C. BADGELEY and 2/Lt	
			TT PRYCE both 6 Glouc also Other ranks Killed 1 wounded 23 missing 1 or 2	
			6/Glouc Regt During a successful night enterprise against the German trenches night 25/26	
	27 "		20 and 21st Bttns. MANCHESTER REGT entered our line and encamped at COUIN	
	28th "		2 Offrs + 12 NCOs proceeded to WISQUES for instruction in Lewis Machine Gun. Casualties Wounded 6	
			20 and 21st Battn. MANCHESTER'S proceeded to trenches for Instruction. Casualty Wounded 2	
	29th "		Casualties wounded 1 - 2 B/6 Bde BOR left for course of Instruction 3rd Army French Mortar School.	
	30th "		Casualties. Killed 5th R Warwicks Lt. HUDSON. Lt. Col SMYTH-OSBORNE A/AQMG joined for duty	

F.O. 1st Dr. (A+P)
S29/Vol IX.

121/7930

WAR DIARY 48th Div. (A-Q)
or
INTELLIGENCE SUMMARY

Army Form C. 2118.

Place	Date	Hour	Summary of Events and Information	Remarks and references to Appendices
BUS-LES-ARTOIS	December 1915 1st		Casualties Nil. The recent severe weather and heavy rains have caused much damage to the roads in the Brit. Area. Sappers being much to repair the traffic. Repairs difficult owing to shortage of metalling. Instructions issued to Bde Commanders as to necessity for clearing drains &	DRO 183(2)
"	2nd		Casualties Nil. Notice received from 7th Corps that owing to the Priest Service being dependent on tides must service will be irregular.	
"	3rd		Casualties. 4/Oxfords hired 4 horses 2.	
"	4th		Casualties. 8/Warwicks K.1. 6/Glos Accidentally injured by local Superior 2. 20th & 21st Batts.	
"	5th (Sunday)		MANCHESTER Regt (30th Div) at separation of Trench Training have finished for COLIN Camps. 1/10 London Batt (56th Div) on conclusion of Training leave Divisional Area. Casualties. 1 SM. 2t Coy RE W.1. 4/R Berks W.2. 20th & 21st Manchester Regt leave Bde Area 202 Fd Coy RE (30th Div) arrive for Training —	
"	6th		Casualties. 2/1 SM N Coy RE W.2. 4/Ox + 3Bucks 2 D. W.1. 5/Gloster W.1. 144 Inf Bde relieve 145th Bde in trenches. Billeting Officers arrive for instructions as follows: Offrs from EDWARDS COVGRAPH Col MOSS to 144 Bde. Col GREG Col DICKSON 143 Bde.	
"	7th		Casualties. 2/1 N Coy RE K.1. 8/Worc W.1. 16 +17th Batt MANCHESTERS arrive for training and camp at COLIN.	

Army Form C. 2118.

WAR DIARY
or
INTELLIGENCE SUMMARY.
(Erase heading not required.)

Place	Date	Hour	Summary of Events and Information	Remarks and references to Appendices
BUS-LES-ARTOIS	DEC 1915 8th		Casualties. 4/9th Line W.I. 6/9th Line W.I. 7/Home W.I. 16th Manchesters W. 1/7th F. DEHIGENS and Lt. P.J. MEAD (latter at duty) other ranks W.1 (at duty). Owing to severe lostage arising from accidental injuries inclusion been issued that COs have to furnish a written report concerning they occur.	SROS 189.
"	9th		Casualties. 6/9th Line W.4. 8/Home K.1. 16th Manchesters wounded to field hosp., other ranks W.4. 5/R. Sussex W.1 (at duty.) Lt/Col WEBBER GSO1 30th Div arrived for attachment to 11th Bn.	
"	10th		Casualties 16th Manchesters W.5 including 2 slightly at duty	
"	11th		Casualties 16th Manchesters W.1.	
SW	12th (SUNDAY)		Casualties. 7/Home K.1. 8/Home W.2 including (1 at duty). Pamphlet COS 307 "Defensive Measures against Gas Attack" issued. The 7th Corps Commander congratulates the Division on the success in repelling the Hunny of last March Feb 9/ 166 & 2 3/12/15 ann the of contaminated	7F Corps
"	13th		Casualties. 17th Manchesters killed 2nd Lt — R.C. JOHNSTON. 7/Home W.1. A division of importance affecting the re-engagement of time expired men in former units today had been 9/The T.F. sending re-enlistment of 9 M.T. ASC who they receive AS rate of pay and lost the Special rates subnets appears to re-enlists him.	
"	14th		Casualties. 7 Warwicks. W. Lt. A.C. DUMAS. 145 Bn. return 144 lost in the Trenches. 16 & 17th Manchesters have trenches. 17th Bn to camp COUN. 16 Bn 3 Coys to LOUVENCOURT 1 Coy to Mill-street farm	ISRO 194.
			St. LEGER (British).	

WAR DIARY or INTELLIGENCE SUMMARY

Army Form C. 2118.

Place	Date	Hour	Summary of Events and Information	Remarks and references to Appendices
BUS LES ARTOIS	1915 Dec. 15th		Cavalletti. 4/R Berks K.1 N.2 (including 1 at duty). Bucks B.n W.1. 117 men from Jackson Examined as to Explication as munition workers. 22 have taken from this Division and sent to HAVRE. All to go for list. 16th & 17th Manchesters have been transferred from on exclusion of these training.	
	16		Cavalletti. 1/Warwick Battn 3" S.M F.A Bde K.1. 2 Battys 149th F.A Bde billet at THIEVRES on arrival for training.	
	17th		Cavalletti. 7/Warwick Regt W.1. 18th & 19th Battn Liverpool Regt arrive for training. 18th + 3 Coys 18th Bde billet LOUVENCOURT. 1 Coy StLEGER. 19th to Camp COIN.	
	18th		Cavalletti. 7/Warwick Regt W.2. Berks Bn W.1. 22 selected members taken forward to HAVRE thro arm. for list.	
	19th		Cavalletti. 2" S.M F.A Bde W.1. Accidentally	
	20th		Cavalletti. M.G. 202 Field Coy R.E billeting LOUVENCOURT left Bn. Area on conclusion of training.	
	21st		Cavalletti. 5/Glouc Regt W.1. 18th Liverpools ditto same K.1. 19th Liverpool W.1.	
	22"		Cavalletti. nil.	
	23		Cavalletti. Lt R.A. LEIGHTON 7 hrs wounded (since dead) 10th Liverpool attached Bge wounded	
	24t		Capt E.B. BEAZELEY. 1/Worwar Other ranks 4. K other ranks 1. Melanie. W.17. Cavalletti. 1/1 S.M Field Coy R.E W.1. 6/Warwick Regt W.1. 7/Warr. W.3	

Army Form C. 2118.

WAR DIARY
or
INTELLIGENCE SUMMARY.
(Erase heading not required.)

Instructions regarding War Diaries and Intelligence Summaries are contained in F. S. Regs., Part II. and the Staff Manual respectively. Title pages will be prepared in manuscript.

Place	Date	Hour	Summary of Events and Information	Remarks and references to Appendices
BUS-LES-ARTOIS	1914 Dec.			
SUNDAY	25"		Casualties. 8/Warwicks K.1. 2/Glouc W.1. Drafts arrived 9/November 20. 5/November 20.	
	26"		Casualties. 3/SM FA Rdn W.1. 4/Glouc W.1. 6/Glouc K.1. W.6. 5/R Sussex W.1. 17/76 R.F.A. W.4	
	27"		Casualties. 5/Warwicks W.1. (at duty). 4/Glouc W.2. self inflicted	
	28"		Casualties. 7/Warwicks W.1. 86th Trench Mortar Battery W.1. (Slightly at duty). 145 Bde relieved 144 Bde in HEBUTERNE and SAILLY. Troop billeted 149 Bde R.F.A. Divn Dist Area on conclusion of Training – Hostile Aeroplane observed over in vicinity of Divl. HQ. No damage to personnel.	
	29"		Casualties. 7/Worc W.1. (Slightly at duty). 4/Oxf. Killed Lt. F.D. DOYNE. 1/Bucks Lt. W.1. Some rough covered [indecipherable] forming 2 km abt 6'6" × 2'6" which have been sent out to certain units by troops in trenches are found to have been of great assistance to the Troops billeted in trenches. They offer the following advantages. Increased warmth, economy of straw and better cleanliness. The features being cavity classified in the trench [indecipherable].	
	30"		Casualties. 5/Glouc W.1. RHA. 4/Oxford W.1. 1/Bucks W.1 slightly at duty – All horses in the Division to be subjected to the Mallein Test which was commenced to-day.	
	31st		Casualties. 86th Trench Mortar Battery W.1 accidentally. A footprint by the Army (cannot to arrange the Recon Parks and arr. supplies from Railhead by Horse Transport (These effecting economy and [indecipherable] of motor during the Winter) When an errand is impracticable, Horses however considered. It is estimated that about 110 waggons from the Parks expect be required to carry on the Scheme for this Division duty. M. Rhonel Mayor. D.A.A. & Q.M.G. 48th (S.M.) Division

1577 Wt.W10791/1773 500,000 1/15 D.D. & L. A.D.S.S./Forms/C. 2118.

489 in. (A+Q) $\frac{\text{ton}}{\text{vol.}}\left|\frac{X}{e}\right|$

ORIGINAL

Army Form C. 2118.

HQ. 48th Div WAR DIARY (A and Q Branch).
or
INTELLIGENCE SUMMARY.
(Erase heading not required.)

Instructions regarding War Diaries and Intelligence Summaries are contained in F. S. Regs., Part II. and the Staff Manual respectively. Title pages will be prepared in manuscript.

Place	Date 1916	Hour	Summary of Events and Information	Remarks and references to Appendices
BOIS-LES-ARTOIS (SATURDAY)	Jan 1st		Casualties 7/Warwicks W.2. 4/Oxf & Bucks L.I. K.3. W.3. 3rd Sm FA Bde W.1. The New Year opens with a continuance of the heavy rains which have fallen incessantly for the past 4 weeks. Roads have been greatly cause considerable anxiety, about the worse in the Bde Area which has become much damaged owing to the heavy traffic over them in the wet weather. Neither labour or material is available in sufficient quantities to repair and maintain the roads. Much good work has been done by the detachment of the 3rd Lowland Bde F.E. A system of block system to govern the traffic moving over our division has been introduced forbids on several roads and has worked well. This enables vehicles to keep to the known metalled portion of the road and saves the heaving army which is found to injure them, vehicles from each other. The section are about 3/4 mile in length and are worked by control posts provided with a telephone or signalling flags.	
(SUNDAY)	Jan 2		Casualties 1/2 S Mid Field Coy RE W.2. No 2 Coy 48 Div Train W.1. 6/Warwicks W.1. 7/Warwicks W.1. 8/Warwicks W.1. R Sussex W.2.	
	Jan 3rd		Casualties 7/Warwicks W.1 Slightly at duty. 4 Ox & Bucks L.I. W.1. 1/6 Lt Bn Blue Regiment W.5 in the Trenches 1/R + 23 OR K 3r Army Trench Mortar School Valenciennes in accordance with the scheme for completing each trg. Bn to 2 Light Mortar Batteries and 1 medium Batty.	
	Jan 4		Casualties 8/Worc R W.1. K 7. W.8.	

Army Form C. 2118.

48th Inf — P.Q. Branch

WAR DIARY or INTELLIGENCE SUMMARY.

(Erase heading not required.)

Place	Date	Hour	Summary of Events and Information	Remarks and references to Appendices
BUS-LES-ARTOIS	1916 Jan 5th		Casualties. 4/Glouc R. W.2. Offrs have asked this day for the formation of Brigade Machine Gun Coys. Reinforcements for the replacement of the Warwicks (Vickers) withdrawn from Bns. have been received and are now used. Transp- Officers report difficulties in finding transport people - Infantry - other units. 2nd Lancashire fusiliers on attachment from 36th Bn arrived and billeted at Sarton.	
	Jan 6th		Casualties. 8/Warwicks W.2. (shell shock). 7/Worc K.1, W.9 (including 4 accidental). 2nd Lanc Fus (private ...) H.Q. + 2 Coys SAILLY. 2 Coys LA HAYE Farm. 1st Kings Own Royal Lanc Regt. 36th Bn arrived for attachment + billeted at LOUVENCOURT.	
	Jan 7th		Casualties. 8/Warwicks W.7 (including 4 from shell shock). With a view of affording recreation to men in rest billetty arrangements are being made to institute a variety troupe in the Division. This will visit the various towns and shelters which have been arranged or constructed as Recreation Rooms. An inter-unit football cup has also been provided by Major General French's comdg the Division and the two commanding Officers.	
	Jan 8th		Casualties. 8/Warwicks W.2.	
	SUNDAY Jan 9th		Casualties. 17th Bn R.G.A W.1. 9th Lond Inf Warwick W.1. The Bishop of BIRMINGHAM visited the division and held a service at THIÈVRES and BAYENCOURT	
	Jan 10th		Casualties. 5/SUSSEX W.2. accidentally. General Sir D.Haig Com'C visited the Division to day. Withers ?	

D.A.A.& Q.M.G. 48th (S.M.) Division

Army Form C. 2118.

HQ Corps

WAR DIARY HQ France
or
INTELLIGENCE SUMMARY.
(Erase heading not required.)

Place	Date 1916	Hour	Summary of Events and Information	Remarks and references to Appendices
BUS LES-ARTOIS	Jan 11.		Casualties: Bar M.G. Coy 143 Bde. W.1 (Shell Shock). 4/OX + Bucks W.1.	
	Jan 12.		Casualties: 4th S.M. FA. Bde W.1. shrapnel in arm. W/R Berks W.1.	
	Jan 13.		Casualties: 5th Warwick W.2. W/R Berks W.1. 4/Oxford & Bucks 1/L.K.1. W.4. 6/Gloucester 1/K.1.	
	" 14.		Casualties: Nil. Lecture at 7 Corps H.Q. Demons from LOOS "A" forming div. G.O.C. 5th A.A. Q.M.G. + 1 A.D.C. to England to be decorated. Brig Gen James 143" Inf Bde assumes command of Div. during absence of G.O.C. Exchange of 5" Hows for 4.5" Hows completed & reported to 7 Corps. L. Col. BATES A.D.B. Remounts W.O. and Sir Meredith Barnwell I.G.R. due at THIEVRES. Inspects horses of D.A.C.	
	" 15.		Casualties: 2/1st P.M. Fusiliers - 86 Trench Mortar Batty wounded. (details on duty) O.R.1. 4 Oxford & Bucks - W.1. A D O S 7 Corps inspects Bands, Grenade Stores - Adjt LEA. Scott Corps. 143 Inf Bde joins AQ JHQ for instruction. One Horse shown re-action Mallein Test.	
	" 16.		Casualties: 8 Worc Regt - W.2. Inspection of Div Train. Transport waggons by B.R.A.M.C. at Commencement. Scheme for drawing supplies from railhead by horse transport worked out + orders issued. Officer i/c 4 RA Courses arr 4th Army School :=	
	" 17.		Casualties: 7 Worc Regt: W 2. = 4 Glos Rgt. W. 1. 7R War R. W. 2. Tour of Horse Transport carried out. DOULLENS to dumps LOUVENCOURT, SLEGGER 9½ miles = 10 minutes 4 to 8 miles. Gen Jenkinson = S.S.D.W. + Col Cockram G.S.O.1 Signals attached for instr. RA. LOOS & Isères.	Malcolm Maj Genl H.Q. III Army.

1577 Wt. W10791/1773 500,000 1/15 D. D. & L. A.D.S.S./Forms/C. 2118.

Army Form C. 2118.

49th Div HQ Branch

WAR DIARY HQ Branch

or

INTELLIGENCE SUMMARY.

(Erase heading not required.)

Instructions regarding War Diaries and Intelligence Summaries are contained in F. S. Regs., Part II. and the Staff Manual respectively. Title pages will be prepared in manuscript.

Place	Date	Hour	Summary of Events and Information	Remarks and references to Appendices
BUS-LES-ARTOIS	18.1.16		Casualties - NIL -. 2nd Lieut JEUDWYN and 2/Lt COCKRANE - leave -. Col. US FRANCE, COL. MAJ. GORDON STEWARD. L/Col. W.G. WALKER - MAJ. STEWARD. Lt. Col. S.D. GORDON arrived for attachment from 66 DIV.	
	19.1.16		Second day of Transport Test. having horse transport -. Trench Mortar Personnel 80, 82, 109 Bde. from VALHEUREUX -. Transport come HAVRE. Casualties - 7 Worc Regt. 1 W accidentally -. RA personnel 80.82 BdeT M to 3rd Army School. with 1-2" and 1-1½" Trench Mortars -. Grenade Stores inspected - AUTHIE, ST LEGER -. Chaff cutting machine wanted at COIGNEUX.	
	20.1.16		Casualties - 4th S.M.R & A. 1 Hun B.R. K.I. - 6 Glos Rgt. 1. W. 1. Self inflicted - 7 Wor Rgt 1 W. Infantry Personnel of 82 T.M.R.Bt returned to units. 16 Essex Rfk. 1/ Kings Own -. 1-2" TM reported to School H Army.	
	21.1.16		Casualties - 6 Glos Rgt W. 1. Col. GORDON - Col. FRANCE, MAJ. WALKER, CO. STEWARD leave for HAVRE -. Remounts 151. arrived -. Reinforcements 500 arrived -. Col LIVESAY, C/M BULLOCK from Course BEAUVAL in RA. return -.	
	22.1.16		Casualties - 6 G.R. War Rgt W. 1. - Bucks Rgt W. 1. - 22 MG Course. WISQUES, parties sent to DOULLENS STN -.	
	23.1.16		Casualties - 8.R. War Rgt. W. 2 - 4 Pontoons. K. 1. Senior Officers Course RA commenced at BEAUVAL.	

Wegner-Moy Capt
for

Army Form C. 2118.

48th Div.

WAR DIARY
or
INTELLIGENCE SUMMARY.
(Erase heading not required.)

Place	Date	Hour	Summary of Events and Information	Remarks and references to Appendices
BUSLES. ARTOIS	24.1.16		Casualties - 4 Oxfords W.1. 4 Berks. W.2 -. G.O.C. D.A.Q.M.G. returned from leave. G.S.O.I proceeded on leave.	
	25.1.16		Casualties: 5/R Warwick W.1. 8/R Warwick K.2. W.9. 5/Glouc K.1.	
	26.1.16		Casualties: 8/R Warwick W.2. /Bucks Batt. K. 2/Lt R.B. Furley. 2/Lt R.B. Furley. 2nd Gen. Two self-inflicted W.1.	
	27.1.16		Casualties. Nil. No news yet of capture of the gas alarm was given two nights about 7pm. The man was thought to be suffering from gas poisoning. It is thought that the gas was generated by the action of urine on chloride of lime which contains iron was put by the 3rd Army for export. 144 Pdrs relieved 145 Brigade in the Trenches.	
	28.1.16		Casualties: 7/R Warwick R. W.2. 4/Glouc R W.1. 8/R Warwick W.3. 6/Glouc R.K.1. 7/WorcR W.1. RR Returned of 95a and 100th T.M. Batteries returned from 3rd Army Trench School	
	29.1.16		Casualties: 7/R Warwick R. W.1. 4/Glouc R. W.2.	
	30.1.16		Casualties: 4/Glouc W.2 - 6/Glouc K.4 (including 2 at duty) - 5/Glouc W.3 (including 1 at duty and 1 accidental) - 7/Worc R attached 89° T.M. Batt. W.1 at duty - 8 Worc R.K.1 - 1st R Bde MG Coy W.1 accidentally.	
	31.1.16		Casualties: 5 R Warwick K.2 including one slight at duty. 5/Worc R W.1.	

(signature)

A.Q. 48th Div:
Vol: XI

Army Form C. 2118.

48th WAR DIARY or INTELLIGENCE SUMMARY.
(Erase heading not required.)

Instructions regarding War Diaries and Intelligence Summaries are contained in F.S. Regs., Part II. and the Staff Manual respectively. Title pages will be prepared in manuscript.

Place	Date	Hour	Summary of Events and Information	Remarks and references to Appendices
BUS-LES-ARTOIS	1916			
	1-2-16		Casualties. 4th S.M. Fd. Bde. K1. W1 — 7R/Warwicks W1 (accidental).	
	2-2-16		Casualties 7R/Warwicks W1. — 8R/Warwick W2 accidentally — 6/Glos W 2/4th F.D. Rgmrs. Other	
			Ranks W 3 — 143 Bde relieve 144 Bde in HEBUTERNE Trenches.	
	3-2-16		Casualties. 8/Worc R. W1 accidental. Consequent on the forthcoming interview of the	
			4th Div from the line following moves take place. Enemy. 6/Glos R COUR to LOUVENCOURT	
			(1st Relief.) 144 Bde MG Coy COUR to BUS, No.100 TM Batty COUR-BUS. 1/Kings Own R	
			(12th Bde) attached 48 (Div) transferred to 48 Div moves from LOUVENCOURT to HEBUTERNE	
COLINCAMPS				
	4-2-16		Casualties Nil. Enemy moves into line. 1st trench party from HEADQUARTERS to BERTRANCOURT	
			2/1st Bus attached from SAULTY and LA HAIE to BERTRANCOURT on relieving 12th Bde.	
			HQ 5/R Sussex from ST. LEGER - SAULTY.	
	5-2-16		Casualties. S/R Warwick W.H. 7R/Warwick 1. 6/R Warwick W1 (accidental). 6R/Warwick (attached	
			143rd T.M. Batty) W1. 4/R Berks W1. 1Kings Own W1 K1. 48th Fd. Am. Col. and the	
			two Cos of 48th and 146th Heavy Battens R.G.A. moved from THIEVRES & ROUTHE	
	6-2-16		Casualties. - 6.R. War. Rgt. K1. W.1. 1st Kmp Own (Rodan. Rgt) W1. — Major Walsh G.S.O.H.Q. leaves to	
			take up appointment A.Q.M.G. 6 Div. — Lieut Ward. takes up duties of A.O.C. RA. 48 Div.	Newington C.M. becoming 48 Div.

WAR DIARY or INTELLIGENCE SUMMARY

Army Form C. 2118.

Place	Date	Hour	Summary of Events and Information	Remarks and references to Appendices
BUS-LES-ARTOIS	1916			
	7.2.16		Casualties – 2 Essex. W.1. – 4" Div: laTke over COUIN. – 1 Batt: 4.5 How: from 37" Bde: joined.	
	8.2.16		Casualties: – 4 Oxford & Bucks. W.2 – 2" Essex Rgt. W.1. – Brig Gen Godley 3 Reserve Bde Lt Col: W.J. Douglas 3/8 R.War: Rgt: + du Col: W.K. Smith 3/4 Blackwatch – or CM W.A. Bourdon 1/5" D.C.L.I. Cut Vam: E.C.R. Hudson – Northern Command – Signalling Instructor – & Capt Russell R.F.A. No 2 Training School, Ripon, – attached for instruction.	
	9.2.16		Casualties 2. S.M. F.Coy RE. K.2. W.1. – 2 Lanc Fus. W.2 (acc) 4 Bucks. K.1. W.1. 5 Gloster. W.1.	
	10.2.16		Casualties – 1/4 2.S.M. Field Coy RE. W.1. – 6. R.War Rgt. K.2. W.4. – 6 Warr attached) 13" M.G. Coy – W.1. – 8. R.War Rgt. K.1. W.3. 5 Glosters Rgt. W.5. – 4 Bucks, W.3. – Kings Dragoon Guards. W.1. Capt V. J.W. Backhouse – Bucks Batt R. – 2" Lanc Fus: K.2. W.2. 2" Essex Rgt. W.1.	
	11.2.16		Casualties – 5" R.War. Rgt. W.1. – 8. R.War Rgt. W.2. – Bucks Bn K.1. W.2. – 4 Bedes W.4 – 4 Oxfords CAPT. I.E. GRIFFIN. W. OR. W.1. 5R. Sussex Rgt Lieut. C.A.M. BINGEN. K. – 1" Kings Own R. Lancaster Regt K.1. W.1. – 2" Essex Rgt. K.1. W.2. – 2 Duke of Wellingtons W.Riding Rgt. W.2. – 2 Lanc Fus: W.1. – 145²⁴ Bde M.G. Coy. K.4. W.1. – moves – 4"/21" Gloster Regt – AUTHIE to SOUASTRE. – Attached officers leave names enlisted on 8" instant. – refugee ballam send gent	

Army Form C. 2118.

WAR DIARY
or
INTELLIGENCE SUMMARY.
(Erase heading not required.)

Instructions regarding War Diaries and Intelligence Summaries are contained in F. S. Regs., Part II. and the Staff Manual respectively. Title pages will be prepared in manuscript.

Place	Date	Hour	Summary of Events and Information	Remarks and references to Appendices
	1916			
BUS-LES-ARTOIS.	12.2.16		Cassulies. — 2ⁿᵈ S.M.B.R.F.A. K.I.W.I. — 2ⁿᵈ DUKE of WELLINGTONS W.I — 5ᵗʰ GLOS: R/R. W.I — 4 OXFORDS. K.I.W.I. BUCKS BN-W.I. — 4ᵗʰ BERKS. W.2. — 5.R.WAR.R/R. W.I. — Moves. 9 ʳ R. SCOTS. BERTRANCOURT to BEAUQUESNE and FAMECHON to MONDICOURT. — 6ᵗʰ GLOS: R/R. LOUVENCOURT to S'AMAND. — COL. BAUMGARTNER. G.S.O.I proceeds to attend French manoeuvres —.	
	13.2.16		Cassulies. — S.R. WAR.R/R. W.I. — R.G.A. 86 T.M. Batt: W.I. — 5 GLOSTERS W.2 — BUCKS. W.I. 4 BERKS. W.2. — 1ˢᵗ K.R.O. OWN. W.I. — 2ⁿᵈ Duke of WELLINGTONS. W.6.-. — Moves —. 144 Bde. HQ. — BUS to BIENVILLERS —. 6 GLOSTERS. S'AMAND to trenches —. 7 WORC R/R. COURCELLES to trenches N. SECTOR, — 8 WORC R/R. BUS to BIENVILLERS...	
	14.2.16		Cassulies 7. R.WAR.Regt. W.4. — 5ᵗʰ CLOSTER Regt. W.I. — 4. BERKS. W.I. — 1ˢᵗ Kings OWN. W.I. — Moves. — Bt. Colonel. A. PEARCE - SEROCOLD 1/4 R. BERKS. Regt. to ENGLAND — Lt. Colonel. S. YOUNG ordered to proceed to ENGLAND on appointment A.D.M.S. 61ˢᵗ Division. —	
	15.2.16		Cassulies — 2ⁿᵈ Bn. R.F.A. 1. Wnd. — 8ᵗʰ Warc. Regt. — 8ᵗʰ Warc. Regt. att'd 144ᵗʰ Bn. M.G. Coy. 1. O.R. Wounded. Moves. Lt. Col. S. Young. R.A.M.C. left for ENGLAND. — 2 Coys. 145ᵗʰ Ind. Bde. to COURCELLES 1 Coy. 145ᵗʰ Ind. Bde. to SAILLY - AU - BOIS — 1 Coy. 145ᵗʰ Ind.Bde HEBUTERNE	

Army Form C. 2118.

WAR DIARY
or
INTELLIGENCE SUMMARY.
(Erase heading not required.)

Instructions regarding War Diaries and Intelligence Summaries are contained in F. S. Regs., Part II. and the Staff Manual respectively. Title pages will be prepared in manuscript.

Place	Date	Hour	Summary of Events and Information	Remarks and references to Appendices
BUS-LES- ARTOIS.	16.2.16.		Casualties – 2nd Essex Regt. 2 Killed, 6 Wnd. – Motor Div. Amm. Col. and 17th Heavy Bde. R.G.A. from AUTHIE to THIEVRES. 132 Coy. R.E. rejoin 37th Division – 9 Officers 350 O. Ranks 4th Entrenching Batn. move to SOUASTRE. – Railhead moved to LABRET.	
	17.2.16.		Casualties – 5th R. Warwickshire Regt. 1 Wnd. – 7th R. Warwickshire Regt. 1 Killed. – 2nd Essex Regt. 2 Wnd. – 11th Lowland Batty. R.G.A. and Nos. 3 & 4 Coys. 48th Div. Train moved to AUTHIE commenced.	
	18.2.16.		Casualties – 7th Warwick Regt. 1 Killed 7 Wnd. – R.G.A. attd 86th T.M. Batty. 1 Wnd. – 4th Gloster. Regt. Killed 1. Wnd 2. 8th Worc. Regt. Wnd. 6. Missing 12. – 8th Wores attd 144th Bde M.G. Coy. Killed 1. Wnd. 1. – 4th Berks Regt. Wnd. 2. – 2nd Essex Regt. Killed 2. Wnd. 3. Missing 1. – 2nd Seve. Pus. Killed 5. Wnd. 4. Missing 1. 85th T.M. Batty. Wnd. 2. Accidentally. Move. Detachment Indian Cav. Corps. 10 Officers 350 O Ranks arrived for work under 7th Corps.	
	19.2.16.		Casualties 7th R. Warwickshire Regt. Wnd. 1. 2nd Seve. Fusiliers. Killed 1. Wnd. 11. Missing 1. Move. Div. Train completed move AUTHIE. 2nd S.M. Fd. Amb. commence move LOUVENCOURT to SARTON. 1 Coy. 5th R. Sussex HERRISART – SOUASTRE 1 Coy. 5th R.S. under ARQUEVES – BERTRANCOURT – 2 Coys. 3rd Lob. Bn. R.E. BERTRANCOURT and SOUASTRE out of Div. Area. Cwt. 5.0 to SARTON.	

1577 Wt.W10791/1773 500,000 1/15 D. D. & L. A.D.S.S./Forms/C. 2118.

Army Form C. 2118.

WAR DIARY
or
INTELLIGENCE SUMMARY.
(Erase heading not required.)

Instructions regarding War Diaries and Intelligence Summaries are contained in F.S. Regs., Part II. and the Staff Manual respectively. Title pages will be prepared in manuscript.

Place	Date	Hour	Summary of Events and Information	Remarks and references to Appendices
BUS-LES ARTOIS	20.2.16		Casualties. 4/Gloucesters Wnd. 1. 8/Worcesters Wnd. 1. 2/Lancashire Fusiliers. Wnd. Capt. J. Collis-Browne. 2/Lieut. H. McNullan - O.R. Wnd. 19 - Killed 10. Missing believed killed 2/Lieut H.S. Carter. O.R. 17. 2nd Duke-Wellington's Regt. Wnd. Capt. E.G. Catacre O.R. 7. Wnd.	
			Move. Lieut. Colonel F. West to Senior A.A. course BEAUVAL.	
	21.2.16		Casualties. 5/Warwicks Wnd. 6. 4/Gloucesters Wnd. 1. Bucks Batn. Wnd. 1. (Slightly at duty) 1/King's Own. Wnd. 2/Lieut P.B. HERLD slightly at duty O.R. Wnd. 5. includes one slightly at duty.	
			Moves. 3rd S.M. Fld. Amb. NAUCHELLES to SOUASTRE. Motor Amb. Workshop NAUCHELLES to SARTON. 1/2 D. Coy. 3rd L&L Bn. R.E. SARTON to BUS - ST. LEGER (Corps Area)	
	22.2.16		Casualties. 7/Warwicks Wnd. 2. 6/Gloucesters Killed 1. Wnd. 1. 2nd Duke of Wellington's Wnd. 2. 2/Lancashire Fusiliers 5 of 17 O.R. reported Missing now reported killed.	
			Moves. Reinforcements arrived LOUVENCOURT 4.30 p.m. afternoon. 7/R. Warwicks 49 - 8/R. Warwicks 159. 4/Gloucesters 121 - 4/Oxford&Bucks 145 - Bucks Bn. 74 - 6/Gloucesters 131. - 1st S.M. M.G. Coy. R.E. 1 Man 6/Sussex Regt. 10 men.	
	23.2.16		Casualties. 4/Gloucesters. Wnd. accidentally. Moves. 107th T.M. Battery arrived COURCELLES. Later 91st 94th and 107th Trench Mortar Batteries moved to ORVILLE.	

1577 Wt. W10791/1773 500,000 1/15 D.D. & L. A.D.S.S./Forms/C. 2118.

Army Form C. 2118.

WAR DIARY
or
INTELLIGENCE SUMMARY.
(Erase heading not required.)

Instructions regarding War Diaries and Intelligence Summaries are contained in F. S. Regs., Part II. and the Staff Manual respectively. Title pages will be prepared in manuscript.

Place	Date	Hour	Summary of Events and Information	Remarks and references to Appendices
BUS-LES-ARTOIS	24.2.16		Casualties. 7th R. Warwicks. 1 Wnd. — 1st King's Own Regt. 1 Wnd. — 2nd Essex Regt. 1 Wnd. —	
	25.2.16		Move. No.4. Coy. 4th Divi. Train moved into AUTHIE for Supply of 12th Inf. Brigade. Casualties. 1st S.M. Bde. R.F.A. 1 Wnd. — 8th R. Warwickshire Regt. 1 Wnd. — 6th Gloucesters Wnd. 3. — 7th Warwicks. Wnd. 2. — 2/Lancashire Fusiliers Killed 1.	
	26.2.16		Move. Orders received for move of Divl. Hdqrs to COUIN. Casualties. 8/Warwicks Wnd. 2. 2/Lanc. Fus. Wnd. 2. Move. The Rev. Dr. Gwynn Deputy Chaplain General arrived.	
	27.2.16		Casualties. 8/R. Warwicks. Wnd. 2. 2/Lancashire Fus. Killed 1. Wnd. 2. 2nd Essex Wnd. 2. 1st K. Own. 2/Lieut. P.B. HERALD reported slightly wounded 21st now to hospital on account of wound.	
	28.2.16		Casualties. 4/Gloucesters. 1 Wnd. Move. Move of Div. Hdqrs. COUIN cancelled.	
	29.2.16		Casualties. 4th S.M. Bde. R.F.A. Killed 1. Wnd. 1. — 8th R. Warwicks Killed 1. Wnd. 3. — 4th Gloucesters Wnd. 1. — 4th Ox fd & Bucks. Wnd. 1. Moves. 144th Inf. Bde. relieved in the line by the 112th Inf. Bde. 37th Division & in future in relief — Bde. Hd. Qrs. Bde. M. G. Company 82nd and 100th Trench Mortar Batteries SOUASTRE. — 4th Gloucestershire Regt SOUASTRE — 6th Gloucesters SAILLY — 8th Worcestershire Regt. BUS.	

1577 Wt.W10791/1773 500,000 1/15 D. D. & L.   A.D.S.S./Forms/C. 2118.

WAR DIARY
or
INTELLIGENCE SUMMARY.

Army Form C. 2118.

Place	Date	Hour	Summary of Events and Information	Remarks and references to Appendices
BUS-LES-ARTOIS	29.2.16		Move (Cont) 7th Worcestershire Regt. 2 Companies SAILLY. Bn Hd. Qrs and 2 Companies COURCELLES. 3rd S.M.P.W. Coy. R.E. Hd. Qrs and 1 Sect. SOUASTRE. 2 Section ROSSIGNAL FME. 1 Section COIGNEAU. Operation Order received re. relief of 12th Inf. Bde. 4th Division by 144th Inf. Brigade.	

48

HQ A&Q 48 Dio
Vol XII

Army Form C. 2118.

48th Div. WAR DIARY A & Q. Rvannes.

or

INTELLIGENCE SUMMARY.

(Erase heading not required.)

Instructions regarding War Diaries and Intelligence Summaries are contained in F. S. Regs., Part II. and the Staff Manual respectively. Title pages will be prepared in manuscript.

Place	Date	Hour	Summary of Events and Information	Remarks and references to Appendices
BUS-LES-ARTOIS.	1.3.16		CASUALTIES. R.G.A. att'd 86 Inverness Coy. 1. Wnd. – 1st King's Own Regt. 1 Killed. Move. Orders re new Division Area Received – 8/War. Regt. arrived Bus.	
	2.3.16		CASUALTIES 1st King's Own. 1 Killed. 1 Wnd. – Move. None.	
Bus.Les.Artois.	3.3.16		Casualties A.S.C. att'd 1st Sn. Bde. R.F.A. Wnd.1. – 7th R. Warwicks Wnd.1. 1st King's Own Regt. Killed 1. Wnd. 6. Move. 1 Sect. 27th Res. Park A.S.C. Rossignal Ferme to Authieule – 1 Coy. 5/R. Sussex Bertrancourt to Bus. 143rd Inf. Bde. 1. Baln. Halloy to 2 Coys. Bayencourt to Souastre. 143rd Inf. Bde. 1st 2 in. Inv. (trans) Bayencourt – Souastre. 144th Inf. Bde. 1 Baln. Sailly to Invincible 1 Baln. Courcelles to Invincible 1 Baln. Bus to Colincamps. 1 Baln. Sailly to Courcelles — Transport (1st Arms). Bde. Hd.qrs + 2 Balns Souastre to Courcelles. Bde. M.G. Coy. and 2 Baln. Souastre to Bus. 145th Inf. Bde. 2 Balns. (1st line Transport) Bus to Bayencourt 2 Baln. (1st line transport) Courcelles to Bayencourt – R.E. 2nd S.M.Rd.Coy. R.E. Transport Rossignal to Souastre. 3rd Fd. Coy. R.E. 2 Rossignal to Courcelles and 2 Souastre to Colincamps — 48th Div. Supply Col. moved to Thievres by 5 wnt.	
Bus.Les.Artois	4.3.16		Casualties 7th Worcestershire Regt. Wnd. 2. –	

1577 Wt. W10791/1773 500,000 1/15 D. D. & L. A.D.S.S./Forms/C. 2118.

WAR DIARY or INTELLIGENCE SUMMARY

Army Form C. 2118.

Place	Date	Hour	Summary of Events and Information	Remarks and references to Appendices
BUS-LES-ARTOIS	4-3-16		Moved. 12th Inf. Bde. Left Division. 1 Battn. SAILLY to MONDICOURT 1 Battn. BERTRANCOURT to HALLOY. 35th and 111th T.M. Batty's to MONDICOURT from SAILLY. Machine Gun Coy. SAILLY to HALLOY. Bde. Hdqrs. BUSVASNE to COLINCAMPS to GRAHAS. 1st S.M. Fd Amb. completed move BERTRANCOURT - BUS. Headquarters and 1 Sect. 27th Res. Park A.S.C. from THIEVRES and ROSSIGNAL FME to AUTHIEULE - Detachment 4th Entrenching Battn. SOUASTRE to BAILLEMENT. 1/1 Lowland Heavy Batty. R.G.A. AUTHIE to GAUDIEMPRE. 114th Heavy Batty. R.G.A. THIEVRES to LA HERLIERE. Own Cos. accompanied batteries.
Casualties 8/R. Warwicks 1 killed 7th Worcesters Wnd. 1.	
	5-3-16		Moved. 7th Corps R.A. Signals Advanced Section left BUS.
Casualties 6/Gloucesters killed 1. 8/Worcesters killed 1.	
	6-3-16		Moved. 50th Seige Batty. R.G.A. SOUASTRE to ORVILLE. 9th West Riding Batty. R.F.A. 49th Div. to action in Div. Area. Waggon Lines ST. LEGER.	
	7-3-16		Casualties 6/Gloucesters Wnd. 3. 8/Warwicks Wnd. 2. Bucks Bn. Wnd. 3. 4/R. Berks Wnd. 1.
Moved. 1 off. 90. O.R. 2nd Lab. Bn. R.E. FRANVILLERS to SARTON.
Casualties R.F.A. 48th Div Am Col. att'd. 4th S.M. Bde. Captain. G.B. Lucas - Lucas. R.F.A. Wounded.	
	8-3-16		Moved. 4th Div. H'dqrs. left COUIN for WARLUZEL - 1 Coy. 3/Monmouth Pioneers arrived BUS. 46th Seige Batty. R.G.A. AUTHIE to COIGNEU and action. 2 Coys Battn. 143 Bde. BAYENCOURT to SOUASTRE. 1 Coy. 5/R. Sussex SOUASTRE - BAYENCOURT.	

Army Form C. 2118.

WAR DIARY
or
INTELLIGENCE SUMMARY.
(Erase heading not required.)

Instructions regarding War Diaries and Intelligence Summaries are contained in F.S. Regs., Part II. and the Staff Manual respectively. Title pages will be prepared in manuscript.

Place	Date	Hour	Summary of Events and Information	Remarks and references to Appendices
BUS-LES- ARTOIS			Moves (cont)	
	8.3.16.		"C" Batty R.M.A. (anti-aircraft) BERTRANCOURT and flowers —	
	9.3.16		Casualties R.F.A. 2nd M. Bde. Wnd. 1. 5th R/Warwicks Wnd. 1. — 8th R/Warwicks Wnd. 1. — 7/Warwicks Wnd. 5.	
			Move. 147 A.T. Coy. R.E. Leave area for WALINCOURT. —	
	10.3.16		Casualties 7th Warwicks Wnd. 5.	
	11.3.16		Casualties NIL	
			Move 25th Anti Aircraft Batty left BERTRANCOURT and from Divisional Area —	
	12.3.16		Casualties R.F.A. 4th PM Bde. Wnd. 2. 3rd S.M. Bde. Killed 3. Wnd. 1. 4/R.Berks. Wnd. 1.	
			Move. 1 Coy. 5/R Sussex BUS to SAILLY.	
	13.3.16		Casualties. R.E. and 48th Div. Sig. Coy. Wnd. 1. — 8th R.Warwicks Wnd. 1. — 4th Gloucester Wnd. 1. 8/Worcesters Killed. 1. Wnd. 1. 4/R.Berks Wnd. 2.	
	14.3.16.		Casualties. R.F.A. R.F.A. Pde. Killed 1. Wnd. 1. 6/R.Warwicks Wnd. 1. 4/Gloucesters. Killed 2/Lieut R.H. Craddock O.R. Wnd. 1. 8/Worcester Wnd. CAPTAIN E.S. JONES. 5/Gloucesters. Killed 1. 4/R.Berks. Wnd. 1. 5/R.Sussex Wnd. 1.	
	15.3.16.		Casualties: 4/S.M. Bde. R.F.A. Wnd. 3. 5/R.Warwicks. Wnd. 4. — 8/R.Warwicks. Wnd. 1. — 4/Gloucesters Wnd. 1. — 8/Worcesters Wnd. 1. Berks Rn. Wnd. 1. 4/R.Berks Wnd. 1.	
	16.3.16		Casualties — 5.R.War:Rgt. W.1. — 7th Worc. Rgt. K. 2nd Lieut. S.E. LLOYD — 6 Glosh Rgt W.7. including 1 slightly at duty 4th Gloster Rgt. W.1. — 4. Oxford W. 2 including 1 slightly at duty. — 4 R Berks W.1. — Buckis Bn W.1 accidentally —.	

1577 Wt. W10791/1773 500,000 1/15 D.D. & L. A.D.S.S./Forms/C. 2118.

Army Form C. 2118.

WAR DIARY
or
INTELLIGENCE SUMMARY.
(Erase heading not required.)

Instructions regarding War Diaries and Intelligence Summaries are contained in F.S. Regs., Part II. and the Staff Manual respectively. Title pages will be prepared in manuscript.

Place	Date	Hour	Summary of Events and Information	Remarks and references to Appendices
BUS-LES-ARTOIS	17.3.16		Casualties. R.G.A. att'd 86th T.M. Battery Wnd. 1. — R.F.A. att'd 86th T.M Battery. Wnd.1. — 7/R Warwicks Killed.1. Wnd.5. 6/Gloucesters Killed.2. Wnd.3. 7/Worcesters Killed.1. Wnd.8.	
	18.3.16		Casualties. 3rd S.M. Bde. R.F.A. Wnd.3. — 4th S.M Bde. R.F.A. Wnd.1. — 1st S.M. P.ds. Coy. R.E. Wnd. 1. — 6/R Warwicks Wnd.1. — 6/Gloucesters Killed.1. — Wnd. Captain. V.L. Young. — 2/Lt. G. BRINDAL — 7/Worcesters Wnd. 1 —	
	19.3.16		Casualties. R.G.A att'd 86th T.M Batty. Wnd.1. 7/R Warwicks Killed.1. 6/Gloucesters Killed 12 — Wnd 2/Lieut. J.G. HOLMAN O.R. 31. — Missing 3 — 7/Worcesters Wnd.5 - 7/Worcesters 82nd T.M Batty Wnd.1 5/Gloucesters Wnd.1. Bucks Bn. Wnd. 12 —	
	20.3.16		Casualties. 3rd R.H.Bde. R.F.A. Wnd.1. – 5/R Warwicks Wnd 1. 7/Warwicks Wnd 3. – 4/Gloucesters Killed 1. Wnd.3. 6/Gloucesters Killed.1. Wnd.1. – Bucks Bn. Wnd.2. – 6/Gloucs. (Missing shown have been shown on 19.3.16	
	21.3.16		Moves. Digging Party – 1st Ind. Cav. Div. and 2nd Ind. Cav. Div. left BUS to GAMACHES. Digging Party 2nd Ind. Cav. Div. arrived BELLE EGLISE and to Billets LOIGNIEUX. Casualties 4/Gloucesters Killed 2. Wnd.9. 5/Gloucesters Wnd.1. — Bucks Bn Wnd.1. — Move — 1 Coy. 145th Inf. Bde. HEBUTERNE to BAYENCOURT.	
	22.3.16		Casualties. 8/Worcesters. Wnd.3. — Moves. 48th Div. Subs. Vet. Sect. SARTON to FAMECHON.	

1577 Wt.W10791/1773 500,000 1/15 D. D. & L. A.D.S.S./Forms/C. 2118.

Army Form C. 2118.

WAR DIARY
or
INTELLIGENCE SUMMARY.
(Erase heading not required.)

Instructions regarding War Diaries and Intelligence Summaries are contained in F. S. Regs., Part II. and the Staff Manual respectively. Title pages will be prepared in manuscript.

Place	Date	Hour	Summary of Events and Information	Remarks and references to Appendices
	Month			
BUS-LES-ARTOIS.	23.3.16		Casualties 8th West Riding Batty. att'd 3rd S.M Bde R.F.A. Killed 2. Wnd. Lt. A.M HAYNES O.R. 2. — 5/R. Warwicks Wnd. Lt. H.R.L.S. GROOM and 2/Lt. E. HOLT O.R. 15. — 7/R Warwicks Killed 2. Wnd 12. — 8/R Warwicks Wnd. Lt. R. ADAMS O.R. 4. — 4/Oxfords Killed. 1. Wnd. 3. — 5/9 Lei'esters Wnd 8. 5/R Sussex Wnd. Killed. 1. Wnd. 6. R.G.A. att'd 86th T.H. Batty. Wnd. 2.	
	24.3.16		Casualties 6/R Warwicks att'd 143rd M.G. Coy. Wnd. 1. 4/Glo'sters Killed 2. Wnd. 1. — 7/Worcesters Wnd. 1. —	
	25.3.16		Casualties. R.E. att'd 62th Div. Sig. Coy. Wnd. 2. — 6/Glo'sters Wnd. 1. — 5/9 Lei'esters Wnd. 1. —	
COVIN.	26.3.16		Casualties. 8/R Warwicks. Killed. 1. Wnd. 2. — 6/9 Leicesters. Wnd. 1. —	
			Move. Div. HQrs. Moved BUS to COVIN. 143rd Div. Supply Column THIEVRES to FAMECHON. Div. Am. Col. THIEVRES to AUTHIE. 145th Inf. Bde. H.Qrs. HEBUTERNE to SAILLY.	
	27.3.16		Casualties 6/Glo'sters. Killed 1. Wnd. 1. 4/Oxfords Bkrs. Wnd. 1.	
			Move. Anglesey Seige Bty. R.E. (A.T.) arrived COIGNEUX from DOULLENS.	
	28.3.16		Casualties. 4/Glo'sters. Wnd. 4. 8/Worcesters. Killed 1. Wnd. 1. — Pioneer Bn. Killed 3. Wnd. 4. —	
	29.3.16		Casualties. 8/Worcesters. Wnd. 1. — Pioneer Bn. Wnd. 1.	
	30.3.16		Casualties 4/Glo'sters Wnd. 1. — 8/Warwicks Killed 1. Wnd. 7. — 12/Yorks & Lancs att'd 8th Warwicks Wnd. 1. — 13/Yorks & Lancs att'd 4/Oxfords Wnd. 1. — 4/R Berks Wnd. 1. —	
			Move. 5/R. Sussex Transpt. BUS to COIGNEUX. — 4/Glo'sters 8/Worcesters Hy. Bdes. M.G. Coy. Transpt to BUS to COVIN.	

Army Form C. 2118.

WAR DIARY
or
INTELLIGENCE SUMMARY.

(Erase heading not required.)

Instructions regarding War Diaries and Intelligence Summaries are contained in F. S. Regs., Part II. and the Staff Manual respectively. Title pages will be prepared in manuscript.

Place	Date	Hour	Summary of Events and Information	Remarks and references to Appendices
COUIN	31-3-16		Casualties 6/R Warwick Wd. 4. — 4/Gloucester Wd. 1. — 8/Worcester Wd. 1. — 8/Worcester Wd. 1. —	

R Mac Gregor aux QMS
for Major General,
Commanding 48th (S.M.) Division.

HQ A&Q 48 Div

Vol XIII

Army Form C. 2118.

48th Div - **WAR DIARY** . A. & Q. Branch
or
INTELLIGENCE SUMMARY.
(Erase heading not required.)

Instructions regarding War Diaries and Intelligence Summaries are contained in F.S. Regs., Part II. and the Staff Manual respectively. Title pages will be prepared in manuscript.

Place	Date	Hour	Summary of Events and Information	Remarks and references to Appendices
COUIN	1-4-16		Casualties 1st S.M.Bde. R.F.A. Killed 1. 2nd S.M. Bde. R.F.A. Wnd. 3. — 2nd/1st S.M. Fd. Coy. R.E. Wnd.1. 6/R. Warwicks Wnd. and missing 2/Lieut. R.B. Piper O.R. Wnd. 2. — 8/R. Warwicks Killed 1. Wnd. 1. — 8/Warwicks Wnd. 1. 7/Worcester att'd 144th Amb. M.G. Coy. Wnd. 1. 7/Worcester Wnd. 1. — Bucks Bn. Wnd. 2.	
	2.4.16		Nova 1st S.N.Fd. Ambulance completed move Bus to SOUASTRE. Casualties 7/R. Warwicks Killed.1. Wnd. 5. — 8/R. Warwicks Wnd. 1. — Bucks Bn. Killed. 4. Wnd. 1. — Move. 1 Battn. 144th Inf. Bde. COURCELLES to COUIN. 1 Battn. 143rd Inf Bde — Trenches to SAILLY. 5/R. Sussex 1 Coy. BAYENCOURT to SAILLY.	
	3.4.16		Casualties. 7/R. Warwicks Killed 2. Wnd. 5. — 6/Gloucesters Wnd. 1. — 8/Worcesters Killed. 1. Wnd. 5. — 4/Oxfords Wnd. 4. — Move. 3rd Fd. Coy. R.E. — HQ & 1 Sect. SAILLY 2 Sects HEBUTERNE. 1 Sect. COUIN. — 1 Battn. 144th Inf. Bde. Trenches to COLINCAMPS.	
	4.5.16		Casualties 5/R. Warwicks Wnd. 2. — 7/Worcesters Wnd. 6. — 4/Oxfords Wnd. 1. Move. Headquarters 144th Inf. Bde. COLINCAMPS to SAILLY — 1 Battn 144th Inf. Bde. ½ to SAILLY ½ to COIGNEUX.	

J. He C/s
for Brig. 7th & 9 Gds Bn

Army Form C. 2118.

WAR DIARY
or
INTELLIGENCE SUMMARY.
(Erase heading not required.)

Instructions regarding War Diaries and Intelligence Summaries are contained in F. S. Regs., Part II. and the Staff Manual respectively. Title pages will be prepared in manuscript.

Place	Date	Hour	Summary of Events and Information	Remarks and references to Appendices
COUIN	5.4.16		Casualties 4/R.S.M. Bde. R.F.A. Wnd. 1. — 4/R.Berks. Wnd. 1. —	
	6.4.16		Moves 1 Battn. 145th Inf. Bde. Hdqrs. & 2 Coys. to COUIN & Coys. BAILEY.	
			Casualties 6/Gloucestershire Regt. Wnd. 2.	
	7.4.16		Moves 1 Coy. No. 3. Entrenching Battn. arrived SOUASTRE from Reserve area.	
			Casualties X Trench Mortar Battery into R.F.A. Wnd. 2. — 2/R Warwicks Wnd. 1.	
	8.4.16.		Casualties 7/Worcester Wnd. 1. 5/R Sussex Wnd. 2/Lieut. E. CARLISH and 1 O.R.	
			Moves 48th Divl. Supply Col. FAMECHON to CANDAS.	
	9.4.16		Casualties 5/R Warwicks Wnd. 1. 7/R. Warwicks Wnd. 3. — 8/Glou'sters Killed. 1. — 8/Warwicks Wnd. 1. —	
			Bucks Bn. Wnd. 1. — 4/R Berks Wnd. 2. —	
			Moves 48th. Divl. Train. AUTHIE to FAMECHON.	
	10.4.16		Casualties 4/Gloucesters Killed 3 Wnd. 11 — 8th Worcester Wnd. 2. — 5/Gloucesters Wnd 3 — 4/Oxfords Killed 1.	
			Wnd. 6. — Bucks Bn. Killed 1. Wnd 3. — Bucks Bn. Wnd. 2/Shelter R. ATTWELL	
	11.4.16		Casualties 4/R.Berks Killed 3, Wnd. 1.	
	12.4.16		Casualties 4/90. Bde. R.F.A. Wnd 1⅓ — 4/R.Berks. Wnd, 3, —	
	13.4.16		Casualties 2/1 Ph Field Coy R.E. Wnd 1, 1/8. Rhn R. Wnd 1, 5ᵗʰ Warwks Wnd 2,	
	14.4.16		Casualties 4/SA Bde. R.F.A. Wnd 1, 5ᵗʰ Rwar R 1 wond , 8ᵗʰ Rwar R Kld 1, 5ᵗʰ Lyts wnd 13, 5ᵗʰ Sussex Kld 2	
			Wnd 7 R/Bks Cpl,	
			? G.W. M.A. 4, L & Bn	

T2134. Wt. W708-776. 500000. 4/15. Sir J.C. & S.

Army Form C. 2118.

WAR DIARY
or
INTELLIGENCE SUMMARY.
(Erase heading not required.)

Instructions regarding War Diaries and Intelligence Summaries are contained in F. S. Regs., Part II. and the Staff Manual respectively. Title pages will be prepared in manuscript.

Place	Date	Hour	Summary of Events and Information	Remarks and references to Appendices
COUIN	14.4.16		Moves. Personnel of 143/1, 144/1, 145/1, X 48 & Z 48 T.M. Batteries to T.M. School, & to be trained & rearmed with 3" (Stokes) & 2" T.M. respectively. Additional personnel in from 143/2, 144/2, & 145/2 STOKES T.M. Batteries to School for training. All mortars 1.5", 3.7" & 4" sent in train. Two STOKES T.M. Batteries & one 2" Medium Battery from 29th Bde arrived to be attached. Two STOKES T.M. Batteries & one 2" Medium Battery from 31st Bde arrived to be attached during the absence of this Bde's T.M. Batteries.	
	15.4.16		Casualties: 6th R.War.R. Wnd 1, 5th Wilts. Wnd 2	
	16.4.16		Casualties: 5th R.War.R. Wnd 2, 7th Worcester Wnd 1, 6th Stokes Wnd 1, 6th Bucks Bn Wnd 1.	
	17.4.16		Casualties: Y 31 T.M. Batty at R.Pn Wnd 3, 8th R.War.R Wnd Capt ARNELL, 18th W.Yorks att. 143 M.I. Bde Wnd Capt D.H. ELLIWELL, 6th Gloster Wnd 1, 5th Glo Kld 1, Wnd 6, 145 Bde M.G. Wnd 1.	
	18.4.16		Moves. 369 Batty R.F.A. to SAILLY (mapa Lieu COIGNEUX).	
			Casualties: 5/R Warwicks Wnd 2. — 6/Gloucesters Wnd 2. — 5/Gloucesters Killed 3 Wnd 2. —	
	19.4.16		Casualties: 7/R Warwick Wnd 1. — 5/Gloucesters Wnd 4. — 1/Oxfords Wnd 1.	
	20.4.16		Casualties: 7/R Warwicks Wnd 1. — 5/Gloucesters Wnd 1. — Bucks Bn Wnd 1. —	
			Moves. 1 Bde 144th & 2nd R.M. to COIGNEUX.	

S.W. Capt
for Bde Mjr M.G.L. 48 Bde

Army Form C. 2118.

WAR DIARY
or
INTELLIGENCE SUMMARY.
(Erase heading not required.)

Instructions regarding War Diaries and Intelligence Summaries are contained in F. S. Regs., Part II. and the Staff Manual respectively. Title pages will be prepared in manuscript.

Place	Date	Hour	Summary of Events and Information	Remarks and references to Appendices
COVIN	21.4.16		Casualties 4/Oxford & Bucks d.I. Wd. 1.—	
			Move. 1 Battn. 144th Inf. Bde. Inverness to Couin.	
	22.4.16		Casualties. 7/Warwicks. Wnd. 7, Bucks Bn. Killed. 3, Wnd. 3.	
	23.4.16		Casualties. 4/Oxford & Bucks d.I. Wd. 5. — Bucks Bn. Killed. 3. Wnd. 5. 4/Royal Berks Wnd. 2/Wnds.	
			J.F.Duff. and 3 O.R.	
	24.4.16		Casualties. 1st S. M. Bde. R.F.A. Wd. 3. — 5/Royal Warwicks Killed. 1. Wnd. 3. — 4/Oxford & Bucks d.I. Wnd. 1.—	
			Bucks Bn. Wd. 3. — 4/Royal Berks Wnd. 3.—	
	25.4.16		Casualties. M.G. Corps. attd 143rd M.G. Coy. Killed. 1. — 5/R Warwicks attd 143rd Inf. Bde M.G. Coy.	
			Wnd. 1. — 6th Gloucestershire Regt Wnd. 1. — 4/R. Berks. Wnd. 6. —	
			Move. 143rd Inf. Bde. 2½ Battns. Trenches — SOUASTRE. 1 Battn COIGNEUX.	
			144th Inf. Bde. 2 Battns. Couin to Trenches 1 Battn. Coigneux Trenches – 1 Battn. Coigneux.	
			SAILLY. 145th Inf. Bde. 1 Battn. BAYENCOURT. 1 Battn. AUTHIE. 1 Battn. COIGNEUX.	
	26.4.16		Casualties. 5/R Warwicks Killed. 1. Wnd. 1. — 6/R Warwicks Wnd. 1.—	
			Move. 1 Battn. Hebuterne Couin to Trenches.	
	27.4.16		Casualties 5/R Warwicks attd 143rd Inf. Bde. M.G. Coy Killed. 1. 6/Gloucesters Regt. Killed	
			Lieut. H.P. Nott OR. Wnd. 2.	

Place	Date	Hour	Summary of Events and Information	Remarks and references to Appendices
COUIN	28.4.16		Casualties. 2nd S.M. Bde. R.F.A. Wnd. 2/Lieut. R.W. Lane. — 8/R. Warwicks Wnd. 1. — 4/Gloucesters Klld. 1. Wnd. 9. Missing 2. — 7/Worcestrs Wnd. 1. —	
	29.4.16		Casualties. X.48. T.M. Bty. attd R.F.A. Wnd. 1. 4/Gloucestrs Wnd. 1. —	
	30.4.16		Casualties :- 6"R.War.R Wnd 4, 8:R.War R Wnd 2, 4/Glos. Wnd. 1, 6: Glos Wnd 3, 7: Worcestrs Wnd 2/Lt J.F. Reading. Wnd 4, 8: Wor Rgt 2/Lt 7207 G.J. Slater Wnd 5	P. Usher Cpl for Div HQ & 145 Bn

WAR DIARY
or
INTELLIGENCE SUMMARY.
(Erase heading not required.)

Army Form C. 2118.

HQ 04R Vol 14

Place	Date	Hour	Summary of Events and Information	Remarks and references to Appendices
COUIN	1.5.16		Casualties :- 3rd C.M. Bde R.F.A wnd 1, 4th Gloster wnd 1, 7th Worcester kld 1 and Capt N.P. Goodwin and 1 O.R.	
	2.5.16		Move. 1 Bn 143rd Inf. Bde into front line, 1 Bn 144 Inf Bde to COUIN. Casualties. Y & S T.M. Batty attacked R.F.A wnd 1, 4th Glos wnd 1, 7 Worcester wnd 1, 6th Sherwd wnd 1.	
			Move. 145th Inf Bde to Trenches MAILLY, 144 Inf Bde HQ to SAILLY, 1Bn to COIGNEUX 2 Bn at COUIN, 1 Bn to AUTHIE.	
	3.5.16		Casualties Y & 48 T.M. Battery attacked R.F.A kld 1, B.9.3 Bgy 48th Div Train from FAMECHON to GEZAINCOURT	
	4.5.16		Casualties 4th S.A Bde R.F.A kld 1, 4th Oxford Bn 2/Lt J.S.C. KING 2/Lt T.D. HUGHES and 1 O.R. wnd 2/Lt R. AFFLECK & 4 O.R., Bucks Bn wnd 1.	
			Move 145 Bde Tps from BAYENCOURT to COUIN, 4th Berks from SAILLY to COUIN, Bucks Bn Trenches to COIGNEUX, 1 Co 5th Surrey HEDAUTERNE to SAILLY. 144th Inf Bde HQ Trenches to HEM BEAUVAL also 1st Fd Amb, 3rd Field Co RE to HEM	
	5.5.16		Casualties. 4th Oxford kld 1, wnd 3; 5th Gloster wnd 1.	
			Move 6th Warwick Trenches to COUIN, 8th Worcester Trenches to AUTHIE. HQ & Tps of 143 Bde to COUIN	

Army Form C. 2118.

WAR DIARY
or
INTELLIGENCE SUMMARY.
(Erase heading not required.)

Instructions regarding War Diaries and Intelligence Summaries are contained in F.S. Regs., Part II. and the Staff Manual respectively. Title pages will be prepared in manuscript.

Place	Date	Hour	Summary of Events and Information	Remarks and references to Appendices
COUIN	5.5.16		Move (continued) HQ & 2 Coys 5th Sussex to AUTHIE.	
	6.5.16		Casualties. No. 2 Coy Train 48th Div Wd 1.	
			Move. 1Bn 143 Inf Bde SOUASTRE to BIVOUAC. 143 Bde Tp SOUASTRE to COUIN. Detach 5th Sussex BIVOUAC N.E. of COURCELLES. 143 Bde Tp SOUASTRE to COUIN. Detach 5th Sussex to HEM. Run FORT DICK and JUNCTION KEEP to SAILLY. HQ & 2 Coys 5th Sussex to HEM.	
	7.5.16		Casualties. 4th Oxfords Wd 3, 5th R. Sussex Wd 1,	
			Move. HQ & 2 Bats 3rd L.A.R.F.A. to St LEGER.	
	8.5.16		Casualties – Nil	
			Move. 1Bn 143rd BIVOUAC near SAILLY to AUTHIE, 1Bn COUIN to BIVOUAC COURCELLES, 1 Bn BIVOUAC COURCELLES to COUIN. 1Bn AUTHIE to BIVOUAC near SAILLY, 144 Inf Bde 1Bn COUIN to FONCLES, 1Bn COIGNEUX to FONCLES, 1Bn FONCLES to COUIN, 1Bn FONCLES to COIGNEUX. Artillery HQ & 3 Bats 2nd Bde R.F.A. to COUIN, HQ & 2 Bats 4th Bde to St LEGER.	
	9.5.16		Casualties. 5/Gloucesters Wd 1. 4/Oxford Bucks Wd 1.	
	10.5.16		Casualties. H.L.	
			Move. 2 Batts. 143rd Inf Bde. From BIVOUAC nr COURCELLES and SAILLY to BIVOUAC nr AUTHIE.	

Army Form C. 2118.

WAR DIARY
or
INTELLIGENCE SUMMARY.
(Erase heading not required.)

Instructions regarding War Diaries and Intelligence Summaries are contained in F. S. Regs., Part II. and the Staff Manual respectively. Title pages will be prepared in manuscript.

Place	Date	Hour	Summary of Events and Information	Remarks and references to Appendices
COUIN.	11.5.16		Casualties. O.B.C. att'd 4/Royal Berkshire Regt. Wnd. 1.	
			Move. 143rd Inf. Brigade & 1 Batln. COUIN & Beaver. AUTHIE to BEZAINCOURT.	
	12.5.16		Casualties. 185 M. Bde. R.F.A. Wnd. 1. V. 42. T.M. Battery att'd R.F.A. Wnd. 1. — Bucks Bn. Wnd. 1.	
	13.5.16		Move. B. Squadron K.E.H. Transferred to 4th Army.	
			Casualties. Bucks Bn. Wnd. 4.	
	14.5.16		Casualties. NIL	
	15.5.16		Move. 48th Div. Cyclist Coy. left Division and Proceeded to BEAUVAL.	
			Casualties. 4th Royal Berks Regt. Wnd. 1.	
			Move. 144th Inf. Bde. Hdqrs. M.G. Coy. T.M. Batteries. 3 Batln. BEAUVAL to COUIN. 1 Batln. COIGNEUX.	
			145th Inf. Bde. 1 Batln. COIGNEUX to AUTHIE.	
	16.5.16		Casualties. Bucks Bn. Killed 1. Wnd. 3. 4/Royal Berks. Killed 1. Wnd. 2/Kent. G.S. Field	
			45 O.R. missing 29.	
			Move. Hdqrs. M.G. Coy. T.M. Batteries 2 Batln. 144th Inf. Bde. COUIN to SAILLY and Ivrenches. Hdqrs. T.M. G. Coy. T.M. Batteries 2 Batln. 145th Inf. Bde. SAILLY and Ivrenches to COUIN.	

Army Form C. 2118.

WAR DIARY
or
INTELLIGENCE SUMMARY.
(Erase heading not required.)

Instructions regarding War Diaries and Intelligence Summaries are contained in F. S. Regs., Part II. and the Staff Manual respectively. Title pages will be prepared in manuscript.

Place	Date	Hour	Summary of Events and Information	Remarks and references to Appendices
COIGN	17.5.16		Casualties 2.48. T.M. Battery. attached R.F.A. Wnd. Lieut. A. PALMER – 8/Worcs. Wnd. 1.	
		Move.	No. 4. Coy. Divl. Train FAMECHON to GEZAINCOURT No. 3. Coy. Divl. Train GEZAIN-COURT to FAMECHON.	
	18.5.16		Casualties 4/Gloucesters Wnd. 1. 8/Gloucesters Wnd. 1.	
		Moves.	146th Inf. Bde. Hdqrs. H.G. Coy. T.M. Battery. 3 Battalions COIGN and 1 Battn AUTHIE. to BEAUVAL.	
	19.5.16		Casualties 8th Worcesters Capt. Killed. 1. Wnd. 4.	
	20.5.16		Casualties 8th Worcesters Bgt. Wnd. 2.	
	21.5.16		Casualties 8th Worcestershire Regt. Wnd. 2/Lieut H.G. CARTER O.R.1. – 6th Gloucesters Wnd. 1. –	
	22.5.16		Casualties NIL.	
	23.5.16		Casualties. 5/R Warwicks. Killed. 2 Wnd. 2. 8/R Warwicks Killed. 2. Wnd. 3. 7/R Warwicks killed. 1. Wnd. 2. 2/Lieut. M.C. KIRBY 7/R Warwicks. attd. (143/2. T.M. Batty) Wnd.– self accidently. 8/Worcester Wnd. 2. – 2nd 9. M. Fld. Coy. R.E. 1 O.R. Drowned in Stoples R. Souke. accidentally drowned.	
	24.5.16		Casualties. 8/Worcesters. Wnd. 3. —	
		Moves.	144 Inf. Bde. 1 Battn COIGN and 1 Battn COIGNEUX to Bivouac 3 mile West SAILLY.	

Army Form C. 2118.

WAR DIARY
or
INTELLIGENCE SUMMARY.
(Erase heading not required.)

Instructions regarding War Diaries and Intelligence Summaries are contained in F. S. Regs., Part II. and the Staff Manual respectively. Title pages will be prepared in manuscript.

Place	Date	Hour	Summary of Events and Information	Remarks and references to Appendices
COUIN	25.5.16		Casualties 2/1st S.M. Fd. Coy. R.E. Wnd. 1.—	
			Moves. 143rd Inf. Brigade GEZAINCOURT to COUIN for Divn. and Reserve No. 2 Coy. Bn. from GEZAINCOURT to AUTHIE.	
	26.5.16		Casualties. Wnd. Lt. G. Davey, 48th Divn. Sig. Coy. R.E.— 7th Worcester Wnd. 1.— Bucks. Bn. attd. 145/1. T.M. Batty. Wnd. 3.— 4/R. Berks Regt. attd. 145/1. T.M. Batty. Wnd. 1.—	
			Moves. 143rd Inf. Bde. COUIN and COIGNEUX to AUTHIE.	
	27.5.16		Casualties. R.F.A. Div. Am. Column attd. 240th Bde. R.F.A. Wnd. 1.— Y.48 T.M. Battery Wnd. 1.— 7/Worcester attd 144/1. T.M. Battery Wnd. 1.— 7/Wounded. Wnd. 2.— 6/Gloucester Wnd. 1.— 48th Divn. Sig. Coy. R.E. Wnd. 1.—	
	28.5.16		Moves 143rd Inf. Bde. COUIN and AUTHIE to GEZAINCOURT.	
			Casualties 4/Gloucester. Killed 3. Wnd. 6.— 7/Worcester Wnd. 1.—	
	29.5.16		Casualties 4/Gloucester. Wnd. 3.— 6/Gloucester H.E.H. SUTTON, O.R. 3.— 7/Worcester. Killed. 1. Wnd. 5.— 6/Gloucester attd 144/2 T.M. Battery Wnd. 2.— 2nd 1st S.M. Fld. Coy. R.E.— Wnd. 1.—	
	30.5.16		Casualties 7/Worcester Killed 1. Wnd. 1.—	

Army Form C. 2118.

WAR DIARY
or
INTELLIGENCE SUMMARY.
(Erase heading not required.)

Instructions regarding War Diaries and Intelligence Summaries are contained in F. S. Regs., Part II. and the Staff Manual respectively. Title pages will be prepared in manuscript.

Place	Date	Hour	Summary of Events and Information	Remarks and references to Appendices
Cavin	31/5/16		Casualties 4/9 Leicesters Wnd. 1.— 7/Worcesters. Killed. 1.— Wnd. 5.— Moves. 143rd Inf. Brigade. GEZAINCOURT to CAVIN and COIGNEUX. 145th Inf. Brigade. BEAUVAL to ST. RICQUIER (Ivanovic Ave).	

S.A.L.
D.A.A. & Q.M.G. 48th (S.M.) Division.

Army Form C. 2118.

WAR DIARY

A+Q Branch

INTELLIGENCE SUMMARY. 48th Division.

(Erase heading not required.)

Instructions regarding War Diaries and Intelligence Summaries are contained in F. S. Regs., Part II. and the Staff Manual respectively. Title pages will be prepared in manuscript.

Place	Date	Hour	Summary of Events and Information	Remarks and references to Appendices
COUIN	1.6.16		Casualties. 240th (Nm) Bde R.F.A. Wnd. 1. B/9 Lowentin attd 144/2 T.M. Battery Wnd.1. Moves. 144th Inf Bde SAILLY and Environs to COUIN and AUTHIE. No. 3 Cav. Div. Train FAMECHON to GEZAINCOURT.	
	2.6.16		Casualties. Nil. Moves. 144th Inf. Brigade COUIN and AUTHIE to GEZAINCOURT. - 1st Sm. Fld Coy R.E. HEM to Bivouac West of SAILLY. 3rd Sm. Fld Coy. R.E. Bivouac W. of SAILLY to HEM	
	3.6.16		Casualties. 5/R Warwicks Wnd. 1. 8/R Warwicks Wnd. 1.	
	4.6.16		Casualties. Wnd. Lieut. E.V. SULLIVAN R.A.M.C. attd 240th S.M. Bn. R.E.O. 5/R Warwicks Wnd. 6. - 7th R. Warwicks Killd. 1. Wnd. 11. - Moves. 144th Inf. Bde. GEZAINCOURT to ONEUX-COULONVILLERS and MAISON ROLLAND 145th Inf Bde. ONEUX-COULONVILLERS and MAISON ROLLAND to ARGENVILLERS and GAPENNES.	
	5.6.16		Casualties. 7th Warwicks Wnd. 1. -	
	6.6.16		Casualties. 5/R. Warwicks Wnd. 1. -	
	7.6.16		Casualties. V. 48. D.M. Battery Wnd. 1. - 5/R/Warwicks Wnd. 1. - 2/Lieut. E.R. CARTER -	

WAR DIARY or INTELLIGENCE SUMMARY

Army Form C. 2118.

Place	Date	Hour	Summary of Events and Information	Remarks and references to Appendices
COUIN.	7.6.16		Casualties (Enc) 5/R.Warwicks Wnd. 2/Lieut. (T. Luine) E.C. WROTH – O.R. 12.– 7.R.Warwicks Killd. 4. Wnd. 3. Drowning (Probably killed.) 1. 8/R.Warwicks Wnd.7.	
	8.6.16		Moves. 242nd S.M.Bde. R.F.A. COUIN to HEM (to exercise ST RICQUIER area). Casualties 6/R.Warwicks Wnd. 2. 242nd S.M. Bde. R.F.A. Moves HEM to St.Ricquier Training area.	
	9.6.16		Casualties 6/R.Warwicks Wnd.1. – 7/R.Warwicks Wnd.4.– Moves Hil.	
	10.6.16		Casualties 6/R.Warwicks Wnd.1. – 8/R.Warwicks Killed 1. Moves. 145th Inf.Bde and 242nd S.M. Bde. R.F.O. from St.Ricquier Training Area to HEM and area OCCOCHES – MEZEROLLES – OUTREBOIS.	
	11.6.16		Casualties 1st F.M.Pld.Cy.R.E. Wnd.1. – 7/R.Warwicks Wnd.1. – 8/R.Warwicks Wnd.1.– Moves. 145th Inf.Bde ten 1 Battn. Occothes area to Couin. (Battn. COIGNEUX 242nd S.M. Bde. R.F.A. HEM to ST. LEGER.	
	12.6.16		Casualties 6/R.Warwicks Killed 1. Wnd.1. – 8/R.Warwicks Wnd.1.– Moves 145th Inf.Bde. COUIN and COIGNEUX to SAILLY and trenches – 143rd Inf.Bde. den 1 Battn from trenches and SAILLY to COUIN – 1 Battn. COIGNEUX	

WAR DIARY
or
INTELLIGENCE SUMMARY.
(Erase heading not required.)

Army Form C. 2118.

Place	Date	Hour	Summary of Events and Information	Remarks and references to Appendices
COUIN	13.6.16		Casualties NIL — Move 6th Bn. R. Warwicks. hire Regt. and 8th Bn. Royal Warwickshire Regt. COUIN to BEAUVAL — 8/Worcestershire Regt. HEM to COIGNEUX all battalions on working parties.	
	14.6.16		Casualties 240th Bde R.F.A. Wnd.1. — Wnd. Major (T)(Captain) T.G.G. RICE 2nd Scottish Rifles attd 1/4th OxfdBucks L.I. — Buchr Bn. 2/Lt. (T.Acain) A.D.B BROWN — Wnd. O.R 3. — 4/Oxford Bucks L.I. Killed 1. — Wnd.1. — 241st S.M. Bde. R.F.A. Wnd. (since 3rd) Lt. Jm. S. HAYES — Wnd. 14/480 Ind Bde. en 1 Both. — YVRENCH and YVRENCHEUX to area OUTRE BOIS - MEZEROLLES- OCCOCHES - HEM.	
	15.6.16		Casualties 240th S.M. Bde. R.F.A. Wnd. 2/Lieut. A.A. LESLIE 242nd S.M. Bde. R.F.A. Killed 6. Wnd.1. 2nd/1st S.M. Field Coy. R.E. Wnd. 5 — 7/Worcesters Wnd.1. —	
	16.6.16		Casualties Bucks Bn. OxfdBucks. d.S. Wnd. 2/Lieut. T.M. ROLLESTON O.R. 6 — missing 1. —	
	17.6.16		Casualties Nil.	
	18.6.16		Casualties in 243rd S.M. Bde. R.F.A. Wnd.1. — 7/R. Warwicks attd 143rd Bde Machine Gun Corp. Wnd.1. 4/Bucks Bn OxfdBucks. L.I. Wnd.1.	

Army Form C. 2118.

WAR DIARY
or
INTELLIGENCE SUMMARY.
(Erase heading not required.)

Instructions regarding War Diaries and Intelligence Summaries are contained in F. S. Regs., Part II. and the Staff Manual respectively. Title pages will be prepared in manuscript.

Place	Date	Hour	Summary of Events and Information	Remarks and references to Appendices
COVIN	19.6.16		Casualties. V/48. T.M.Batty. and R.F.A. Wnd.1. — Bucks Bn. Wnd.2. —	
"	20.6.16		Casualties. 4th Ox&Bucks L.I. Wnd.2. — 1/Royal Bucks Regt. Wnd.2. —	
"	21.6.16		Casualties. 242nd Sh.Bde. R.F.A. Wnd.1. — Bucks Bn. Wnd.1. —	
"	22.6.16		Casualties. Special Brigade R.E. Wnd.1. — 7th Warwicks Wnd.1. — Bucks Bn. Wnd.5. — 5/Royal Sussex Wnd.1. —	
			Move. 143rd Inf: Bde. (less 2 Battns. (6th & 8th R.Warwicks) to SAILLY and environs. 145th Inf: Bde. Brigade Trenches to COVIN. 144th Inf. Bde. COIGNEUX and Bivouacs in wood SAILLY-au-BOIS.	
	23.6.16		Casualties. 48th D.A.C. Killed.1. — 7th R.Warwicks Wnd.3. — 5/R.Leicester Wnd.1. — 5/R.Sussex Wnd.1. —	
	24.6.16		Casualties. 7/R.Warwicks Wnd.1. Machine Gun Corps. and 144th Inf.Bde.M.G.Coy. Wnd.1. —	
	25.6.16		Casualties. 240th Sh.Bde. R.F.O. Killed.1. Wnd.4. — 242nd Sh.Bde. R.F.O. Wnd.3. — 48th D.A.C. Wnd.2. — V.48th T.M.Batty and R.F.A. Wnd.2. 2/Lieut. E.V.F. RUSSELL — 5/R.Warwicks Wnd.2/Lieut. F.C.ALABASTER — O.R.1. — 7th/R.Warwicks Killed 2. Wnd.10. 5/R.Sussex Wnd.1. 7/R.Warwicks Killed.2. — Wnd.	
	26.6.16		Casualties. 242nd Bde.R.F.A. Wnd.4. — 5/R.Warwicks Wnd.7. — 7/R.Warwicks Killed. 2. — Wnd. 2/Lieut. W.A.IMBER. — O.R.9. —	
	27.6.16		Casualties. 242nd Sh.Bde. R.F.A. Wnd.3. — 243rd Sh.Bde. R.F.O. Wnd.1. — V.48. T.M.Batty. and R.F.A.Wnd.1.	

HQ and 2 & 8 Army Form C. 2118.

Vol 15

WAR DIARY
or
INTELLIGENCE SUMMARY.
(Erase heading not required.)

Place	Date	Hour	Summary of Events and Information	Remarks and references to Appendices
COIGN	27.6.16	-	Casualties (Coys) 5/Royal Warwicks Wnd. 2/Lieut R. HAMBIDGE and 2.O.R.— 7/Royal Warwicks Wnd.— Lieut A.J. FIELD — 2.O.R.— 5/Royal Sussex Killd. 2 - Wnd. 2 .—	
"	28.6.16.	.	Casualties. 240th R.M. Bde R.F.A. Wnd.1.— 5/R Warwicks Wnd. 2/Lieut F.W. MARVIN O.R.15. Missing. 4.O.R.— 7/R Warwicks Wnd 13.— 8/R Warwicks 5/Royal Sussex Regt Killed.1. Wnd. 5.	
"	29.6.16		Casualties. 7/R Warwicks Wnd.1.— 5/Royal Sussex Killed.1. Wnd.1.— 1 man 5/Royal Warwicks reported missing 28-6-16 now returned wounded.—	
"	30.6.16		Casualties. 164 Seige Battery R.G.A. att'd X.48. T.M.Batty Wnd.1.— 5/R Warwicks Wnd.1. 4/9 Glo'sters. Wnd.2. 7th R. Warwicks Wnd.2. Wnd.3.—	

VIII Corps.

Division came under
orders of X Corps
16.7.16.

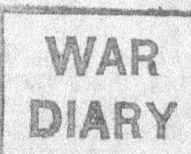

A. & Q.

48th DIVISION

JULY

1916

SECRET.

WAR DIARY.

48th (S.M.) DIVISION "A" & "Q"

PERIOD 1st to 31st JULY 1916

VOLUME XVI

Place	Date	Hour	Summary of Events and Information	Remarks and references to Appendices
COUIN	1-7-16		Moved. Div. Hdqrs - 144th, 145th Ind. Bde. 5/Royal Sussex, 2nd and 3rd S.M. Fld. Coy. R.E., 1 Sect. 2nd Fd. Amb., 1 Sect. 3rd Cav. Amb., 13th Motor M.G. Battery, Hotchkiss Section, Lancashire Hussars COUIN and SAILLY areas to MAILLY-MALLET - Div. Hdqrs. CAFÉ JOURDAIN - Remainder bivouac P.18.a. due South West MAILLY-MALLET. Casualties: 240th S.M.Bde. R.F.A. Wnd. 3. 242nd S.M.Bde. R.F.G. Wnd.3 - 48th Div. A.A.C. Wnd.2. R.F.G. attd. Y.48. T.M. Battery Killed 1 - 46th Seige Battery R.G.A. attd. Y.48. T.M. Battery Wnd. 2. 5/R.Warwicks Wnd. 2/Lt. P.A. GROVE 2/Lt. H.H. PINE and 10. O.R. 7/R.Warwicks Killed Capt. N.C. MURRAY and 3. O.R. Wnd. - 7/R.Warwicks attd. 143rd M.G. Company Wnd. Lt. S. HOWATT O.R. 1 - 4/Glosters Killed 1. Wnd. 2.	
MAILLY-MALLET	2-7-16		Casualties 240th S.M.Bde. R.F.A. Wnd. 3. - 8/Worcs. attd. X.48. T.M. Battery Wnd.2. 2/Lieut. V.R. FOX. - SMITH 5/R.Warwicks Killed 1. Wnd. Captain W.C. GELL O.R. 10. - 7/R.Warwicks Killed 7. Wnd. 20.	
			Moves. 144th and 146th Inf. Bdes. less 1 Battn. each to Trenches near MESNIL. Operations Cancelled. 10.30 p.m. and Units returned to Bivouac MAILLY-MALLET	
"	3-7-16		Casualties. R.F.A. attd Y.48 T.M.Battery Killed 1. 21st Coy. R.G.A. attd Y.48. T.M. Battery Wnd.2. - 7/R.Warwicks Wnd. 1 - 5/R.Warwicks attd 143rd Bde. T.M. Battery Wnd.1. - 8/R.Warwicks attd. 143rd T.M. Wnd. 1.	

Place	Date	Hour	Summary of Events and Information	Remarks and references to Appendices
MAILLY-MAILLET	3.7.16		Casualties (Cont.) 6/Glosters. 1. Slightly Wnd. 7/Warwicks. Wnd. 1.— No. 4 Coy. No. 5. Special Bn. R.E. Wnd. Lt. M.H. VERNON. O.R. 13. Missing. 1.	
			Moved. Div. Hd qrs. 144th 145th Inf. Bdes. 2nd & 3rd M. Cav. Cos. R.E. 5/Royal Sussex Regt. 1 Sect. 2nd/2nd. Fld. Ambulance. 1 Sect. 3rd/3rd. Fld. Ambulance. 13th Div. M.G. Battery. Hotchkiss Section. Seven Hussars. No. 2 & 3 Coys. Div. Train. marched to COUIN.	
			Hd qrs. & No. 4 Coy. Div. Train M.V. Vet. Section COUIN to FAMECHON. 6/R. Warwicks. BERTRANCOURT and MAILLY MAILLET to COUIN	
COUIN.	4.7.16		Casualties. 4/Royal Berks. Wnd. 1.—	
			Moved 145th Inf. Bde. Hd qrs. and 2 Battns. to SAILLY and Trenches. 144th Inf. Bde. Hd qrs. and 1 Battn. to COURCELLES. 2 Battns. to Trenches. 1 Battn. OISNEUX. 143rd Inf. Bde. and Hd qrs. 2 Battns. to COUIN.	
	5.7.16		Casualties. 5/R. Warwicks. Wnd. 2/Lieut. S.C. SQUIRES O.R. 2. 6/Glosters. Wnd. 2. 4/Oxfords. Wnd. 3.	
			Moved. 2 Battns. 145th Bn. COUIN to SAILLY Bivouacs.	
	6.7.16		Casualties. 6/Glosters. Killed 1. Wnd. 16.— 8/Warwicks. Wnd. 6. 5/9/Warwick. Killed 1. Wnd. 1.— 4/Oxfords killed 1. Wnd. 2. 4/R. Berks. Wnd. 1.— 5/R. Sussex Wnd. Captain E.S. RICHARDSON.— O.R. Wnd. 3.—	

Appendix A.

The 6th R. Warwicks and 8/R. Warwicks suffered following casualties during attachment to 11th Inf. Bde 4th Division during attack on enemy position North of BEAUMONT-HAMEL.

6/R.Warwicks — Killed. Captain. A.B. RABONE — 2/Lieut. H.L. FIELD - 2/Lieut. J. BAIKWILL
2/Lieut. A.V. ROSE - 2/Lieut. W.P. WHEELER — Wounded Lieut. K.W. BROWN. Lieut W.H.B.
BAXTER — Captain. J.N.G. STAFFORD — Lieut E. WYNNE-JONES — 2/Lieut. A.H. DOWNING
Lieut. A.D. WILCOX - 2/Lieut. K.T.C. HEARNE. Capt. A.B. TURNER — Major F.H. DEAWIN
— Lt. Col. W.H. FRANKLIN. — Lieut F.L. MORGAN.— Missing Captain J.E.B. DIXON
2/Lt. C.T. MORRIS-DAVIES. — 2/Lieut. R. PRICE — Wounded and Missing 2/Lieut.
C.R.C. MARTIN. — 2/Lieut. S.S. WINCKLEY - 2/Lieut. A.E. CLARKE. O.R. killed 43.
Wnd. 173 - Missing 234.

8/R.Warwicks. Killed. Lt. Colonel. E.A. INNES C.M.G. — Lt. C. HOSKINS — Lt. J.G. FUSSELL
Lt. A. PROCTER - 2/Lieut. F.W. WAREHAM 2/Lieut. F.R. KEY. Wounded Major J.N. TOWNSEND — 2/Lt. J. TEAGUE
2/Lt. R.H. FISH. — Lt. H. MARTIN-JONES — Lt. L.W. AUSTER - Lt. L. GRIFFITHS - 2/Lt. F. HEATH - Captain. F.W. WALSH RAMC
Captain S.W. LUDLOW Captain. S.W. MARTIN. — Chaplain S.H.N. COXON. — Lt. R. ADAMS - Lt. D.R. ADAMS - 2/Lt. E.R.
SHUTTEWORTH - 2/Lt. S.W. PEPPER. — 2/Lt. J. TURNER - 2/Lt. J.H. ANSTEY - Missing; Wounded Major A.A. CADDICK - 2/Lt. F. BRETTELL
M.532 — ? ellised killed ?. S/Lt. F.B. FREEMAN — O.R. Killed 52 Wounded 238 Missing 273

Place	Date	Hour	Summary of Events and Information	Remarks and references to Appendices
COUIN.	7/7/16		Casualties. 48th Div. Ammn. Col. Att. Y.&8. T.M. Batt. Killed. 1. 122 Batt. R.F.A. Att. Y.&8. T.M. Batt. Wounded. 1. 34th Bay. R.G.A. Att. Y.&8. T.M. Batt. Wounded. 1. 122nd Heavy Batt. R.G.A. Att. Y.&8. T.M. Batt. Wounded. 1. 48th Div. Ammn. Col. Att. Y.&8. T.M. Batt. Wounded. 1. 241st Bde. R.F.A. att. Y.&8 T.M. Batt. Wounded. 2. 6th Gloucesters. att. 144th T.M. Batt. Wounded. 1. 6th Gloucesters. Wounded. Capt. E.Y.Y. BIRD. Lieut. H.E. TUCKER. 2nd Lieut. J.A. FLETCHER. 2nd Lieut. G.A.B. MONTAGUE. 10th Devon Regt. Att. 2nd Lieut. A. FOWLES. and 7. O.R. 7th Worcesters. Killed. 6. wdn. 7. 8th Worcesters. wdn. 3. Rolies. 1. 5th Gloucesters. wdn. 1. (Slightly at Duty) 4th Oxfords. wdn. 7. 5th Bn. James. Killed 1. wdn. 4. Artillery.	
" "	8.7.16		Moves. Two Companies 5th Sussex from SAILLY proceeded to MAILLY MAILLET. Casualties. 8th Worcester Regt. Wnd. 2/Lieut. S.W. Lewis. O.R. 11. — 4/Royal Berks. Wnd. 1. — 5/9 Worcester Wnd. 1. — 5/Royal Sussex W.nd. 1.	
" "	9.7.16		Casualties. 243rd S.M. Bh. R.F.A. Wnd. 1. — R.S.&J. att. 4/9 Worcesters Killed. 2/Lieut. H.P. FISHER. 4/9 Worcesters Killed, 5. Wnd. 1. — 7/Worcesters Killed. 1. — 5/9 Worcestrs. Wnd. 2. — 4/R. Berks Wnd. 3. — Berks Bn. Wnd. 1. Wnd. 6. — 5/Sussex Wnd. 1.	

Place	Date	Hour	Summary of Events and Information	Remarks and references to Appendices
COUIN	10.7.16		Casualties. 243rd S.H. Bde. R.F.A. Wnd.1. Bucks. Bn Wnd.2 — 4/Royal Berks. Wnd.1. —	
	11.7.16		Casualties. 4/Gloucs. Wnd.2. 7/Warwicks. Wnd.2. — Bucks Bn. Wnd.5. — 5/Ghurkas. Wnd.1. — 4/R.Berks. Killed.1. Wnd.2. — 4/Oxfords. killed 2. Wnd.6. — 5/R.Sussex Wnd.3. —	
	12.7.16		Casualties. 7/Warwicks. Wnd.2. — 5/Gloucesters Wnd.2. — Bucks Bn. Wnd.1. — 4/R.Berks Wnd.5. — 5/Royal Sussex Killed.2. Wnd.10.	
	13.7.16		Casualties. 5/Gloucs. Wnd.1. — 5/R.Sussex Killed.1. Wnd.8. Move. 143rd Inf. Bde. COUIN to BOUZINCOURT	
	14.7.16		Move. 4/Royal Berks + Bucks Batt; from SAILLY BÉTHUNES to SENLIS. 4/Gloucesters + 7/Worcesters from COURCELLES + COIGNEUX to BOUZINCOURT. No. II Field Coy R.E. from ROSIGNOL FARM to ALBERT BOUZINCOURT. 144+145. Bde. H.Q. to BOUZINCOURT. Casualties. 6/Gloucesters. Wnd.16. Among 3. 6/Worcs. died. 144ᵗʰ T.M.Battr. wounded. 2. 7/Worcester. off. 144. T.M. Batt. wounded. 1. 8/Worcesters Killed. 9. 2ⁿᵈ Lieut. A.S.CLOTTERBUCK wounded. 2ⁿᵈ Lieut R.L.HANCOCK. O.R. wounded. 9. 2ⁿᵈ Lieut. N.D.HOUGHTON. O.R. wounded. 5. 4.Oxfords. wounded. 2ⁿᵈ Lieut. H.JEFFERSON. O.R. 2. 5ᵗʰ Warwicks wounded. 3. 7/Warwick. wounded. Lieut.Col. J.M.KNOX.	

Place	Date	Hour	Summary of Events and Information	Remarks and references to Appendices
COUIN	15-7-16		Moved 3rd Rl. Sussex, two Comp-anies from SAILLY LORETTE to BOUZINCOURT. 8th Worcesters, 1st Worcesters, 144 Bde. M.G. Coy, 144 T.M. Battr, 4 1/2 Field Amb., from COUIN to BOUZINCOURT. 3rd Field Coy. R.E. from COURCELLES to BOUZINCOURT. 1st Field Coy. R.E. from DELL to BOUZINCOURT. Casualties 242nd R.F.A. Brigade, wounded, 7. 4th Oxfords, killed 1, wounded 2nd Lieut G.M. RAWLINSON. O.R. 1 missing 2. Following casualties recurred to 143 Bde: att. 25th-Div. on 14-7-16. 7th Warwicks, killed 2nd Lieut H.A.L. BULLOCK, 2nd Lieut F.G. BAKER, 2nd Lieut J.Y. JONES, 2nd Lieut F. FORMAN, all att: from 3rd DORSET Regt. O.R. 68. wounded Capt. D.M. GREG, 2nd Lieut P.E. EDKINS, 2nd Lieut A. SYMES all att. from 3rd DORSET Regt. O.R. 97. missing 31. wounded 9 missing 29. 5th Warwicks wounded 2. 143 Bde M.G. Corps wounded 2nd Lieut F.C.E. STANTON, O.R. 2 missing 1. 36. wounded 40. 7th Warwicks killed Lieut E.W. FOWLER, O.R. 8 wounded 1, 5th Warwicks killed	
BOUZINCOURT	16-7-16		Moved Div. H.B. from COUIN to BOUZINCOURT	

Place	Date	Hour	Summary of Events and Information
BOUZINCOURT	17-7-16		Casualties. 6th Warwick. Wounded 2. 7th Warwick. Wounded 3. 8th Warwick. Wounded 10. 4th Gloucesters. Killed. Lieut E.E. POLACK. Lieut A.D. ANDERSON. O.R. 12. Wounded. 2nd Lieut. C.F. HOLLARD, W.A. SIMMONDS. H. MERRICK + Lieut. H.C. CRUMP. Wounded 170. 2nd Lieut. R.F. ROSSITER. N.S.L.I. attd. 4th Gloucesters Wounded. 7th Worcesters. Killed. 2. Wounded. Lieut. W.C. CASSELS. + 10. O.R. 4 th Suffolks. Wounded. 1. 2nd Lieut. G.M. RAWLINSON. 4 th Norfolks. Reported Wounded. 15-7-16. died of wounds.
			GROVE. 5th Suffolk. BOUZINCOURT TO ALBERT.
			WOUNDED. 30 Prisoners. Guardsmen in Action 6/7 Warwick Regt.
" "	18 7 16		Casualties. 6/R Warwick, 2/Lieut. R.M.C. BATTEN Northants Regt. attd Wnd. 7/R. Warwick Adenia B.B. Schofield 3 rd Dorset attd. Wnd. Lt. (T. Capn) N.C. HINDY 7/R Warwick. attd 14 st T.M. Batty. Wnd. 8/R. Warwick. Killed O.R.S. Lt. R.A. BLOCK 2/Lt. W.L. BLOVET. Wnd. O.R. Wnd. 28. Lt. F.H.M. HARRISON 2/Lt. G.G. WILSON Northants. Regt. attd. Wnd. 2/Lt. P.A. RAINE 3/5.Staffords attd 8/Warwick. Wnd. 2/Lt. F.O. TOWNEND. 5/Middlesex attd 8/Warwick Wnd. Butler Bu. Killed. 1. Wnd. 2/Lt. C. HACE Wnd. O.R. 35. Missing. 2/Lt. R.C. NORWOOD O.R. Missing 19. 8/R Sussex Wnd. 4 ~ 7/Worcs. Killed. 8. Wnd. 83. Missing 2. 7 th Worcs. attd 144 Inf. Bgde. Killed. 3. Wnd. 1. 6/Gloucs. attd

Place	Date	Hour	Summary of Events and Information	Remarks and references to Appendices
BOUZINCOURT	19.7.16		144th Ind.Bde J.H.Barry. Wnd. 3. 2/Lt. E.G.M.King (K.S.L.I.) attd 4/Gloucesters 4/Gloucesters Missing. 35. Casualties. 5/Royal Sussex Killed. 2/Lieut. J.A.SYMONDS Wnd. 2/Lts. L.A. HONEY – A.ADAMS – O.R.7. 5/Glosters Wnd. O.R.1. – 4/Oxfords O.R. killed 10. Wnd. 2/Lt. H. JEFFERSON and 2/Lt. C.FENWICK. 15/Middlesex attd) O.R. Wnd. 84. Missing. 141 – 5/R. Warwicks killed Captain D.G. GUNT. Captain C.V. SUCKLING – 2/Lt. R.J.H. SIMPKIN – O.R. 35. – Wnd. 2/Lt. R.S. TURNER - 2/Lt. R. HEGAN O.R. 63. Missing. 4 – 2/Lt. A.S. EIGHTEEN E. Surrey Regt. attd 5/R. Warwicks Wnd. – 1/4th S. Lancs. attd 5/R. Warwicks Killed 1 – Wnd. 2. – 6/Welsh Regt. attd 5/R. Warwicks Killed. 2 – Wnd. 6. – 6/R. Warwicks Killed 5. Wnd. 47 – Lt. V.A. CARR 3rd Connaught Rangers attd 143 T.M. Battery Wnd. – 2nd Bn. Fld. Coy R.E. Wnd. 4. – 7/Worcesters – killed 2/Lt. J.W. GORRIE O.R. 26. – Wnd. 58 – Missing. 2. – Wnd and Missing 2/Lt. H. GOUGH – 7/Worcesters attd 144 T.M. Battery Wnd.1. – 6/Glosters Wnd. 4. – 4/Gloster. Killed 2. Wnd. 18 – M.G. Corps. attd 144th M.G. Coy Wnd. 2. MOVE. 143rd Inf. Bde. from the line to Divn Reserve at BOUZINCOURT. 145th Inf. Bde. BOUZINCOURT to the line.	

Place	Date	Hour	Summary of Events and Information	Remarks and references to Appendices
BOUZINCOURT	2/7/16		Casualties. 1st S.M. Field Coy. R.E. wounded: 1. 2nd S.M. Field Coy. wounded: 2 Lieut. G.S. PERRY & 2nd Lieut. L.M. WATTS, wounded. O.R.5. 2/1st S.M. Field Coy. R.E. wounded: O.R.3. 105th Field Coy. R.E. att: wounded O.R.1. 5th Somerset wounded: O.R.2. 5th Scot. Rifles Pioneers att: Killed O.R.2. wounded O.R.1. 111th R.F.A. B'de att: wounded: O.R.1. 112th R.F.A. B'de att: Killed O.R.2. wounded: O.R.3. 6th Warwick Killed O.R.3. wounded O.R.16. 7th Warwick Killed O.R.1. wounded O.R.7. 5th Warwick wounded O.R.4. missing O.R.1. 8th Warwick Killed O.R.1. wounded O.R.1. 144th F.A. M.G. Coy. wounded O.R.2. 4th Gloucester Killed 4. O.R. wounded 60. O.R. missing 1. 5th Gloucester Killed O.R.3. wounded O.R.7. 4th Berks wounded O.R.8. Bucks Batt: wounded O.R.1. of 19. O.R. of Bucks Batt. reported missing on 4.15 p.m. 10th 2.O.R. have rejoined. one of them wounded. Moved 5th Somerset H.A.T. 2½ Coy a, 7 & 2nd Field Coy R.E. from ALBERT to M.I.Gd.6. Casualties 2nd/1st Som Fd Coy R.E. Wnd 1. — 105 Fd Cy R.E. att'd killed 1 — Wnd 1. — 7/R Warwicks att'd 143rd M.G. Cy. Wnd 1. — 7/R Warwicks att'd 143rd In Bailey Wd. 1. — 8/R Warwicks att'd 143rd Tm Bailey Wnd 1. — 5/ Somerset Wnd 1. — 2/ W. R. Fd Ambulance Wnd 11 — 6/ Gloster Killed 7 Wnd 2/Lieut. SUTTON-SMITH, DURANT — O.R.74 — Remaining Captain R.E. ELLIOTT O.R. 14 — 7/W rnrs killed 2/Lt WAREHAM — O.R.1 — Wnd 16. — Wnd missing 2/Lt FAIRBROWN	

Place	Date	Hour	Summary of Events and Information	references to Appendices
BOUZINCOURT	21-7-16		Casualties (contd) 8/W'ssters Wnd. Lt. C.R. PAWSEY - 2/Lt. C.T. LODGE - O.R. 16. - M.P. Cpls. and 144 Inf. Bde. Bn. Cy. - Wnd. 1 - 4/R Berks. Killed 12 Wnd. 17 - 5/Gloster Wounded Captain H.C.B. SESSIONS and 2/Lt. P. BADHAM O.R. 37 - Missing Lt. W. FREAM. Lt. C.V.H. PUCKERIDGE. - 2/Lt. S. - FARRIMOND - O.R. 44. - Bucks Bn. Killed 2/Lt. C.W. TRIMMER 2/Lt. C.G. ABBEY O.R. 7. Wnd. 2/Lieut. H.C.E. MASON - 2/Lt. H.V. SHEPHERD. 14th missing and Wnd. O.R. 123 - Missing Captain L.W. CROUCH 2/Lieut. H.E. MOLLOY - Captain Q.G. JACKSON. 2/Lt. R.C. RIGDEN - 2/Lt. J.P. CHAPMAN - 2/Lieut R.E.W. YOUNG. Missing O.R. 1. 72 - 5/4 (attn alto) 145 M.G. Coy Killed 2/Lieut. R.C. MADGER Wnd. O.R.1.	58
	22-7-16		Worcesters 1st Gloucesters arrive L.O.R. missing. 1.O.R. & 14 men reported missing on 31st 2. have rejoined. 8th Worcesters wound No. O.R. 4. 1st Gloucesters about 144 to 1st M.G. by return. 1 O.R. 4 1st Worch. noon. L.O.R. 4. 8th Worcs. noon. 10 A. 5th Gloucester killed 4 O.R. 1 O.R. 4 1st Worch. noon. got Lieut N.E. KNIGHT noon. 2nd Lieuts. H.G. DURRANT and F.R. BELL + died of wounds. got Lieut N.E. KNIGHT noon. 2 Lieuts. L.15. LONDON. moon. O.R. 10. 2.3. O.R. morning. O.R. 9. 5th Gloucs. Killed 2nd Lieut. L.15. LONDON. moon. O.R. 10. 1st 7th Field Coy. R.E. morn. O.R. 9. 2nd 7th Field Coy. R.E. moon. O.R. 2. 2nd 7th. Field Coy. R.E. moon. O.R. 1. 2nd C.A.F.A. Bde. killed O.R. 1.	
	23-7-16		Casualties. Owing to heavy fighting, the following defaults are wanting for today's diary at present return.	

Place	Date	Hour	Summary of Events and Information	Remarks and references to Appendices
BOUZINCOURT	23.7.16	—	Casualties (Cont.) 8/R.Warwicks Wnd.2.— 1st S.M. R&S.Cry. R.E. Wnd.1. 2nd S.M. R&S.Cry. R.E. Wnd.1. Killed 1.— 3rd P.W. Res. Cry. R.E. Killed 1. Wnd. Lieut. R.J. Watts. O.R.7.— 2nd S.M. P.G.A.W.L. Wnd.5.— 111th Bde. R.F.A. att'd Wnd.3.— 8/Warwicks Wnd.5.— 6/Gloucesters att'd 144th T.M. Battery Wnd.2.— 4/Gloucesters Killed 4.— Wnd 2/Lieut. S.W. Fraser R.S.L.I. att'd Wnd.35. O.R.— Missing 2/Lieut. D.F. Maclean R.S.L.I. att'd Missing O.R.1.— 6/Gloucesters Wnd. Lt. W.H. Anderson 2/Lieut. M. Durant — 2/Lieut. C.H. Carruthers — 2/Lieut. W.H. Coombes — 2/Lieut. L.A.H. Stovell 3rd Devons att'd. Missing Major C.E. Coates. Lieut. R.E.P. Parramore 1st Devons att'd 2/Lieut. H. Corbett 3rd Devons att'd 2/Lieut. H.C.P. Balderson 8th Devons att'd - 2/Lieut. G.T.C. Dillon — 7/Warwicks att'd 144th T.M. Battery Wnd. O.R.2. 2nd M.P.I. Casualties 5/R.Warwicks Killed 2/Lieut. P. Matts 7/R.Warwicks Wnd. 2/Lieut. A.J.B. Vincent 3rd Berwicks att'd O.R.7.— 8/R.Warwicks att'd 143rd M.G. Cry. Killed 2/Lieut. D.E. Bennett Wnd. O.R.6. 5/R.Warwicks att'd 143rd Bedford R.Bn. Killed.1. Wnd.2.— 7/R.Warwicks att'd 143rd M.G. Cry. Wnd O.R.1.— Missing Pan Carlos att'd 143rd M.G. Cry. Wnd.1.— 4/Gloucesters Killed 1.	58
	24.7.16		Wnd. 2/Lieut. C.H. Symes O.R.20. Missing 3.— Lt. C.M. Coste. Hunts Cyclists att'd 4/Gloucesters Missing— M.G. Crps. att'd 144th Bde. M.G. Cry. Wnd.1.— 6/Gloucesters. Killed 2. Wnd. 133 Missing. 74.— 4/Royal Berks Killed. 2/Lieut. N. Clayton.—	

Place	Date	Hour	Summary of Events and Information	Remarks and references to Appendices
BOUZINCOURT	24/7/16		Casualties 4/Royal Berks. (Coms) 2/Lieut. G.T. WANSFORD Wnd - 2/Lieut. W.O. DOWN 5/9/Loucesters Wnd. Captain. R.J.C. LITTLE — Captain L.R.C. SUMNER — Captain F.W. COLE - Captain R.M.F. COOKE - Lieut. H.S. KING 2/Lieut. L.J. CLAYTON. 2/Lieut. W.B. LYCETT Monctrands Regt attd 2/Lieut. W.J. PEARCE — Bucks. Bn. Wnd. Captain E.V.D. BIRCHALL Captain O.Y. VINEY — Lieut. E.N.C. WOOLLERTON — 4/Oxfords Killed Captain J.E. BLAKE O.R. 36. Wnd. Captain M.W. EDMUNDS — 2/Queens T.H. HALL — E.E. SMITH — S. SMITH and M. HUTCHINS 5th Batt. Queens attd — O.R. 123. Missing Captain B.B.B. BROOKES O.R. 63. — 5/R Sussex Killed 1. Wnd. 2/Lieut. A.G.F. KENNEDY O.R. 16. — 242nd Sm. Bde. R.F.A. Wnd O.R.1. — 3rd Sh. Fn. Cy. R.E. Wnd. O.R.1. — 110th R.F.A. Bde. attd Wnd. Lieut. C.E.L. LYLE. 25th Div. Arty. attd. 4/Royal Berks. O.R. Killed 23 Wnd. 87 Missing 9 - 5/Glouters. Killed 9 - Wnd. 102 - Missing 28.	587
	25.7.16		Casualties 4th R. Berks. Killed 2/Lieut. H.S. TEED. Wounded 2/Lieut. H.B.F. WENNY and 145th Bde. M.G. Coy. Wnd O.R. 3. — Bucks Bn. Killed O.R. 8. Wounded O.R. 72. Missing 2 — 4/R Royal Berks. attd 145th Bde. M.G. Coy. Wnd Lt. C.T. KAVENHOVEN — 6/R. Warwicks. Wnd O.R. 3. 7/R. Warwicks attd 143rd Bde M.G. Coy. Wnd O.R. 2. — 5/R Warwicks Killed 3	

Place	Date	Hour	Summary of Events and Information	Remarks and references to Appendices
BOUZINCOURT	25/7/16		Casualties (Cont) Wnd. O.R. 5.— 8/Warwicks Wnd. O.R. 4.— 4/Gloucesters Killed Lieut. G.G.D. MASTER — 7/Worcesters Killed O.R. 2. Wnd O.R. 6.— 2/5th Fd. Amb. Wnd O.R.Z. 178th Fd. Amb. Wnd O.R.1.— 242nd Bde R.F.O. Wnd 2/Lieut A.E. MANDER. 243rd Bde R.F.A. Killed Captain O.E. STONE — Wnd O.R. 2.— 4/R Berks Killed 2—Wnd 59- Missing 2.— 1st Sth Fd: Coy. R.E. Wnd. O.R. 2.	
	26.7.16		Casualties. 5th Warwicks. Killed O.R.1. Wounded O.R.11 Missing O.R.1. 1/5th Lancs Wt. 5/5th Warwicks Wounded: O.R.1. 1/6th Welsh. Wd. 6/8th Warwicks Wounded: O.R.4. 6/5th Warwicks Wounded: 2nd Lieut. H.S. POWELL. Wounded O.R.3. 8/5th Warwicks. Wounded O.R.4. 1/6.7/5th Mr. Ly. 5/6th Warwicks att. worn O.R.1. 6/6th Warwicks att. Killed Lieut. A. POTTING 7/6th Warwicks att. worn O.R.1. 14. 3. T.M. Batt. 7/6th Warwicks att. worn O.R.1. 8/6th Warwicks att. worn O.R.1. 7/6th Warwicks att. worn Capt: H.G.M. M.O. D.R. worn 3. 3/6th Jeoman. worn: 3rd Lanc. R. Russ 14 Warwicks O.R.7. Signals Ly. H.Q.2. worn: O.R.1. 242nd R.F.A. Wd. worn: D.F.C.3. Moves. 145th Inf. Bde. BOUZINCOURT → FRANCE, to ARQUEVES. 2nd T.M. Batt. Ly. A.T. BOUZINCOURT to LILLE VILLERS. 1st Horn Amb. BOUZINCOURT to ARQUEVES 2nd T.M. Bde Ly. A.T. BOUZINCOURT to FRANCE.	583
	27.7.16		Casualties. 242nd R.F.A. Wd. worn: 2nd Lieut: A.C. STEPHEN 3rd 7/6th Fus Amb. worn. O.R.1.	

Place	Date	Hour	Summary of Events and Information	Remarks and references to Appendices
BOUZINCOURT	27.7.16		Casualties (cont:) 5th Jumper. nothing. 2nd Lieut J.W.HERBERT. O.R.21. 112th N.F.a Bte. Nil. Killed. O.R.1. 3rd Glo. Rifles. nothing. O.R.3. 5th Glo. Res. adt. 146th - 15th - 16th G. Coy. nothing. O.R.2. N.Z.a. adt. 1.48. T.M.Batt. nothing. O.R.1. 40th Div. Amn. Sub. nothing. (Gas affected) No. 28564. Gunner E.WRIGHT. 1st S.Gr. Field Coy. R.E. nothing. 2nd Lieut. E.M.BROWNE nothing. O.R.35. Moved - 6th Glo. afrom BOUZINCOURT to HÉDAUVILLE. 144th Inf. Bde. less 6th Glo. HQrs & 9th Worcesters from Trenches to HÉDAUVILLE. No 4 Coy. Sioux. FORCEVILLE to ARQUEVES. 14f. Cy. Sioux. FORCEVILLE to TANMAS. 143rd Inf. Bde. Trenches to BOUZINCOURT.	584
LE PLOUY DOMQUEUR	28.7.16		Casualties 5/R. Warwicks. Wd. 2. 7/R.Warwicks killed others. A.C.P.LOVETT. O.R. 13. Wd. 2/dwin. E.F.FABIAN O.R.34. Division O.R.2. - 2/R.Warwicks AUTHI1143d TM Battery Wd. 1. 48th Div. Sig. Coy. Wd. 1. - 6/9 Lancers. Wd. 2 LPoint: L. Savin. Move. Bri. HQrs. - BOUZINCOURT to LE PLOUY DOMQUEUR. 143rd Inf. Bde. BOUZINCOURT to area COULONVILLERS - 145th Inf. Bde. ARQUEVES and BEAUVILLERS to BEAUVAL and BEZAINCOURT - HEM area with 2nd F.A. Coy. R.E. No 2. Coy Amn. Train - 144th Inf. Bde. HEDAUVILLE to ARQUEVES with 2nd SAA Fd. Ambce. Train Bns. 2nd Cys. - HANGEST. FORCEVILLE ARQUEVES.	

Place	Date	Hour	Summary of Events and Information	Remarks and references to Appendices
LE ROUX-DON QUEUR	29.7.16		Consult in. 5/R Sussex Wd. 2/Lieut. L.V. Michele. I.O.R. — 5/R Warwicks Wd. 1. — 6/R Warwicks Wd. 3. — 2/R Warwicks Actd. 2. 6/R W. Colt. T.A. Wilson. Charge D R13. Move 145th Inf Bde. No. 2 Cas. Coy. Div Train, 1st Fd Amb. BEAUVAL G area ORAMONT — No 2 Bde Coy. R.E. BEAUVAL area to MAISON ROLAND — 144th 3rd Bde (Chan 8th Warwick Regt) 2nd Fd Amb. 3rd Fd Amb. Helge Div. Train (Chan 2th Coy) Sh. Mor & Vet Sect. from ARQUEVES- RAINCHEVAL and VADENCOURT to BEAUVAL area — 48th Div R.A. from action near POZIERES to area AMPLIER (Amm & Bde). 5/R Sussex Regt. — 1/13 Fd Corp RE AVELUY to DON QUEUR — 48th Div. Supply Column LEALVILLERS — St. OUEN.	585
	30.7.16		Operation 144th Inf. Bde. Less 8th Worc. Helping Div. Train. 3rd Fd. Amb. Mob. Vet. Section from ARQUEVES area to FRANSU area — Royal Artillery 48th Div. AMPLIER Area to St. OUEN.	
	31.7.16		Nil.	

48th Division.

A？ & Q.

48th DIVISION

AUGUST 1916

Army Form C. 2118.

WAR DIARY
INTELLIGENCE SUMMARY. 48th Division

Army Corps

(Erase heading not required.)

Vol 17

Place	Date	Hour	Summary of Events and Information	Remarks and references to Appendices
LE PLOUY DOHQUEUR	8.8.16		Division in Rest Area — ST.OUEN — DOMART — COULONVILLERS — Fine weather. 5/R.Sussex Regt. DOHQUEUR to BOUZINCOURT to AVELUY by Buses — 1st and 2nd S.M.Fld.Coys. R.E. joined 2nd Fld.Coy. R.E. at LONGVILLERS. Orders received for Move of Division to area BEAUVAL — GEZAINCOURT — CANDAS — LEALVILLERS.	
	8.8.16			
BEAUVAL	9.8.16		Moves. 48th Div. H.Qtrs — 145th Inf.Bde. — 1st,2nd and 3rd S.M.Fld.Amb — BEAU LE-PLOUY — CRAMONT and DOHQUEUR to BEAUVAL. 143rd Inf. Bde. COULONVILLERS to GEZAINCOURT. 144th Inf.Bde (1st Bn. and 2/Worc. Regt. FRANSU and SURCAMPS to AUTHEUX and LONGUEVILLETTE. 1st 2/1/1:3". S.M.Fld.Coys. R.E. LONGVILLERS to AUTHIEULE. 48th Div. R.A. and D.A.C. ST.OUEN to AMPLIER. Casualties. 3/Wilts attd BUCKS Bn. Wnd. 2/Lieut. F.NIALL. 15th Middlesex attd Bucks Bn. Wnd. 2/Lt. M.E. MILROY O.R. Wnd.1. —	
			Casualties. Killed. 2/Lieut. G.A. ALINGTON O.R.1. Wnd. Lieut. F.H. SANGER-DAVIES O.R.1. all s/R.Sussex	
BEAUVAL	10.8.16		Moves. 145th Inf.Bde. BEAUVAL to VARENNES — 144th Inf.Bde. and 2/Worc. AUTHEUX and LONGUEVILLETTE to PUCHEVILLERS — 143rd Inf.Bde. GEZAINCOURT to ARQUEVES and LEALVILLERS — 1st 2nd 3rd S.M. Fld.Amb. from BEAUVAL to VARENNES — PUCHEVILLERS and ARQUEVES — 1st 2nd 3rd S.M. Fld.Coys R.E. AUTHIEULE to ACHEUX. 48th Div. Supply Column ST.RICQUIER (C.44) to BEAUVAL — and Div. Train GEZAINCOURT to FOREVIELLE.	

WAR DIARY or INTELLIGENCE SUMMARY

Army Form C. 2118.

Place	Date	Hour	Summary of Events and Information	Remarks and references to Appendices
BEAUVAL	11.8.16		Casualties - 5/R.Sussex Regt. Wnd. O.R. 7	
			Move - 145th Inf. Bde. VARENNES to BOUZINCOURT and Vicinity	
	12.8.16		Casualties. 243rd Div. Bde. R.F.A. Wnd. Captain J.W. Sutherland - 5/R.Sussex Wnd. 1.	
			Move. 144th Inf. Bde. PUCHEVILLERS to HEDAUVILLE and FORCEVILLE. 1 Bde to BOUZINCOURT - 2in R.A. AMPLIER to BERTIN and BOUZINCOURT area.	
BOUZINCOURT	13.8.16		Casualties. 4/Oxford & Bucks. O.R. Killed 5 - Wnd. 12 - 110th Bde. R.F.A. 12th Div. Otkd. Wnd. 1. - 5/R.Sussex Wnd. 5.	
			Move. 48th Div. Hdqrs. BEAUVAL to BOUZINCOURT - 1st 2nd 3rd S.A. Pk Cos. R.E. ACHEUX to AVELUY and BOUZINCOURT - 145th Inf. Bde to Via Senechan. 144th Inf. Bde. HEDAUVILLE and FORCEVILLE to BOUZINCOURT and Vicinity. 48th B.G.C. AMPLIER to BOUZINCOURT area.	
BOUZINCOURT	14.8.16		Casualties. 8/Warwick Regt. Wnd. 3. - 4/OH(?) J.J. Bucks. Wnd. Lt. C. LAKIN Wnd. Merkens 2/Lt. J. PEARSON - Lt. J.V. KING. 6/Middlesex - Lt. A.W. CARTER 8/Middlesex and J. Mining Lt. W.G. WAYMAN. 7/L.W. HUNTER - 4/R.Berks killed Capt. R.G. ATTRIDGE - 2/Lt. R.G.W. O'HARA - 3/V.E. Summerall - 2/Lt A.W. BEASLEY.	
			Move. 143rd Inf. Bde. Un 2 Batts. LEALVILLERS and ARQUEVES to VARENNES and BOUZINCOURT. Hdqrs. BOUZINCOURT - 2 Batts. VARENNES.	

WAR DIARY or INTELLIGENCE SUMMARY

Army Form C. 2118.

Place	Date	Hour	Summary of Events and Information	Remarks and references to Appendices
BOUZINCOURT	14.8.16		Casualties (Cont.) 4/Royal Berks killed Wnd. Capt. C.A.L. LEWIS — Capt. W.E.M. BLANDY — 2/Lt. C.H. TAYLOR — Missing 2/Lieut. A. BARTRAM — 145th Bde. M.G. Coy. Killed 2 — Wnd. 3. 5/R Sussex Wnd. 1. — Rat. inoculated O.R. — 4/O.Y H/B wtn. 1350 O.R. 4/R Berks 120 O.R.	
-Do-	15.8.16		Casualties. 1st Sm. Fd. Coy. R.E. — Wnd. 2/Lieut. H.S. KING O.R. I. — missing O.R. I. — 2nd Sm. Fd. Coy. R.E. killed O.R. I. — 3rd Sm. Fd. Coy. R.E. Wnd. 2. — 9th Devons attd 144th Bde. M.G. Coy. Wnd. 2/Lieut. E. BARRINGTON — 6/Glosters O.R. killed 4 Wnd 9. — 7/Worc Regt. attd 144th M.G. Coy. Wnd. 3. O.R. 6/Glosters O.R. killed 5. Wnd. 11. — 145th Bde. M.G. Coy. O.R. Wnd. 2 — 145 Tr/ Mor. Battery O.R. Wnd. 1. missing 1. — 4/Royal Berks Died miss. 2/Lieut. A BARTRAM was killed — O.R. killed 22. — Wnd 74 — Missing 50. — 5/Royal Sussex Wnd O.R. 10. — 27/Fd. Coy. R.E. attd. O.R. killed 1. — Wnd. 1. —	
			Moves 2 Batln. 143rd Inf. Bde. VARENNES to BOUZINCOURT	
-Do-	16.8.16		Casualties 1st Sm. Fd. Coy. R.E. Wnd. 1. — 2nd 9th Fld. Coy. R.E. Wnd. — 70th F. Amb. Cy. R.E. Wnd. 4 — Bucks Bn. Wnd 2/Lt. D. FALLON — Lt. F.D. EAGLE. — Capt. V.C. HEATHCOTE — HACKER — 2/Lt. F.C. DIXON — 5/4 Oxon killed 2/Lt. D.G. DURRANT — Wnd. 2/Lt. T.H.A. WOOD — 3rd Northumberland Regt. attd 2/Lt. R.L. HARMSWORTH — 2/Lt. N. VARPS — 2/Lt. P. CHAPMAN — Lt. G. HAWKINS — 4/Royal Berks. Wnd. O.R.I. — O.R. 50 Casualties 5/Royal Sussex Wnd. Capt. S. SMITH — 2/Lt. W.E. STINSON — O.R. killed 6. Wnd. 15 — 4/Glosters attd 144th M.G. Coy. Wnd. 1 — 6/Glosters attd 144th M.G. Coy. O.R. Wnd. 1 —	

WAR DIARY or INTELLIGENCE SUMMARY.

Army Form C. 2118.

Place	Date	Hour	Summary of Events and Information	Remarks and references to Appendices
BOUZINCOURT	17.8.16		Casualties 3rd M.G. Coy. R.E. Wnd. 2. — 2nd S.M. Fd. Coy. R.E. Wnd. 2/Lieut. L.M. WATTS O.R. 6. — 5/R.Warwicks. Wnd. 1 — 6/Warwicks Killed O.R. 3. — 2/Lieut. A.P. HAGG — 4/R.Scots Fusiliers att'd 2/6 B.T.M. PURCHASE 3rd Buff. att'd O.R. 10 — 7/R.Warwicks Wnd O.R. 2. — 4/Oxfd&Bucks L.I. Killed O.R. 10. Wnd Lieut. G.H. GREENWELL O.R. 22. Missing 5. — 1/4th O.R. Killed O.R. 25. Wnd 98. Missing 26. — 4/R.Berks. Wnd O.R. 3 — M.G. Corps att'd 145th Bde 2nd R.Cay. Wnd O.R. 2 — Bucks Bn. 1st O.R. Killed 15. Wnd. 153. Missing 28. — 5/Glosters Killed 2 Wnd. 104 — Missing 25. — 4/Glosters Killed 1 Wnd. m. W. Killed 6. — Wnd.Lieut. McCRUMP Lieut. R.H. DOWN — O.R. 85 Missing 7/R. Birds. 2/Lt. H.G. BAKER — O.R. 20 — 5/R. Sussex Rel'd 2. Wnd 26. —	
BOUZINCOURT	18.8.16 to 28.8.16		Missing. During this period the Division was engaged in heavy fighting in the neighbourhood of OVILLERS – LA BOISSELLE – THIEPVAL – and POZIERES and the following casualties occurred ※ 5/Royal Warwicks Officers Killed 2 – Wnd 4 – O.R. Killed 13 Wnd. 123 Missing 5. — 6/R.Warwicks Officers Killed 6. Wnd 4 — O.R. Killed 39 Wnd. 141 Missing 14. — 7/R.Warwicks Officers Killed — Wnd. 4 — O.R. Killed 17 — Wnd. 141 — 8/R.Warwicks Officers Killed 3. Wnd 3. Missing 1 — O.R. Killed 18 — Wnd. 149. Missing 116. 4/Glosters Officers Wnd 6 – Missing 2 – O.R. Killed 20 Wnd. 147. Missing 20 — 6/Glosters	※ Appendix = 22 H –

WAR DIARY
or
INTELLIGENCE SUMMARY.

Army Form C. 2118.

Place	Date	Hour	Summary of Events and Information	Remarks and references to Appendices
BOUZINCOURT			Officers Killed 1 - Wnd 2 - Missing 2 - O.R. Killed 11 - Wnd 107 - Missing 30 - 7/Worcesters Officers Wnd 2 - O.R. Killed 23, Wnd 54, Missing 8 - 8/Warwicks O.R. Killed 3 Wnd 7 - 5/Gloucs - Officers Killed 4 - Wnd 8 - Missing 1 - O.R. Killed 16 - Wnd 220 Missing 34. 4/Oxford Bucks L.I. Officers Wnd 6 - Missing 2 - O.R. Killed 34 Wnd 183 Missing 52. 1/Bucks Bn. Officers Killed 2, Wnd 6. - O.R. Killed 38 Wnd 213 - Missing 43 - 4/R Berks - Officers Killed 5 Wnd 8 - O.R. Killed 49 Wnd 167 Missing 56 - 5/R Sussex - Officers Wnd 2 - O.R. Killed 13 Wnd 61 - Casualties 242nd Bde R.F.A. Wnd 30. Captain T.B Pritchett - 240th Bde R.F.A. Wnd. O.R. 4 - 4/Glouc Wnd 1 -	
	3/8/16.		Moved I.H. following morning to Arch Have - Aug 26th 144th Inf Bde Bouzincourt to Forceville - Aug 27. 146th Inf Bde: Forceville to Hailly - Hallett and Ivanhoes Aug 28th 143rd Inf Bde Sus 7 & 8th R. Warwicks from Bouzincourt to Varennes 7th & 8th R Warwicks to Warthimont Wood Bus. - 145th Inf Bde Trenches to Bouzincourt - 1st Fld Ambulance - Bouzincourt to Bus - 2nd Fld Ambul. Varennes to Vauchelles - 3rd Fld Ambulance Louvencourt to Bertrancourt - 5/R Sussex Avelay to Vauchelles - 3rd Fld Coy R.E. Avelay to Englebelmer N 12th Fld Coy	

Army Form C. 2118.

WAR DIARY
or
INTELLIGENCE SUMMARY.
(Erase heading not required.)

Instructions regarding War Diaries and Intelligence Summaries are contained in F. S. Regs., Part II. and the Staff Manual respectively. Title pages will be prepared in manuscript.

Place	Date	Hour	Summary of Events and Information	Remarks and references to Appendices
Moves (cont.)			R.E. AVELUY to AUTHIE and BUS. — Cav. 29th. 143rd Inf. Bde. VARENNES to AUTHIE. — 145th Inf. Bde. BOUZINCOURT to BUS. Div. Hdqrs. BOUZINCOURT to BERTRANCOURT on Aug. 28th.	

[signature]
Major General
Commanding 48th (S.M.) Division

1 / 2

Unit	Date	Officers K	Officers W	Officers M	Other ranks K	Other ranks W	Other ranks M	Names of Officers
5 Warwicks	19/8/16 20/8/16	2	3	-	14	99	5	2/Lt W E Curtis (K) 2/Lt L P Kyd (K) Capt H L R J Groom (W) 2/Lt S Coulson (W) 2/Lt W S Townsend (W)
	24/8/16	-	-	-	4	23	-	
	25/8/16	-	-	-	-	1	-	
	28/8/16	-	1	-	-	-	-	2/Lt G Buck attd 4 Berks
		2	4	-	18	123	5	
6 Warwicks	18/8/16	-	-	-	3	11	-	
	19/8/16 20/8/16	6	3	-	29	104	14	Capt R C Lowe (K) Lt C J Crockett (K) 2/Lt R J Hacco (K) 2/Lt J Omar (K) 2/Lt G B Pearson (K) 2/Lt A Skillington (K) Capt E B Hargreaves (W) 2/Lt H V Shelton (W) 2/Lt G J Seddon (W)
	23/8/16	-	-	-	-	6	-	
	24/8/16	-	1	-	-	1	-	2/Lt W S Cattell
	25/8/16	-	-	-	6	5	-	
	26/8/16	-	-	-	1	7	-	
	27/8/16	-	-	-	2	7	-	
		6	4	-	39	141	14	
7 Warwicks	18/8/16	-	-	-	-	4	-	
	19/8/16 20/8/16	-	2	-	4	76	-	Lt W E Murray 2/Lt R G Pirie
	21/8/16	-	-	-	4	29	-	
	22/8/16	-	-	-	-	9	-	
	23/8/16	-	1	-	-	-	-	Capt R B Mason - Won 18th
	25/8/16	-	1	-	3	7	-	Capt R Godfrey-Payton
	28/8/16	-	-	-	6	16	-	
		-	4	-	17	141	-	
8 Warwicks	19/8/16	-	1	-	-	4	-	2/Lt R H Hinton
	20/8/16	-	-	-	-	1	-	
	21/8/16	-	-	-	8	9	-	
	22/8/16	-	-	-	-	13	-	
	25/8/16	-	-	-	3	12	-	
	26/8/16	-	-	-	-	7	3	
	28/8/16	3	3	1	7	144	73	Lt R C Denison (K) Lt R G Day (K) 2/Lt L P Barton (K) Capt S H H Eaton (W) 2/Lt C M Holmes (W) 2/Lt R G Snowden (W) 2/Lt H S Toogood (M)
		3	4	1	18	190	76	

2

Unit	Date	Officers			Other ranks			Names of Officers
		K	W	M	K	W	M	
4 Glosters	16/8/16	-	3	2	5	46	20	2/Lt Helcrust (W) 2/Lt R.H. Dowen (W) 2/Lt R Bird (W) 2/Lt H.G. Bakin (M) 2/Lt E.J. Lissimore (M)
	22/8/16	-	-	-	12	60	-	
	23/8/16	-	1	-	5	60	-	2/Lt L.H. Scalles
	26/8/16	-	1	-	-	-	-	Capt. G. Ginterbock (S at duty)
	30/8/16	-	1	-	-	1	-	2/Lt E Davis
		-	6	2	22	167	20	
6 Glosters	21/8/16	-	2	1	6	50	20	2/Lt W.E. Hawkins (W) Lt J.V. Blad (W) 2/Lt B.A. Woodford (M)
	22/8/16	1	-	1	2	40	10	Lt J.K Gilman (K) 2/Lt E.B. Clarke (M)
	23/8/16	-	-	-	3	12	-	
	26/8/16	-	-	-	-	5	-	
		1	2	2	11	107	30	
3 Worcesters	21/8/16	-	1	-	8	15	-	G.J.O Melhuish
	22/8/16	-	-	-	12	30	8	
	25/8/16	-	-	-	3	6	-	
	28/8/16	-	-	-	-	2	-	
	29/8/16	-	-	-	-	1	-	
	30/8/16	-	1	-	-	-	-	Lt J.C.H. Hill (W on 25)
		-	2	-	23	54	8	
8 Worcesters	24/8/16	-	-	-	-	1	-	
	25/8/16	-	-	-	-	3	-	
	26/8/16	-	-	-	-	1	-	
	30/8/16	-	-	-	3	2	-	
		-	-	-	3	7	-	
5 Glosters	18/8/16	1	5	-	3	104	25	2/Lt D.G. Durrant (K) 2/Lt J.A. Gleave, 2/Lt R.C. Harmsworth 2/Lt N Vears, 2/Lt L Chapman J.G Hawkins
	19/8/16	-	-	-	-	14	-	
	20/8/16	-	-	-	-	4	-	
	23/8/16	-	1	-	-	4	-	2/Lt K.E Church
	25/8/16	-	-	-	-	3	-	
	27/8/16	-	-	-	-	8	-	
	28/8/16	3	2	1	13	80	9	Lt C.L. Moore (K) J.G.W Winterbotham (K) 2/Lt R.S Apperley (K) 2/Lt N.G.N Smith (W) 2/Lt L.T Bigger (W) 2/Lt G Byrun (M)
		4	8	1	16	220	34	

Unit	Date	K	W	M	K	W	M	Names of Officers

3

Unit	Date	Officers K	Officers W	Officers M	Other ranks K	Other ranks W	Other ranks M	Names of Officers
4" Oxf & Bucks	14/8/16	-	4	2	25	98	26	2/Lt C Lakin (W) 2/Lt G Pearson (W) 2/Lt V King (W) 2/Lt R W Carter (W) 2/Lt A Wayman (M) 2/Lt L C Hunter (M) Lt C H Greenwell
	17/8/16 18/8/16	-	1	-	5	36	2	
	24/8/16				1	13		
	25/8/16		1		2	23	4	
	29/8/16				1	13	-	
		-	6	2	34	183	32	
Bucks Bn	16/8/16	-	4	-	15	153	28	2/Lt D Fallon Lt L D Earl Capt V C Heathcote-Hacker 2/Lt L C Dixon
	24/8/16 25/8/16	2	2	-	23	60	15	2/Lt E W Bates (K) 2/Lt W R Heath (K) 2/Lt M Bowen (W) 2/Lt H W Breton (W)
		2	6	-	38	213	43	
4" R Berks	14/8/16	4	3	-	28	81	34	Capt R G Attride (K) 2/Lt P C W O'Hara (K) 2/Lt A W Beasley (K) 2/Lt R Bartram (K) Capt C A L Lewis (W) Capt W S M Blandy (W) 2/Lt B H Taylor (W)
	16/8/16					1		
	17/8/16					3		
	18/8/16		1					Lt E C Smith
	19/8/16	1	3		9	30	-	Lt L E Ridley (K) Capt G H W Cruttwell Capt C N Lacy Lt G A C Wix
	20/8/16					2		
	21/8/16				3	2		
	23/8/16		1		9	48	22	Lt L O Garside
		5	8	-	49	167	56	
5" Sussex	16/8/16		2		6	15		Capt S Smith 2/Lt W E Stinson
	17/8/16				2	26		
	18/8/16				1	1		
	19/8/16				2	8		
	22/8/16				1	3		
	24/8/16				1	5		
	28/8/16					3		
		-	2	-	13	61		

48th. DIVISION

A. & Q.

48th. DIVISION

SEPTEMBER 1 9 1 6.

CONFIDENTIAL.   48th Division.
                                                            7766 A.X.

D.A.G., G.H.Q.,
    3rd Echelon.

        Herewith original and duplicate copies of War Diaries
for month of September, 1916, for "A" & "Q" Branch, 48th
Division.

        Kindly acknowledge.

                                                    Major-General.
October 1st, 1916.   Commanding 48th Division.

WAR DIARY
A ＆ Q or Branch
INTELLIGENCE SUMMARY

Army Form C. 2118.

Place	Date	Hour	Summary of Events and Information	Remarks and references to Appendices
BERTRANCOURT	Sept 1st 1916		Casualties 5/R.Warwick Wnd O.R.3 — 48th Bde. Wnd O.R.1 — 2/3rd Bn R.F.A. Missing 1. — 2/Warwicks O.R. Wnd 10. — 7/Warwicks attd. 143rd B. Wnd 1. — 6/Gloucesters attd. 144th B. Wnd 1. — 6/Gloucesters Wnd 1. — 6/9 Gloucesters killed 1. — Wnd 2/Lieut A.C. Stevenson O.R. 4. 6/9 Gloucesters Wnd 1. — 7/Worcesters killed 1. — Wnd 1 — No. 38 & 48th Divl. Sig. Cay. R.E. Wnd 1. —	
			Horses — Nil.	
	2/9/16		Casualties 4/6 Gloucesters killed 1. — 4/6 Glosters Wnd 1. — 4/6 Gloucesters Wnd. Lieut. F.D. Andrews Minor. 5/R Warwick Wanderout Wood to Sarton. 6/R Warwicks Warnemont Wood to Vauchelles. 7/R Warwicks Wanderout Wood to Authie. 8/R Warwicks Warnemont Wd nord to Thievres. 123rd M.G. Coy. Authie to Thievres	
	3/9/16		Casualties 4/R Warwicks killed 1. Wnd 7 — 4/R Gloucesters killed 5 Wnd 6 — 4/Warwicks Wnd 2. 7/Worcesters attd 144 Inf. Bty wnd. Captn B.H. Bright O.R. 2 — 2 Pr. Corp attd. 144 R. Coy. Wnd 1. No. 3 Sec. 48th Div. Sig. Coy. R.E. W 1. — R.W.P. Devas. 48 M.M.G. 48th Div. wnd — Sec. Moves 48th Divl. Hdqrs. Bertrancourt to Beauval.	
BEAUVAL	4/9/16		Casualties 240th Bn A.L R.E.A. Wnd 2. 2/Lieut C.H. Taynton O.R. 10. — 241st Bn R.F.A. Wnd O.R. 1. — 242nd Bn R.F.A. Wnd 2 — 243rd R.F.A. OR Wnd 1. — DAC OR Wnd 1.	

WAR DIARY or INTELLIGENCE SUMMARY

Army Form C. 2118.

Place	Date	Hour	Summary of Events and Information	Remarks and references to Appendices
BEAUVAL	4.9.16		Casualties (Cav). 243rd Bde RFA. (2.11d 1.wd.6. (on 3-9-16).	
	5.9.16		Casualties. 4/9 Lincoln West — 6/9 Yorkshire Rifles 2 — Wnd 2 — 4/9 Lincoln killed 1 — Wnd 2 — 6/9 Lincoln Killed 1 — Wnd 2 — 7/9 tracto killed 1 — Wnd 2. Support 2-Bn 145th Inf. Bde Bus to Ivergny 2 Bn 144th Inf. Bde Ivergny to Bus. Connection Nil.	
	6.9.16		Moves 145th Inf. Bde and 1 Battn — to MAILLY-MAILLET. 144th Inf. Bde — less 2 Battns to BUS.	
	7.9.16		Casualties 6th & 7th 243 Bde RFA. wounded OR 2 & one Casualties 6 num 7th to Oxfords wounded OR 2 in Berks RR Killed OR.1. wounded OR 1. -. 2-5th Battn Regt reported missing on 29/8/16. No. A.790. now reported wounded. Moves 1st Field bank from BUS-les-ARTOIS to SARTON. 2nd Field Amb. from VAUCHELLES to WARNIMONT WOOD. 3 Field Amb from BERTRANCOURT to BUS-les-ARTOIS. Capt. DAVENPORT reports to AUSTRN. REGT. and assumes command. Capt DOBIN joins 2nd A. Inf. Bde.	

WAR DIARY
or
INTELLIGENCE SUMMARY.
(Erase heading not required.)

Army Form C. 2118.

Instructions regarding War Diaries and Intelligence Summaries are contained in F. S. Regs., Part II. and the Staff Manual respectively. Title pages will be prepared in manuscript.

Place	Date	Hour	Summary of Events and Information	Remarks and references to Appendices
BEAUVAL	8.9.16	-	Casualties - Bucks Bn. O.R. Wounded 1.	
	9.9.16	"	Casualties - 4. R. Berks Regt - Killed - O.R. 1 wounded O.R. 1.	
	10.9.16	"	Casualties - Bucks Bn. wounded O.R. 3 - 4 R. Berks - Killed O.R. 1. wounded O.R. 1.	
			Move - 145th Bde from MAILLY to BUS and WARNIMONT WOOD.	
	11.9.16	-	Moves - 5 R. Sussex Regt - VAUCHELLES to LONGUEVILLETTE	
			1st 2nd and 3rd Fwd Coy R.E. " "	
			No 1 Coy DUFTRAIN - VARENNES to GEZAINCOURT	
			No 4 " " " "	
			143rd Inf Bde - AUTHIE division to GEZAINCOURT.	
			145" Inf Bde - BUS " to BEAUVAL	
			1st Trench Mortar SARTON to GEZAINCOURT	
			2" " " BUS to BEAUVAL	
			Casualties - Nil.	
	12.9.16		Casualties - 4th Ox Bucks L.I. Missing + has R.E. BEAUVAL-LONGUEVILLETTE 1st	
			H.E.A.	

WAR DIARY
or
INTELLIGENCE SUMMARY.

Army Form C. 2118.

(Erase heading not required.)

Place	Date	Hour	Summary of Events and Information	Remarks and references to Appendices
BEAUVAL	13.9.16		Moves: Bde H.Q & 131 -- Bus to Amplier and Onward. 3 Field Ambce units -- No 3 Coy Train -- Varennes to Orville -- in morning 69th Bde R.V. to Sarton.	
			Casualties - Nil.	
	14.9.16		Casualties - Nil - Moves Nil.	
	15.9.16		Casualties - Nil - Moves - 5th Sussex Regt. to Senlis.	
	16.9.16		Casualties Nil - Moves Nil.	
	17.9.16		Casualties 291st Bde RFA W.d 1 -- 243rd Bde RFA w.d 1 -- 2/R S Sussex W.d 2/ Accid.	
			J.E.C. Langham Killed O.R.1 W.d OR.17	
BERNAVILLE	18.9.16		Casualties Nil.	
			Moves 48th Div H.Q's Beauval to Bernaville - H.Q. Co 48th Div train Varennes to Candas.	
			143rd Inf Bde Gezaincourt Comm. & Beaumetz - Prouville and Bernaville area --	
			144th Inf Bde Amplier & Occoches - Mezerolles - Autheux area - H.Q R.E Auth.	
			Amplier area La Mon Plage - 4th Sou R.E. K Occoches - Mezerolles area -	
			145th Inf Bde - Beauval to Bernaville and Candas - Fienvillers area - Train -	
			No 2 Coy. Amplier to Lanches - No 3 Coy. Occoches - No 4 Coy. Candas - Majveles.	
			Beauval to Candas- H.Q Ft Amm & Fienvillers.	

WAR DIARY
or
INTELLIGENCE SUMMARY.
(Erase heading not required.)

Army Form C. 2118.

Place	Date	Hour	Summary of Events and Information	Remarks and references to Appendices
BERNAVILLE	19.9.16		Casualties 240th Bde R.F.A. Killed Major G.D. BROWNE — Lieut R.W.F. WYATT — Wnd. Captain W.B. LAWRENCE — Rank & Files R.F.A. Wnd. 1 — 241st Bde RFA Wnd. Captn H.H. do " VALANEY	
	20.9.16		Moved HQrs 2 Coy Div: Train & Batches to PROVILLE. No moves.	
	21.9.16		Casualties 7/R Warwicks Wnd 1 —	
	22.9.16		Nothing to report	
	23.9.16		Casualties S/R Sussex Regt. O.R. Wnd 4 —	
	24.9.16		Casualties 241st Bde. RFA Wnd 2	
			Moved 7/R Warwicks BEAUVAL to PROVILLE — HQrs R.E. HEZECQUES to BERNAVILLE	
			HQrs Divl Train CANDAS to BERNAVILLE — N°1 Cy R.E. OUTREBOIS to CANDAS — 2nd/43rd	
			Fd Coy. R.E. OUTREBOIS and OCCOCQUES to BERNAVILLE	
	25.9.16		Casualties 241st Bde. R.F.A. Wnd. 1 —	
			Moved 143rd Inf. Bde HQrs PROVILLE to RIBEAUCOURT	
			Casualties Nil.	
	26.9.16		Moved 8/Warw Regt. OUTREBOIS to DOMESMONT and EPECAMPS.	

T.131. Wt. W708—776. 500000. 4/15. Sir J.C. & S.

Army Form C. 2118.

WAR DIARY
or
INTELLIGENCE SUMMARY.
(Erase heading not required.)

Instructions regarding War Diaries and Intelligence Summaries are contained in F.S. Regs., Part II. and the Staff Manual respectively. Title pages will be prepared in manuscript.

Place	Date	Hour	Summary of Events and Information	Remarks and references to Appendices
BERNAVILLE	27.9.16	-	Casualties 242nd Bde. R.F.A. Wnd. O.R. 1.	
	28.9.16	-	Nil.	
			Casualties 5/R.Sussex Wnd. 2/Lieut. H.M. Whitehead O.R.1 — 241st Siege Bty. R.F.A. Wnd O.R.5.	
			Move 3/R.Warwicks Beaumetz to Martigny-les-Jongleurs —	
	29.9.16		Casualties 243rd Bde. R.F.A. killed near Colincamps CFB West — 240th Bde. R.F.A. Wnd. Knit.	
			E.R.L. Tiernan 243rd Bde. R.F.A. O.R. killed in Wd.3 — 240th Bde R.F.A. Wnd 2. 5/R.Sussex	
			Regt. Wnd 2.	
			Moves 143rd Inf Bde. Ribeaucourt and Prouville, Heuzecourt Area to Oneux Mondicourt	
			Gorenflos — Halloy. — No.2 Cy Div Train — Mt Renault Fme to Halloy — 145th Inf Bde.	
			Candas and Fienvillers Area to area Warluzel — Humbercourt — Sombrin — No.4 Cy.	
			Div. Train — Candas to Warluzel — H.Q. 48th Div A.E. Candas to Sombrin. 2nd Hvy.	
			R.E. Bernaville to Couturelle. 3rd S. Midld Cy R.E. Abbeville to Sus-St-Leger — 8/Worcs Regt	
			Beauvoisines Bouquemaison Outrebois	
			Casualties 5/R.Sussex Regt. Wnd. 1. 240th Div. Bde. R.F.A. Wnd 7.	
HENU	30.9.16		Move 48th Div. H.Qrs. Bernaville to Henu — 144th Inf Bde. Area Authieux — L'Heureuse —	
			Outrebois to area Sus-St-Leger — Ivergny — Beauvoisin — No.3 Cy. Div. Train Outrebois	
			la Thierry — 42nd H.F.A. Vet. Section (Candas to Grincourt — 1st Sth. Midld. Ambulance — Barlette and Ribeaucourt	
			to Neuvillette —	

T2131. Wt. W708-776. 500000. 4/15. Sir J. C. & S.

Army Form C. 2118.

WAR DIARY
or
INTELLIGENCE SUMMARY.
(Erase heading not required.)

Place	Date	Hour	Summary of Events and Information	Remarks and references to Appendices
HQ	3rd		March (cont.) 2/8th Battn. Outlying Pickettes to our Warwicks - 4/5th South West Berkshire to Warincourt- 1st/24 8th Middlesex- Havoy to Souatre- Sailly - Bayencourt and St Amand - 5/10 Sussex Regt. At Hdqt 16 Bayencourts	

R. J. Hulham
Brig. Major
for Brigadier-General
Commanding 148th Br. H. Division

Vol 19

War Diary -
"A" & "Q" Branch 48 Division
October 1916
Volume XIX

Army Form C. 2118.

WAR DIARY
INTELLIGENCE SUMMARY

(Erase heading not required.)

Instructions regarding War Diaries and Intelligence Summaries are contained in F. S. Regs., Part II. and the Staff Manual respectively. Title Pages will be prepared in manuscript.

Place	Date	Hour	Summary of Events and Information	Remarks and references to Appendices
HENU	1.10.16		Casualties. Nil.	
			Moves. 5/R. Sussex Regt. BAYENCOURT to SOUASTRE - No 2 Cay. Div. Train HALLOY to HENU - 144th Inf. Bde. SUS-ST-LEGER - IVERGNY - BEAUDRICOURT to HALLOY - GRENAS - MONDICOURT - No 3 Coy. Div. Train IVERGNY to HALLOY - No 4 Coy. Div. Train WARLUZEL to WARLINCOURT - 145th Inf. Bde. Area WARLUZEL - COULLEMONT - HUMBERCOURT to WARLINCOURT - GRINCOURT - ST AMAND - 1st Aus. Amn. VAUCHELLES to ST AMAND. 2nd Fd. Amb. to CUIN. 2nd Fd. Amb. to SOUASTRE - 1st Hd. Coy. R.E. to GAUDIEPRÉ. 2nd Fd. Coy. to SAILLY 3rd Fd. Coy. to GRENAS.	
	2.10.16		Casualties. 6/R Sussex Regt. Wnd. Cpl. T.W. ROSE. O.R. 1 —	
			Moves. 48th Div. R.A. BOUZINCOURT - HDqrs - HENU - 240th, 241st, 243rd + DAC. to WARLINCOURT - 242nd Bde - to ST AMAND.	
	3.10.16		Casualties. 5/R Warwicks O.R Wnd. 1 - 7/R Warwicks O.R Wnd. 1.	
			Move. 2 Batln. 144th Inf. Bde. from HALLOY Area to ST AMAND and SOUASTRE.	
	4.10.16		Casualties. 8/R Warwicks Wnd. 1 - 7/Yorks (Pion. attd) Wnd. 1 —	
			1 Batln. 144th Inf. Bde. ST AMAND to HALLOY	

Army Form C. 2118.

WAR DIARY
or
INTELLIGENCE SUMMARY
(Erase heading not required.)

Place	Date	Hour	Summary of Events and Information	Remarks and references to Appendices
HENU	5.10.16		Casualties - 8/R Warwicks Wnd 1. 8/R Warwicks Killed 1. Wnd 2. - 241st Bde R.F.A. Wnd 2. —
Moves. 1 Battn 145th Inf. Bde. ST. AMAND to Trenches - 1 Battn. 145th Inf. Bde. WARLINCOURT to SOUASTRE - Brigadier's H.Qrs. M.G. Coy. T.M. Batty + 3 Batts 143rd Inf. Bde. 143rd Inf. Bde. ST. AMAND 1 Battn Trenches - 145th Inf. Bde. H.Qrs. M.G. Coy. T.M. Batty. 1 Battn SOUASTRE - 2 Battn WARLINCOURT. 1 Battn Trenches.	
	6.10.16		Casualties - 8/R Warwicks Killed 1. Missing 1. 8/R Warwicks Killed 1. Wnd 5 5/R Sussex Wnd 7.
Moves. Nil.	
	7.10.16		Casualties. Nil.
Moves. 144th Inf. Bde. HALLOY to LAHAIE 2 Battn - 1 SOUASTRE and 1 HALLOY to Trenches - 143rd Bde Concentrated at ST AMAND 145th Inf. Bde SOUASTRE 2 Battn WARLINCOURT - Supply Column at LUCHEUX.	
	8.10.16		Casualties 8/R Warwicks Wnd 1. — 6/Gloucs Wnd 1. — 5/Inf Bde. Wnd 1 —
Forestry wnd 3 / Lincolns Wnd 1. 7/Bedns Wnd 2. —
Moves. Nil.	
	9.10.16 to 13.10.16		No moves of a big nature occurred - and the Division remained in present positions. The following Casualties occurred.	

WAR DIARY
or
INTELLIGENCE SUMMARY

Army Form C. 2118.

Place	Date	Hour	Summary of Events and Information	Remarks and references to Appendices
HENU	18.10.16		5/R Warwicks Wnd.1. — 6/R Warwicks Killed 3 - Wnd 11. — 8.R Warwicks Wnd 2 — 4/5 Glo'sters.Killed 1. Wnd.6. — 6/Glo'sters. Wnd. 2/Lt. G. KINNEIR — 5/9 Glo'sters - Wnd 4 — 4/Royal Berks - Killed 1- Wnd.7. 6/R. Sussex Wnd.5 — 240 Sh.Bde RFA Wnd.1 — 241st Sh.Bde RFA. Wnd.1 — 242nd Bde RFA Killed 1 Wnd 3. 243rd Sh Batty Wnd.1. — X 48 Tr.M. Batty Wnd.1. — Y 48 Tr.M. Batty Wnd.1 — 143rd Tr.M.Batty Wnd 1 offrs & 8 oth.ranks Wnd 2. 145th R. Eng. Wnd.1 — 2/1st S.M. Fld. Cmp.R.E. Killed 1 wnd.1. — 1st Staff.Coy R.E. Killed 1 — 48th Div. Train A.S.C. 2/Lieut H BUETTELL A.S.C. Wnd - Taking supplies to HEBUTERNE — Moves — NIL — Casualties NIL	
	19.10.16		Moves 7/R & 8th R Warwicks St AMAND to SOMBRIN - 7th Wor. from Trenches to HUMBERCOURT Hdqrs 145th Inf Bde and 4/Royal Berks Bouastre to WARLUZEL and WARLINCOURT Bucks Bn. WARLINCOURT to WARLUZEL 4/Oxford Bucks WARLINCOURT & WARLUZEL 5/9 Glo'sters. HENU to WARLINCOURT. Casualties NIL 8/10 men Wnd.5.	
	20.10.16		Moves. Hdqrs. 143rd Inf Bde. St AMAND to GRANDE ROULLECOURT - 5th & 6th R Warwicks 143rd Inf. Bde. Coy to Tr. Battery from St AMAND to GRANDE ROULLECOURT 144th Inf Bde Hdqrs LA HAIE Free to SUS. ST. LEGER - 4/6 Glo'sters. Trenches to Trenches area WARLINCOURT - 6/R Glo'sters. St AMAND to IVERGNY area / Wor. from HUMBERCOURT and B/Wars. from BOUASTRE to IVERGNY area	

Army Form C. 2118.

WAR DIARY
or
INTELLIGENCE SUMMARY

(Erase heading not required.)

Instructions regarding War Diaries and Intelligence Summaries are contained in F. S. Regs., Part II. and the Staff Manual respectively. Title Pages will be prepared in manuscript.

Place	Date	Hour	Summary of Events and Information	Remarks and references to Appendices
HENU	20.10.16		144th T.M. Battery HEBUTERNE to SOUASTRE — 144th M.G. Coy. to IVERGNY Area — 5/9 Lincolns a/R Bosn. 14/5th T.W. Poetry & M.G. Coy. WARLINCOURT to WARLUZEL Area — 5/R. Sussex Regt. SOUASTRE to WARLINCOURT — M. & S. Coy. R.E. LA HAIE to WARLUZEL No.2 Cy. HENU to SOMARIN Area T/o. 3 Cy. SOUASTRE to IVERGNY Area — 1st Fld. Ambs. St Amand to SOMARIN Area — T/o 2 & 3 Cup Ams. Train WARLINCOURT to SOMARIN and IVERGNY Area —	
HENU	21.10.16		H.dqrs. 48th Div. HENU to DOULLENS — 4/9 Lincolns. WARLINCOURT to IVERGNY Area — 144th M.G.Coy. Bally. SOUASTRE to SUS-ST-LEGER — 2/3rd Fld. Coy. R.E. from HENU and 3rd Fld. Coy R.E. from SOUASTRE to WARLINCOURT — 2/3 Sth. Md. Ambulance COUIN to COUTURELLE — H.dqrs. North Cup. Div. Train WARLINCOURT to COUTURELLE	
DOULLENS	22.10.16		H.dqrs. 48th Div. Train COUTURELLE to DOULLENS — 145th Infantry Bde. Group (Worcesters. 2nd Bn. Rifle Brigade, Div. Train 1st M.Fld Coy R.E.) to BEAUVAL — 8th Mx. Fd. Amb. COUTURELLE to BEAUVAL. Capt. S.A. GABB. D.A.D.M.S. & left for 2nd Corps. Capt. O.W. HALL O.C. 48th Div Supply Col. to BEAUVAL. Capt. I. LEA joined Div adjutment. WHITE (Bonin Pity) joined Xtra Ch/T. GABB, Capt. E.I. LEA joined Div adjutment. Moves. 48th Div. HQ, 48 Div R.E.M.A., 48 Div Sig. Co., 48 Div San Sect., 48 Div Salvage Co. to BAISIEUX. 145 Inf Bde Group (145 Inf Bde, 2nd S.M. Fld Amb, No 4 Co. Train, 1st S.M Fld Co. R.E.) to TALMAS.	
BAISIEUX	23.10.16			
BAISIEUX	24.10.16		Move 145 Inf. Bde Group (as above) to BEHENCOURT & LA HOUSSOIE. Mob Vet Sec, HQ 48 Div Train, Co Train, 1st Line T/p of 143 & 144 Bde Gps + 1/2 Lon Tp 5th Survey to TALMAS.	

2449 Wt. W14957/M90 750,000 1/16 J.B.C. & A. Forms/C.2118/12.

WAR DIARY or INTELLIGENCE SUMMARY

Army Form C. 2118.

Place	Date	Hour	Summary of Events and Information	Remarks and references to Appendices
BAISIEUX	25/10/16		Move 143 Bde Gp (143 M Bty, 1 Sm Fd Amb, 2nd & 3rd Coy R.E. No 2 Coy Train) to FRANVILLERS. HQ Btn to BAISIEUX. 144 Inf Bde, 2 S.M. & Amb. 2 S.M.? Coy R.E. No 3 Coy Train to BRESLE. 5th R. Surrey to BAISIEUX via MOTT VL Sd. HQ 4/8 Div Train to BAISIEUX. 1/7 Coy R.E. to FRICOURT F.W.	
BAISIEUX	26/10/16		143 & 144 Bdes to BECOURT. 2 & 3 Coy R.E. to HAMETZ WOOD (S13d 2.2.) 1st & 7 Coy R.E. & S.R. Surrey Regt (incl 6 Pnrs 150 R) to X 28 c, 10 officers & 50 O.R. to S13 d 6.2. 3 St. Amb. to BECOURT. Left Sec to III Corps M/Adw Unit. Casualties 2 & 2 Bde R.F.A. 4 O.R. Wounded.	
BAISIEUX	27/10/16		5,6,7. R War Regt to HAMETZ WOOD, 3 Inf Amb. to Tents Bart Sh BECOURT. 2nd D. Coy to FRANVILLERS. Casualties - Nil	
BAISIEUX	28/10/16		No news or casualties	
BAISIEUX	29/10/16		Casualties X TM Batty 2 O.R. wounded, 1/4 RGA, 1/4 RFA ? Turvey ? Wood ?	
BAISIEUX	30/10/16		? News ? ? Casualties In N.S. CATTELL 4/ NORTHANTS altered 1/6 R War Regt accidental S/W. Casualties 2 & 1 Bde R.F.A. - 4 O.R. wounded including 2nd Bdy. Norts 4/8 Div HQ, No R.E. Pct Vet Sn. to MILLENCOURT CAMP, 1/4 S.R. Gpron to MILLENCOURT Village, 1/4 Coy Bde Train ALBERT. HQ Div Train ALBERT. No 3 Coy Cav to E3d South of main ANIENS road. A. F. Div S. Col to FRANVILLERS. Div Salvage Coy to ALBERT.	

Commanding 48th (S.M.) Division

Vol 20

War Diary.

"A" "Q" Branch. 48th Divn,

November 1916.

Volume XI.

Army Form C. 2118.

WAR DIARY
or
INTELLIGENCE SUMMARY

(Erase heading not required.)

Instructions regarding War Diaries and Intelligence Summaries are contained in F. S. Regs., Part II. and the Staff Manual respectively. Title Pages will be prepared in manuscript.

Place	Date	Hour	Summary of Events and Information	Remarks and references to Appendices
MILLENCOURT	1/9/16		Casualties 241 Bde RFA. 1 OR wounded accidentally. 5pm 2/4th TMB5 1 OR killed RBA. 1 OR wounded RBA. Moves 6 Gloucester Regt to STOTTS Redoubt (Reserve Post area) 8 Worcester Regt to CONTAL MAISON & Ox & Bucks R.I. to DINGLE Camp (Reserve Post area) 14th 145 Inf Bde Killed wood, 2/3rd 145 Inf Post & 2 Bn 1 Inf Bde to forward area trenches.	
MILLENCOURT	2/9/16		Casualties 6 R Warwicks 2 OR wounded. Includes 1 slight at duty. Moves 5 R War Regt. Moves 5 R War Regt PEAKE WOOD Camp 14.3 Approx HQ MILL to SHELTER WOOD Camp. HQ 145 Inf Bde HQ MARTIN PUICH	
"	"		HQ 145 Inf Bde HQ MARTIN PUICH	
LOZENGE WOOD	3/9/16		HQ War HQ RE Bn Salvage Coy to LOZENGE wood 1st 7 Coy RE Bn 3 Secns to BAZENTIN LE PETIT, 3 Secns 1st 7 Coy RE to MARTIN PUICH, 2 Coy RE to SHELTER Valley, 3 Coy RE to BAZENTIN LE PETIT 14.5 Inf Bde Mg Coy Killantho Wood Bn in Reserve Post area 14.3 Inf Bde HQ to MARTIN PUICH 14.3 Inf Bde HQ to SHELTER Wood. 1st SM Pl down 14.4 Inf Bde HQ to MARTIN PUICH. 14.3 Inf Bde HQ to ALBERT - Another MEAULTE wood 14.3 - 145 to CONTAL MAISON. Details for few to CHAPES SPUR on BECOURT - LA BOISSELLE Road and 1st line transport to CHAPES SPUR on BECOURT - LA BOISSELLE Road. 9 Worcesters 5 Gloucester 2 OR killed & OR wounded Casualties 6 Gloucesters 10 OR wounded - 9 Worcesters 6 OR wounded 5 Gloucesters 2 OR killed & OR wounded.	
LOZENGE WOOD	4/9/16		Casualties 6 Gloucester 5 OR & wounded. 4 OR wounded includes (at duty) 6 Gloucester 2 OR killed & OR wounded. 5 R Warwicks 1 OR wounded. Move NCO.	

2449 Wt. W14957/Mg0 750,000 1/16 J.B.C. & A. Forms/C.2118/12.

WAR DIARY or INTELLIGENCE SUMMARY

Army Form C. 2118.

Place	Date	Hour	Summary of Events and Information	Remarks and references to Appendices
LOZENGE WOOD	5/10/16		Casualties 2/Lt J.G. GREENWAY 7 OR accidentally wounded 7 Rwn Regt. 2/Lt F.J. STOMP 4 Gloucester Regt slightly wounded at duty. 2/Lt E.J. HUBBARD 3 R.W. Surrey Regt attached 144 MG Coy killed 4 Gloucester 6 Gloucester 5 OR wounded 144 MG Coy 2 OR killed 4 Ox & Bucks Lt. 1 OR wounded Mince hill.	
LOZENGE WOOD	6/10/16		Casualties 6 November 3 OR killed 6 November 3 OR killed 4 OR wounded 6 OR wounded. 6 November 3 OR killed 4 OR wounded 4 Lt T.J. I GORE (MG coy) 144 MG Coy 2 DR wounded 145 MG Coy wounded gunshot wound forearm 2/Lt T.H. MITCHELL 5/DCLI. 4 M MGB Lt. 6 OR killed 9 OR wounded 7 November 1 OR wounded at duty B Gloucester Ryl B Gloucester Reserve Post area, 4 Ox Bucks Lt. 4/B Bests moved to forward area	
LOZENGE ATTN	7/10/16		Casualties. 8 November 1 killed 9 OR wounded 2/Lt N.H. GRIFFITHS MG 2/Lt NEEH RTM (?) 2/Lt RAIKIES RF. 4B November attacked B Gloucester wounded 2/Lt wounded in the 4/OR being 3 OR B November moved yesterday to Pre detail area. 6 Gloucester to front area to Bde reserve area. Eftine & Courcelette to front area. Casualties 7 Rwar Regt 2 OR wounded, 6 R.W. Ref. 1 OR wounded B Gloucester 4 OR killed 7 Rwar Regt 144 MG Coy 2 OR killed 1 wounded 4 Ox & B.L.I. Walked 3 Bomaunt (Pouchs 1? 4 OR wounded 144 MG Coy 2 OR killed 4 OR wounded 14 April at duty.	

Army Form C. 2118.

WAR DIARY
or
INTELLIGENCE SUMMARY
(Erase heading not required.)

Instructions regarding War Diaries and Intelligence Summaries are contained in F.S. Regs., Part II. and the Staff Manual respectively. Title Pages will be prepared in manuscript.

Place	Date	Hour	Summary of Events and Information	Remarks and references to Appendices
LOZENGE WOOD	8/11/16		Casualties 7 R Wn Regt 2 OR wounded. 4th Gloucester 85 killed 1 wounded 2 slight at duty, 7th W Yorks Regt OR 2 killed 1 wounded 2 slight at duty. 2 Worcesters OR 6 wounded. Bucks OR 3 wounded, 4 R Berks OR 2 wounded. 5 R Sussex OR 1 killed 3 wounded. 2nd R Bde R 2nd OR 5 wounded. Prisoners 8 November × 21.6 (Stotts Redoubt) to New BAZENTIN LE PETIT, 6 from line front area (Stands de SARS to STOTTS REDOUBT.	
LOZENGE WOOD	9/11/16		Casualties. Officers 2 Lieut. F.M. MATTHEWS killed 8/11/16 by Capt. E.C. NORREY + 2/Lt Mg 7th PPW wounded – 4th Gloucester Regt – 7 R War Regt OR 2 wounded 1 slight at duty, 143 MG Bg 14 killed 1 wounded, 4 Gloucester Regt OR killed 3 wounded 9, 3 wounded, 8R wounded, 4 R Berks OR 2 wounded, 25 G Bat MTR 1 wounded, 4 Bn Bucks Bn OR 6 wounded, 4 R Berks OR 2 wounded, 2 R Bde Rg × OR 1 killed 2 wounded, 5/8 RF. Attached MR 1 Kings ---- wounded, 7 R Bde Rg × OR 1 killed 2 wounded. OR 1 wounded accidental self inflicted. James Reed 6 November to Scots Regt.	
LOZENGE WOOD	10/11/16		Casualties 5 R Warwickshire Regt 7 OR wounded, 4th Gloucester Regt 2/Lt R Clark killed of gt N.H. Austin MC wounded 9-11-16, 7 OR killed 8 OR reported to missing 14.4.16(?) 3 OR wounded at Buck fr. 15 OR wounded 1 RBerk Bn OR 1 killed 2/13 wounded, 3 OR wounded at bk stall shock. 4 Ox & Bucks fr. 1 OR wounded, 1 R Bucks Bn OR 1 killed. 5 R Berkshire OR 7 wounded, 14 ----- wounded (Shell Shock). 2/Lt ----- wounded boy 2 R Berkshire OR 2 wounded 1 slight at duty 5 R ------ OR 1 slight wounded at duty 2/S R 14 killed 8 wounded 1 slight at duty. 2/Lt	

OSIGUN (MCO)

WAR DIARY or INTELLIGENCE SUMMARY

Army Form C. 2118.

Place	Date	Hour	Summary of Events and Information	Remarks and references to Appendices
LOZENGE WOOD	10/9/16		continued. Moved 143 Bgde HQ to MARTIN PUICH, 144 Bde HQ to SHELTER WOOD, 5 Shetlrs from JUNGLE CAMP & 22 R.F.S. from to SHELTER WOOD Camp (Reserve Post and Dump) 4 Offr & Bucks Bn from front area to BAZENTIN LE PETIT moved with 10 in numbers. S2 B/X 12a 1/5 Bucks Bn from front area to new camp PEAS DROP Camp X 16 D 8. 1/4 R Berks Regt front area to LOWER WOOD Camp X 12 A 59, 10 Gn in numbers X 6a/t 55. 145 Regt MG Gy YTH by to PEAS DROP camp from front area. 2 secs 143 MG Gy remain in line. 145 Bde MG Regt by YTM Bg to 2 secs. 145 MG Gy remain in line. 145 Post at all Bathing Hrs by MTM Bg to forward area. 144 Gy Offr & 2 men then, 5 lancers in flame throw to PEAS HORR camps R.E. etc of lancers men across SCOTTS Rdge New Camps for reinforcements available at THE DINGLE & arrangements to 15 b 9 13 → 1 14 3 R.P. B.C.	
ALBERT WOOD	11/12/16		quiet - nil except tactical changes in forward area. Casualty. 2/Lt. F. W. LANDS 4 R.P. Berks Regt wounded 9/9/16 not previously reported, 5 R Warks Rgt OR 2 killed 5 wounded 1 R War Regt OR 2 wounded 2 R War Rgt OR 5 wounded & R War Regt OR 2 wounded 572 1 wounded 5/Glo T.M. B.S. (attached) 10 OR wounded. accidental & effects etc.	
LE SARS WOOD	13/9/16		Arres - nil Casualties. 5 R War Rgt OR 2 killed 6 wounded, 4 R War Rgt OR 3 wounded 7 R War Regt OR 2 killed 16 wounded 1 shell shock 8 R War Regt OR 1 killed 2 wounded, 1 R Bks Rgt 2 w T Gy R 1 Offr Killed. Lieut W MICHELL-CLARKE OR 2 killed 2 wounded includes 1 slightly at duty	

2449 Wt. W14957/M90 750,000 1/16 J.B.C. & A. Forms/C.2118/12.

WAR DIARY or INTELLIGENCE SUMMARY

Army Form C. 2118.

Place	Date	Hour	Summary of Events and Information	Remarks and references to Appendices
LE MESNIL WOOD	13/7/16		Casualties 5 Warwicks OR 1 wounded, 7 R War Regt OR 6 wounded, 8 R War Regt OR 2 killed 13 wounded, 8 R War Regt OR 2 killed 4 wounded, 144 MG Coy OR 1 wounded (2 accidental), 5/ Gloucesters OR 1 accidental, 4/2 Berks OR 1 wounded accidental, 12 w/6 1/5 H. Coy 2 OR wounded 1 Sgt (in 12 in) 5 R Sussex 2 OR wounded, 2 m/ S.M.G. Bty OR 1 wounded. Attached 1/3 R.M.S. Regt OR 1 killed.	
LE MESNIL WOOD	14/7/16		Miners None. Casualties Officers Capt F.H. Richards 102 R.M. RFH - slightly at duty. 1/5 R. Sussex Regt 2 Lt N.G. Baker killed. 2 Lt M.S. Wilkinson wounded. Both 6" R War Regt. 6" R War Regt 2 wounded, 7 R War 1 wounded, 6 R Sussex Regt 4/5/1/6. Other Ranks. 7 Lancaster Regt 1 killed & wounded 6 R Berks 1 self inflicted 5 R Sussex 1 wounded. 7 Lancaster Regt 1 killed & wounded 6 R Berks 1 self inflicted. 7 3 for Regt 3 killed 9 killed 7 wounded 2 missing believed killed. 6 R War Regt from reserve Bde area to forward area, 6 R Berks for reserve. 6 Gloster from Reserve Bde area to forward area. 8 R War Regt from forward area to Reserve Bde area.	
LE MESNIL WOOD	15/7/16		Casualties Officers Capt R.S. Partridge 6 R War Regt wounded. M.M. Park 6 R War Regt B includes 1 Signed at duty. 7 R War Regt 1 wounded 1 missing believed killed.	

WAR DIARY or INTELLIGENCE SUMMARY

Army Form C. 2118.

Place	Date	Hour	Summary of Events and Information	Remarks and references to Appendices
	13/11/16 (continued)		8 R War Regt OR 4 killed 2 wounded, 1 wounded. 5 Gloucesters Regt 3 OR wounded, 2 Wilts Regt 1 OR wounded, 10th R.Bde F.A. 2 OR wounded. 7th R Regt OR 1 killed 1 wounded. During the 14th & 15th R Bns to MARTINPUICH, HQ 143 & 2/R Bn H & 1 company Bucks Bn to Pioneer Post area relieved by 1 Bucks Bn to front area. 8 R War Regt to Pioneer Post area relieved by 4 Ox Bucks from BAZENTIN LE PETIT and to Pioneer Post area relieved by 14 5/6 G 7 R War Regt to Pioneer Post area relieved by 14 5/6 G 7 MBS from Pot area.	
LOZENGE WOOD	16/11/16		Casualties 8 R War Regt 2 Lieut W.A BUTLER 2/5 Staffords attd to 8 War Regt. 1 OR DOW, 1 OR wounded 5 Gloucesters Regt 8 OR 2 killed. 1 Bucks Bn 2 Lieut D. FALLON wounded, 5 R Warwickshire Regt 1 OR wounded Move — nil	
LOZENGE WOOD	17/11/16		Casualties — Officers — Capt. C.E.P HENDERSON (killed) Lt. R.G. FARINGTON (wounded) both 7th R. Bde, 2/Lt. R.S.G LAKE, killed 17/11/16 R.F.A (attd HT Bn) 7th R. War R. 1 OR wounded Bucks Bn. 1 OR wounded 7th R Lan R 1 wounded, 7th Lan R 1 (attd) 1 OR wounded Move — nil	
LOZENGE WOOD	18/11/16		Casualties — Officers 5th R. War R. 1 (2/Lt G.E AUSTIN slightly on duty), 14th Ox Bucks L.I 1, (Lt R S G LAKE) killed 17/11/16 OR 5th R War R 1 killed 4 wounded officer, 1 wounded, 7th R Lan R 1 killed, 8th R Lan R 1 wounded, 1/4 Ox Buck L.I 2 Killed 4 wounded Relieved by Brigade blown to pieces by whizz bang, 5 Gloucs. 1 wounded, 1/4 Ox Bucks L.I. 2	

WAR DIARY
or
INTELLIGENCE SUMMARY

Army Form C. 2118.

Place	Date	Hour	Summary of Events and Information	Remarks and references to Appendices
(Contd.)	18/11/16		1 Killed 10 wounded, 1/4th R. Berks, 5 wounded, 1/5 T.M.By. 5 wounded (Bucks Bn. attd T.M.Bx.), 70 1KTB de R.F.A. (att/d) 1 Killed, 2 wounded, 7 1 2nd de R.F.A. (att/d) 1 Killed, 2 wounded, 104 1KTB de R.F.A 1 Killed.	
	19/11/16		Move. 7th Howse Bde to forward area, taking over left Battle section from 3/OFord Div. in Moves. Casualties. Officer - 5th Glosters 1 wounded slightly (Lt. G. G. Howard) 4th R.Berks 1 wounded (2/Lt. R. M. Turner). O.R. 5th War. R. 2 Killed, 7th Worcesters 9 Killed 25 wounded, 1/6th T.M.By. (5 Glos. 1 wounded), 4th R. Berks 1 Killed, 6 wounded, 4th R. Barns 1 Killed, 14 wounded, 146th T.M.By. (5 Glos. 1/4th Ox & Bucks Lt. 3 Killed, 6 wounded, 2nd R. Dublin Fus. (attd 145 Bde H.Q.) 1 wounded. 70 1KTB de R.F.A (attd) 1 Killed, 23rd D.A.C. 1 Killed 1 wounded. Moves. 146 th Inf. Bde H.Q. to forward area (Martinpuich), 145 Bde. Shelter Wood, 5th Worcesters to Forward area (Rt. Support) 4 R. Berks to Peake Wood (Right Camp). 5th War. R. to Acid Drop Camp.	
LONGE WOOD	20/11/16		Casualties Officers 7/ 1KTB R.F.A. attached. Lieut. H. W. Deacon wounded on 7/11/16 at duty. 1 Worster O.R. 1 wounded, 5 Gloucester Regt. 2 wounded 1 missing believed/ accidental missfire 5 Gloucester 1 killed 7 wounded to 4th Bucks Lt. 2 Killed 8 wounded. Moves. 4 th Bucks Regt to Peake Wood centre (November area) 5 Gloucesters to Middle Wood 6/7 Northamptons area Worcesters to Gloucesters to forward area Peake Ravine area 144 T.M. B y. M.G. Cy. to Forward area relief of 145 Bde remainders.	
LONGE WOOD	21/11/16		Casualties Lieut W. D. Scott 1/4 Ox/Bucks Lt. wounded 21-11-16 - Other Ranks. 6 Glos. in left wounded 7 Worcester B.R. 1 Killed 5 wounded Worcesters /wounded, 4 Ox/Bucks Lt B.R. 1 Killed 4 wounded 144 M.G. Cy. 1 wounded, 4 Ox/Bucks Lt. B.R. 1 Killed 4 wounded. Moves Nil.	

WAR DIARY or INTELLIGENCE SUMMARY

Army Form C. 2118.

Place	Date	Hour	Summary of Events and Information	Remarks and references to Appendices
Loz ENGR NOYR	22/4/16		Casualties. 6 Gloucesters OR 1 missing 8 Worcesters OR 2 wounded 3 missing, Berks Regt OR 3 wounded, 145 Bde MG Coy OR 1 killed 1 wounded 2/4 & 7th Bty RFA OR 1 wounded (Regt #) attached 7 & 8 Bde RFA 4 wounded 1/4 R.O.RFA 3 killed 1 wounded	
Loz ENGR WOOD	23/4/16		Casualties Officers (attached units) 2 Lieut H.S. JOHNSON 1/4 Bn RSR RFA M 23/4/16 1 Gloucesters 4 Worcesters 1 wounded, 6 Gloucesters 1 killed 5 wounded Attached 4 R Berks 1 killed 4 wounded 145 MG Cy 1 wounded — attached units 1/4 Bde RFA 1 killed 1 wounded — 1/24 RGA Regt 2 wounded Orders. Two Coy of 6th Bn Reserve area to front line, 8 Worcester Regt to support Coy line from area — 6 Gloucester 7 Worcester from Reserve area to Bde Reserve Rifle area.	
LOZENGE WOOD	24/4/16		Casualties 7 Worcester OR – 1 killed 2 wounded 1 missing, 5 Gloucesters from front line M. HESHLER wounded OR 6 wounded including 1 self inflicted 4/R Berks Regt OR 1 killed 1 wounded Orders 1/4 Ox Bucks to Relieve Res Rue 1/5 Oxon to HILLSWORTH, 1/5 OB/B to forward area, 8 Worcester Regt to 8 Worcester to Reserve Post area, 6 Worcester Regt to forward area & Gloucester to Reserve Rue Area	

WAR DIARY or INTELLIGENCE SUMMARY

Army Form C. 2118.

Place	Date	Hour	Summary of Events and Information	Remarks and references to Appendices
LOZENGE WOOD	26/11/16		Casualties Capt W N Bush (1/4th R Warwick Regt wounded, other Ranks 5 R War Regt O.R. 5 wounded, 8 R War Regt 1 wounded, 1/43 M.G. Coy 3 killed & 5 laterRegt. 4 Gloster Regt O.R. 1 Killed 6 King's Rifles 1 killed & wounded, 144 M.G Coy 1 killed 5 wounded (2 stretcher party) 5 Glosters 1 wounded, Brooks Bn O.R. 1 wounded, 4 R Berks 3 killed 8 wounded. 6 Yorkshires 7 Pents R. Ref. 1 killed 6 wounded. Moves — Nil.	
LOZENGE WOOD	26/11/16		Casualties — 2/Lieut. H.L. HELSDON 3rd Dorset Regt attd 1/7 R. Warwick Regt Killed Lieut. F.W. JONES 1/7 R. Warwick Regt wounded. Other Ranks 7 R Warwick Regt. O.R. 5 wounded. Moves Nil	
LOZENGE WOOD	27/11/16		Casualties — 5th R. Warwick Regt. O.R. 2 killed, 1 wounded — 6th R. Warwick Regt. O.R. 1 killed, 1 wounded — 7 R. Warwick Regt killed, 4 wounded. Moves — 9th T.B. to Reserve Area, 5th Glosters Regt from MIDDLE WOOD (X.12.c.5.4) to SCOTTS REDOUBT SOUTH (X.21.d.6.9) – Bucks Batt. from SCOTTS REDOUBT SOUTH (X.21.d.6.9) to MIDDLE WOOD (X.12.c.5.4)	
LOZENGE WOOD	28/11/16		Casualties.— 2nd Lieut. L.W. PINNICK 1/8 R. Warwick Regt wounded, 2 Lieut R.G. CARNALL 9 D.C.L.I. attd. 143 Machine Gun Coy — Other Ranks — 5th R. Warwick Regt. O.R. 2 killed 6 wounded 6th R. Warwick Regt. 1 wounded 8 R Warwick Regt. 1 killed, 7 wounded — 4th Oxford and Bucks L.I	

WAR DIARY or INTELLIGENCE SUMMARY

Army Form C. 2118.

Place	Date	Hour	Summary of Events and Information	Remarks and references to Appendices
	28/11/16 cont'd		2 wounded. Moved. In 13th Res. area – 7th Worcester Regt. from ACID DROP SOUTH (X.16.d.9.1) to New Camp, SHELTER WOOD SOUTH (X.21.c.7.4). Surplus Personnel of 143rd and 145th Bdes from CHAPES SPUR to ACID DROP SOUTH (X.16.d.9.1), 4th Berks Regt. PEAKE WOOD (X.22.d.3.8) to SHELTER WOOD NORTH (X.22.c.4.9), 8th Worcester Regt from SHELTER WOOD (X.22.c.4.6) to SCOTTS REDOUBT NORTH (X.21.b.6.0), 6th Gloucester Regt from BAZENTIN (57.a.8.2) to VILLA CAMP (NEW) (X.11.c. scattered)	
LOZENGE WOOD	29/11/16		Casualties 7th R. War Regt. O.R. 1 wounded. 8 R. War Regt. O.R. 3 wounded. 4th Ox & Bucks O.R. 1 wounded. Killed & wounded. 145 M.G. Coy. O.R. 1 wounded. Moves – 5 platoons from SCOTT'S REDOUBT SOUTH to SCOTT'S REDOUBT SOUTH. From forward area to SCOTT'S REDOUBT SOUTH.	
LOZENGE WOOD	30/11/16		Casualties:- Lieut. C.S. NASON 1/5 Gloster. Regt. wounded – other Ranks 5th R. Warwick Regt. O.R. 1 wounded. 6th R. Warwick Regt. 1 killed, 8 wounded. 8th R. Warwick Regt. 1 wounded – 143rd Machine Gun Coy. 1 killed – Moves – Nil. –	
LOZENGE WOOD				

J.W. White Capt.
for Major General
Commanding 48 Division
30/11/16

Secret

War Diary
48' (S. M.) Division (A&Q)
1st to 31st December 1916

Volume XVII

WAR DIARY or INTELLIGENCE SUMMARY

Army Form C. 2118.

Place	Date	Hour	Summary of Events and Information	Remarks and references to Appendices
LOZENGE WOOD	1916		Casualties 1/7 R. War Regt OR 6 wounded. Batt'lion 143 MG Coy O.R. 1 killed 1 wounded. 1/5 Gloucester Regt OR 1 killed 3 wounded. 1st S.M. Coy R.E. OR 1 wounded. Moves 1/6 Gloucester & 1/7 Worcester Regts to front area. 1/7 + 1/8 Worcesters to Batt Reserve area at VILLA Camps I + II. 1/6 central in SHELTER WOOD SOUTH.	
LOZENGE WOOD	2/12/16		Casualties 6th R. Warwick Regt 2 killed 2 wounded all O.R., 143 MG Coy M. 5 wounded, 4 Gloucester Regt OR 1 wounded, 6 Gloucester Regt MR 1 wounded, 7 Worcester Regt OR 2 killed & 2 wounded, 8 Gloucester Regt MR 3 killed 5 wounded, 4 R Berks OR 1 wounded, 1/5 MG Coy MR 1 killed 2 wounded, 1/1 SM Coy RE, Re OR 1 wounded. Moves 143 Inf Bde to SHELTER WOOD in place 144 Inf Bde to forward area. 4 Gloucesters & 1 Worcesters to forward area replied by 5/6 R War Regt to Reserve Bde area. MG Coy TM Bty 143 replaced in forward area by 144 Inf Bde.	
LOZENGE WOOD	3/12/16		Casualties – Other Ranks. 5th R Warwick Regt. O.R. 4 wounded, 6th R Warwick Regt. 1 killed, 1 wounded, 143rd Trench Mortar Battery, 7 Worcester Regt. 1 wounded – 7 Worcester Regt. 1 wounded – 7 Gloucester Regt. 1 killed, 2 wounded – 7 Gloucester Regt. 1 wounded – 5 Gloucester Regt. 4 wounded – 8 Worcester Regt. 5 wounded – 5 Gloucester Regt. 4 killed, 1 wounded – 5 R. Essex Regt. 1 wounded –	

WAR DIARY
or
INTELLIGENCE SUMMARY

Army Form C. 2118.

(Erase heading not required.)

Place	Date	Hour	Summary of Events and Information	Remarks and references to Appendices
LOZENGE WOOD	3/9/16		Moves – Bucks Batln. from VILLA WOOD area to forward area – 5th Gloster Regt. from forward area to VILLA WOOD area –	
LOZENGE WOOD	4/9/16		Casualties 7th Gloucester O.R. 9 wounded + 2 missing (probably killed) 4/9/16. R. Warwicks M. wounded. Horse Wd	
LOZENGE WOOD	5/9/16		Casualties Other Ranks. 7th Worcestn. Regt. O.R. 1 killed – 8th Worcester. Regt. 1 killed, 3 wounded. Bucks Batln. 1 killed, 1 wounded – 4th R. Berks. Regt. 1 killed, 5 wounded – Moves. 7th R. Warwicks from VILLA CAMP to forward area, 7th Worcester Regt. from forward area to VILLA CAMP, 8th R. Warwick Regt. from SHELTER WOOD CAMP to forward area, 8th R. Worcester Regt from forward area to SHELTER WOOD CAMP.	
LOZENGE WOOD	6/9/16		Casualties – Other Ranks – 7th Worcester Regt. O.R 3 wounded – 7th Warwick. Regt. O.R. 2 wounded. Moves – 144th Inf. Bde to SHELTER WOOD in place of 143 Inf Bde to forward area – 5th R. Warwicks and 6th R. Warwicks to forward area replaced by 8th Worcestn Regt. and 6th Gloster Regt. to Reserve Brigade area. 144th Machine Gun Coy and T.M. Battery replaced in forward area by 143rd Bde units	

WAR DIARY
or
INTELLIGENCE SUMMARY
(Erase heading not required.)

Army Form C. 2118.

Place	Date	Hour	Summary of Events and Information	Remarks and references to Appendices
LOZENGE WOOD	7/12/16		Casualties – Other Ranks – 8th R. Warwick Regt. 1 wounded – 8th Worcester Regt. 8 wounded – 6th O.& Bucks L.I. 1 wounded – 5th R. Sussex Regt. 1 wounded – Moves – N.L.	
LOZENGE WOOD	8/12/16		Casualties – Other Ranks – 5th R. Warwick Regt – O.R. 1 killed, 4 wounded – 7th R. Warwick Regt. 1 wounded – 8th R. Warwick Regt. 1 wounded – 6th Gloucester Regt. 3 wounded – 4th Oxford & Bucks L.I. 1 wounded – Moves – 4th R. Berks Regt. from Scotts Redoubt South to Forward Area – Bucks Batt – 4th R. Berks Regt. from Forward Area to Scotts Redoubt South –	
LOZENGE WOOD	9/12/16		Casualties Other Ranks. 8th R. Warwick Regt. 2 wounded – 4th R. Berkshire Regt. 1 killed, 2 wounded – 249th Bde R.F.A. 1 wounded – Signal Coy R.E. 2 wounded – Moves – Nil –	
LOZENGE WOOD	10/12/16		Casualties – Other Ranks – 5th R. Warwick Regt – O.R. 1 wounded – 6th R. Warwick Regt. 1 wounded – 8th Royal Warwick Regt. 1 wounded – 4th R. Berks. Regt. 3 killed, 6 wounded – Moves – 7th R. Warwick Regt. from Forward area to SHELTER WOOD SOUTH – 8th R. Warwick Regt. from Forward area to VILLA CAMP – 6th Gloucester Regt. from VILLA CAMP to Forward area – 7th Worcester Regt. from SHELTER WOOD to Forward area –	
LOZENGE WOOD	11/12/16		Casualties – Other Ranks – 5th R. Warwick Regt. O.R. 3 killed, 4 wounded – 6th Gloucester Regt. 1 killed, 2 wounded – 4th R. Berks. Regt. 1 wounded – 5th R. Warwick Regt. from Forward area to BOWEER CAMP – Scotts Redoubt N. 6th R. Warwick Regt. from Forward area to Reserve Area relieved in Forward area by	

Army, Form C. 2..

WAR DIARY
or
INTELLIGENCE SUMMARY

(Erase heading not required.)

Instructions regarding War Diaries and Intelligence Summaries are contained in F.S. Regs., Part II. and the Staff Manual respectively. Title Pages will be prepared in manuscript.

Place	Date	Hour	Summary of Events and Information	Remarks and references to Appendices
(Contd)	11/12/16		144 M.G. Coy and T.M. Batty – 4th Gloucestr. Regt. from Bn Res area to forward area vice 8th Worcestr Regt. 8th Bn Res. area – (Casualties) admitted in Bn relieved. Nos. 22 O.R. R.A.M.C. attached to 7th R. Warwickshire Regt. 1 wounded. S.W. Mn. 2-2.	
LOZENGE WOOD	12/12/16		Casualties. 2nd Lieut. A.M. KIRKWOOD, 4th Oxford and Bucks L.I. wounded – Other ranks – 4th Gloucestr. Regt. 3 killed, 1 wounded – 6th Gloucestr Regt. 1 killed, 8 wounded. 7th Worcestr Regt. 4 wounded. 8th Worcester Regt. 1 wounded. 4th Oxford and Bucks L.I. 1 killed, 8 wounded. 5th R. Warwick Regt. 1 killed, 8 wounded. Moves. 4th Oxford and Bucks L.I. from Bn Res. area to forward area vice 4th R. Wks. – 7th R. Wks. and 5th Glouctr Regt from Middle Wood (×1946) to Scotts REDOUBT S. (×26661)/in Bucks Balley.	
LOZENGE WOOD	13/12/16		Casualties. 2nd Lieut H.R. PAXTON. 8th Oxford and Bucks L.I. wounded. Other Ranks – 5th R. Warwick Regt. 1 wounded – 8th Worcester Regt. – 8th Worcester Regt. 1 wounded – 144 M.G. Coy wounded – 4th Oxford and Bucks L.I. 2 killed – Moves. Nil.	
LOZENGE WOOD	14/12/16		Casualties – Other Ranks. – 4th Gloucestr Regt. – 6th Gloucestr Regt. 1 wounded. 7th Worcestr Regt 1 wounded, 1 missing. – 8th Worcestr Regt. 1 killed, 5 wounded – 5th R. Warwick Regt. 1 wounded. Moves. 5th Gloucestr Regt from Bn Res. area to forward area vice 4th Oxford and Bucks L.I. 5th R. Warwick Regt. from Scotts REDOUBT N (×1872) to ALBERT. 6th R. Warwick Regt. (× H.R.(×H.07) from SCOTTS to BECOURT. 8th R. Warwick Regt. VILLA CAMP (×19258) to ALBERT. 4th Oxford & Bucks L.I. from SCOTTS REDOUBT.S (×26.61) to BECOURT. Bucks Balley from MIDDLE WOOD (×1946) to BECOURT. 4th Bucks Regt from SHELTER WOOD W. (×11489) to BECOURT.	
LOZENGE WOOD	15/12/16		Casualties – 2nd Lieut P.J. BRETHERTON, 5th Gloucestr Regt wounded. – Other ranks – 8th R. Warwick – 1 wounded. – Moves – 4th Gloucestr Regt from forward area to SCOTTS REDOUBT S. (×26661) – 6th Gloucestr Regt from forward area to SHELTER WOOD N (×11489) – 7th Worcestr Regt. from forward area to MIDDLE WOOD (×18a.6). Relieved by 15th Division.	
LOZENGE WOOD	16/12/16		Casualties. 144 M.G. Coy. O.R. 7 killed, 2 wounded – 5th Gloucestr Regt. 2 wounded – Bucks Balley – 1 missing. 240 Bde R.F.A. 2 wounded – Move. 8th Worcestr Regt from forward area to MAMETZ WOOD (×26a.6) 5th Gloucestr Regt from forward area to VILLA CAMP (×19a.58). 4th Gloucestr Regt from SHELTER WOOD N to MAMETZ WOOD (×23a.16). S (×26.6) to MAMETZ WOOD (×23a.1). 6th Gloucestr Regt from SHELTER WOOD N to ALBERT. 5th Gloucestr Regt from VILLA CAMP (×19a.58) to	
ALBERT			7th Worcestr Regt from MIDDLE WOOD (×18a.6) to ALBERT. 143rd H.Q. to MILLENCOURT. BECOURT. Disturbed 14 Gun from LOZENGE WOOD (×17×612) to ALBERT. 143rd H.Q. to MILLENCOURT. 144th H.Q. to BECOURT.	

Army Form C. 2118.

WAR DIARY
or
INTELLIGENCE SUMMARY
(Erase heading not required.)

Instructions regarding War Diaries and Intelligence Summaries are contained in F. S. Regs., Part II. and the Staff Manual respectively. Title Pages will be prepared in manuscript.

Place	Date	Hour	Summary of Events and Information	Remarks and references to Appendices
ALBERT	17/12/16		Casualties - Nil. Moves Nil.	
ALBERT	18/12/16		Casualties - Nil. Moves Nil.	
ALBERT	19/12/16		Casualties - Nil. Moves Nil.	
ALBERT	20/12/16		Casualties - other ranks - 5th R. Surrey Regt - 1 wounded - Moves - nil	
ALBERT	21/12/16		Casualties - other ranks - 242nd Bde R.F.A. 1 wounded - Moves Nil.	
ALBERT	22/12/16		Casualties - Nil. Moves Nil.	
ALBERT	23/12/16		Casualties - other Ranks 246th Bde R.F.A. 1 wounded - Moves: 4th & 5th Gloucester Regt from MAMETZ WOOD (X23a.) to FRICOURT CAMP (X28a.3.4.) - 5th Worcester Regt from MAMETZ WOOD	
ALBERT	24/12/16		(X23a.) to FRICOURT CAMP (X28a.3.4.) Casualties. Nil. Moves Nil	
ALBERT	25/12/16		Casualties. Nil. Moves 8th Gloucester Regt from MAMETZ WOOD (X23a) to FRICOURT CAMP (X28a.2.3.)	
ALBERT	26/12/16		Casualties - other ranks - 242nd Bde R.F.A 2 wounded - Moves - nil	
ALBERT	27/12/16		Casualties - other ranks - 5th Royal Sussex Regt - 1 wounded - Moves - Nil	
ALBERT	28/12/16		Moves. 143 Inf Bde complete to WARLOY, 145 Inf Bde complete to BRESLE, HQ, HQ Coy & TM/135 1/4th Gloucester and 7th Worcester Regt to MILLENCOURT, 1st Lynes Ambulance to BECOURT CHATEAU. Casualties. 6th & 5th SR Sussex Regt 1 O.R. 50-5	
ALBERT	29/12/16		Moves. 4 & 5 Bns Gloucester Regt from FRICOURT FM camps to BECOURT. Casualties Nil.	
ALBERT	30/12/16		Moves 4 & 5 Bns Gloucester Regt from BECOURT to BAIZIEUX. Casualties Nil	
ALBERT	31/12/16		Moves - Nil. Casualties Nil.	

M.N.H. Clark Capt
for Major Front Comdr
48 Div——

2449 Wt. W14957/M90 750,000 1/16 J.B.C. & A. Forms/C.2118/12.

Army Form C. 2118.

WAR DIARY
or
INTELLIGENCE SUMMARY
(Erase heading not required.)

Instructions regarding War Diaries and Intelligence Summaries are contained in F.S. Regs., Part II. and the Staff Manual respectively. Title Pages will be prepared in manuscript.

Place	Date	Hour	Summary of Events and Information	Remarks and references to Appendices
LOZENGE & BAZENTIN WOOD	1916		Casualties 1/F R War Regt O.R. 6 wounded Batttn 143 M.G. Coy O.R. 1 killed 1 wounded 1/6 Gloucester Regt O.R. 1 killed 3 wounded 1st S.H. Coy R.E. O.R. 1 wounded. Moves 1/6 Hampshire & 1/6 Worcester Regt to front area, 1/7 & 1/8 Warwickshire to Bde Reserve Area at VILLA Camp X — 11 C central — SHELTER WOOD SOUTH	
LOZENGE WOOD	2/1/16		Casualties 6th R Warwick Regt 2 killed 2 wounded all O.R. 143 M.G. Coy O.R. 1 wounded 4 Gloucester Regt O.R. 1 wounded 6 Gloucester Regt O.R. 1 wounded Worcester Regt O.R. 2 killed 2 wounded 1 Gloucester Regt O.R. 3 killed 1 wounded 4 R Berks O.R. 1 wounded 143 M.G. Coy O.R. 1 killed 2 wounded 174th Bty 12 O.R. 1 wounded Moves 143 Bde to SHELTER Wood in place 146 Bde to forward Area 143 & Gloucester Regt & Worcester to forward area relieved by 5th R. Devon Regt & Gloucester MG Coy 174 Bty 146 replaces in forward area by 143 Bty 146 to Reserve Bat Area.	
LOZENGE WOOD	3/7/16		Casualties Other Ranks. 5th R Warwick Regt O.R. + wounded 1st R Warwick Regt 1 killed, 1 wounded. 143 Trench Mortar Batty 6th R Warwick Regt 1 killed, 1 wounded 1/5 Gloucester Regt. 1 wounded — 7 Worcester Regt. 1 killed, 2 wounded — 4 Gloucester Regt. 1 wounded — 5th Gloucester Regt 4 1 wounded — 8th Worcester Regt. 5 wounded — 6th Gloucester Regt. + 1 wounded — 5th R Sussex Regt. 1 wounded killed, 1 wounded — 5th R Sussex Regt. 1 wounded.	

WAR DIARY
or
INTELLIGENCE SUMMARY

(Erase heading not required.)

Army Form C. 2118.

Place	Date	Hour	Summary of Events and Information	Remarks and references to Appendices
LOZENGE WOOD	3/9/16		Moves – Bucks Batts. from VILLA WOOD area to forward area – 5th Gloucester Regt. from forward area to VILLA WOOD area.	
LOZENGE WOOD	4/9/16		Casualties. 1st Gloucester O.R. 9 wounded + 2 missing from patrol 4/9/16. R 48 T.M.Bty. O.R. wounded.	
LOZENGE WOOD	5/9/16		Casualties. Other Ranks – 7th Worcester Regt. O.R. 1 killed – 8th Worcester Regt. 1 killed, 3 wounded – Bucks Batts. 1 killed, 1 wounded – 4th R. Berks Regt. 1 killed, 5 wounded – 7th R. Warwicks 2 wounded. Moves – 7th R. Warwicks from VILLA CAMP to forward area, 7th Worcester Regt. from VILLA CAMP, 6th R. Warwick Regt. from SHELTER WOOD CAMP to forward area, 6th Gloucester Regt. from forward area to SHELTER WOOD CAMP.	
LOZENGE WOOD	6/9/16		Casualties – Other Ranks – 7th Worcester Regt. O.R. 3 wounded – 7th Warwick Regt. O.R. 2 wounded. Moves – 144th Inf. Bde to SHELTER WOOD in Reserve. 143rd Inf. Bde to forward area – 5th R. Warwicks and 6th R. Warwicks to forward area replaced by 8th Worcester Regt and 6th Gloucester Regt to Reserve Brigade area. 144th M.G. machine gun Coy and T.M. Battery replaced in forward area by 143rd Bde units.	

WAR DIARY or INTELLIGENCE SUMMARY

Army Form C. 2118.

(Erase heading not required.)

Place	Date	Hour	Summary of Events and Information	Remarks and references to Appendices
LOZENGE WOOD	7/7/16		Casualties, Other Ranks - 6th R. Warwick Regt. 1 wounded - 8th Gloucester Regt. 3 wounded - 6th Ox & Bucks L.I. 1 wounded - 5th R. Sussex Regt. 1 wounded - Divers. N.C.	
LOZENGE WOOD	8/7/16		Casualties - Other Ranks - 5th R. Warwick Regt. O.R. 1 killed, 4 wounded - 7th F.R. Warwick Regt. 1 wounded - 8th R. Warwick Regt. 1 wounded - 6th Gloucester Regt. 3 wounded - 4th Ox & Bucks L.I. 1 wounded - Moves - 4th R. Berks Regt. from Scotts Redoubt South to forward area - Bucks Bn from forward area to Scotts Redoubt South.	
LOZENGE WOOD	9/7/16		Casualties - Other Ranks. 8th F.R. Warwick Regt. 2 wounded - 4th F.R. Berkshire Regt. 1 killed, 2 wounded - 240 F.R. Bde R.F.A. 1 wounded - Signal Coy R.E. 2 wounded - Moves - Nil.	
LOZENGE WOOD	10/7/16		Casualties - Other Ranks - 5th R. Warwick Regt - O.R. 1 wounded - 6 F.R. Warwick Regt. 1 wounded - 8th Royal Warwick Regt. 1 wounded - 4th R. Berks Regt 3 wd Batt. 1 wounded - Moves - 7th R. Warwick Regt from forward area to SHELTER WOOD SOUTH - 8th R. Warwick Regt from forward area to VILLA CAMP - 6th Gloucester Regt. from VILLA CAMP to forward area, 7th Worcester Regt. from SHELTER WOOD to forward area.	
LOZENGE WOOD	11/7/16		Casualties - Other Ranks. 6th R. Warwick Regt. O.R. 3 killed, 4 wounded - 7th Gloucester Regt. 1 killed, 2 wounded - 4th R. Warwick Regt. 1 wounded - 6th Gloucester Regt. 2 wounded - Moves - 8th R. Warwick Regt from forward area to PIONEER CAMP, 5th R. Warwick Regt from Reserve line relieved 8th forward area by	

WAR DIARY or INTELLIGENCE SUMMARY

Army Form C. 2118.

Place	Date	Hour	Summary of Events and Information	Remarks and references to Appendices
(Cont'd)	11/9/16		2/Lt M.G. Coy and T.M. Battery of 5th Gloucester Regt from Bde. H.Q. sent to forward dug out. 8th Worcester Regt to Brig: for Inns of Court Billets) abandoned 2/Lt Pallister wounded T.R. Rankin wounded 2nd R. Rankin wounded Capt. T.M. Bren wanted Major C—	
LOZENGE WOOD	12/9/16		Casualties. 2nd Lieut. A.H. KIRKWOOD, 4th Oxford and Bucks L.I. wounded. Other ranks 4th Oxford and Bucks — 2 killed, 5 wounded. 6th Gloucester Regt — 1 wounded. 5th Gloucester Regt — 1 wounded. 2/Lt — killed, 1 wounded. Bucks — 1 killed, 1 wounded, 3 missing. 4th Oxford and Bucks L.I. from Bde. dug out to forward area. 4th T.R. Rankin and 4th R.W.F. and 5th Gloucesters Regt from Middle Wood (bomb) to Scotts Redoubt S (K055) and Bucks Trench.	
LOZENGE WOOD	13/9/16		Casualties — 2nd Lieut. H.A. PORTON, 5th Oxford and Bucks L.I. wounded — Other Ranks — 5th R. Berwick R.S.F. — 1 wounded. 8th Worcester Regt — 5th forward Regt - 1 wounded — 1st R. Coy — 1 wounded — 5 A/wounded 4th Bucks L.I. — 1 killed — M.G. & M.L.	
LOZENGE WOOD	14/9/16		Casualties — Other Ranks — 4th Gloucester Regt — 1 wounded — 5th Gloucester Regt — 1 wounded, 3 Patricks 5th Worcester Regt wounded — 8th Worcester Regt 4 wounded, 5th R. Sussex Regt 1 wounded — 4th Bucks L.I. Bde. 3 — 5th Bucks Regt from Bde. Res. area to forward area 4th Ox. (Infantry) Trenches ? R. Warwick Regt from Scotts Redoubt N (K0715) to ALBERT, 5th Worcester Regt from 8th Worcester Regt VILLA CAMP (X19a0) to ALBERT, 4th Oxford & Bucks L.I. from Scotts Redoubt. S (X11-0) to BECOURT. Bucks Trench from MIDDLE WOOD (X1940) to BECOURT. 4th Bucks Regt from SHELTER WOOD N (X1149) to BECOURT.	
LOZENGE WOOD	15/9/16		Casualties. 2nd Lieut. P.J. BRETHERTON, 5th Gloucester Regt wounded — Other Ranks — 5th T.R. Warwick Regt 1 wounded. Mores. 4th Gloucester Regt from forward area to Scotts Redoubt S (K0662). (8th Gloucester Regt from forward area to SHELTER WOOD N (X1149) 7th Worcester Regt from ridge in MIDDLE WOOD (X1940). Relieved by 6th Division.	
LOZENGE WOOD	16/9/16		Casualties. 144 M.G. Coy O.R. 7 killed, 2 wounded. 144 Tr Bn— ... wounded. Mores. 8th Worcester Regt from forward area to MAMETZ WOOD (X?a?). 5th Gloucester Regt from forward area to VILLA CAMP (X19a0) 5th Warwick Regt from SHELTER WOOD N to MAMETZ WOOD (X3415) 5th (qui) Gloucester Regt from MAMETZ WOOD (X?a?) 5th Gloucester Regt to ALBERT. 5th Gloucester Regt from VILLA CAMP (X19a0) to	
ALBERT	17/9/16		7th Worcester Regt from MIDDLE WOOD (X1940) to ALBERT, 143 Tr Bn M.Gr? MILLENCOURT. BECOURT Divisional H.Qrs from LOZENGE WOOD to BECOURT. 144 Bde. Tr? PALLISER 143 Tr Bn H.Qrs. to BECOURT.	

WAR DIARY
or
INTELLIGENCE SUMMARY

(Erase heading not required.)

Army Form C. 2118.

Instructions regarding War Diaries and Intelligence Summaries are contained in F. S. Regs., Part II. and the Staff Manual respectively. Title Pages will be prepared in manuscript.

Place	Date	Hour	Summary of Events and Information	Remarks and references to Appendices
ALBERT	17/4/16		Casualties - Nil. Moves Nil.	
ALBERT	18/4/16		Casualties - Nil. Moves Nil.	
ALBERT	19/4/16		Casualties Nil. Moves Nil.	
ALBERT	20/4/16		Casualties Other ranks - 5th R. Sussex Regt. 1 wounded - moves nil	
ALBERT	21/4/16		Casualties other ranks. 3rd & 2nd R.F.A. 1 wounded - moves nil	
ALBERT	22/4/16		Casualties Not Reported	
ALBERT	23/4/16		Casualties Not Reported	
ALBERT	24/4/16		Casualties. Other Ranks. 2nd & 5th Bde R.F.A 1 wounded - 1 Miss. d. 4th Gloucester Regt from MAMETZ WOOD Camp (X19 a 3) N Edmunds Regt from MAMETZ WOOD (X22a 3) 5 R Fusiliers Camp at R27 d 2.5	
ALBERT	25/4/16		Casualties Nil Moves Nil	
ALBERT	26/4/16		Casualties. Other Ranks. 4th Gloucester Regt from MAMETZ WOOD (X22a 3) 5 R Fusiliers Camp (X22a 63)	
ALBERT	27/4/16		Casualties - Other Ranks - 2, 4 & 2 Bde R.F.A. 2 wounded. moves nil.	
ALBERT	28/4/16		Casualties - Other Ranks. 5th Royal Sussex Regt. 1 wounded. moves nil.	
ALBERT	29/4/16		Moves. 143rd Inf Bde complete to WARLOY, 145th Inf Bde complete to BRESLE HQ, MGs + TMBs/144th Inf Bde, and 7th Worcester Regt to MILLENCOURT. Casualties Staff + 5th R Sussex Regt 1 OR gas.	
ALBERT	29/4/16		Moves 4/5th Gloucester Regt from FREICOURT MENTS to BECOURT. Camelon nil.	
ALBERT	30/4/16		Moves 4/5th Gloucester Regt from BECOURT to BAZIEUX. Casualties nil.	
ALBERT	5/5/16		Moves - Nil. Casualties Nil.	

D M Hart Capt
for M. Gen Front Commd
46 Divn

2449 Wt. W14957/M90 750,000 1/16 J.B.C. & A. Forms/C.2118/12.

Vol 22

War Diary

"A" & "Q" Branch 48th Divn.

January 1917

Volume XXI

WAR DIARY or INTELLIGENCE SUMMARY

Army Form C. 2118.

Place	Date	Hour	Summary of Events and Information	Remarks and references to Appendices
NEUFCHÂTEL to BAIZIEUX	1/1/17		Div HQ to BAIZIEUX. Casualties nil. 1/4th Rly T 242 Bde RHA 1 OR killed	
BAIZIEUX	2/1/17		Moves – nil. Casualties 243 Bde RFA OR 1 wounded.	
BAIZIEUX	3/1/17		Moves – nil. Casualties 48th D.A.C. 5 O.R. wounded (Jan 31.16)	Pk
BAIZIEUX	7/1/17		Moves – 1st Line Tp of 143 & 144 Inf Bde + No 2 & 3 Coys of 48 Div Train to ST SAUVEUR by march route	144
BAIZIEUX to HALLENCOURT	8/1/17		Moves – 1st Line Tp of 143 & 144 Inf Bde + No 2 & 3 Coys of 48 Div Train to AREA 5 (143 Bde & No 2 Coy Train to WANEL + SOREL AREA, 144 Inf Bde & No 3 Coy Train to HUPPY area) 1st Line Tp of 145 Inf Bde + No 4 Coy 48 Div Train to ST SAUVEUR by march route. 143 Inf Bde to WANEL + SOREL area by Tactical Train. 2 Sec 1st Fd Amb to HUPPY. Div HQ to HALLENCOURT. 144 Inf Bde to HUPPY area by Tactical Train.	33L
HALLENCOURT	9/1/17		Moves - 1st line Tp of 145 Inf Bde + No 4 Coy 48 Div Train to YONVILLE area by march route. 145 Inf Bde + 1 Sec 2nd Field Amb to YONVILLE AREA by Tactical Train. 48 Supply Col to HALLENCOURT. 1 Sec 3rd Fd Amb from HUPPY to AIRAINES	PL
HALLENCOURT	12/1/17		Casualties 2/1 S.M. Field Tp R.E. O.R. 2 wounded.	PLL
HALLENCOURT	13/1/17		Moves # Field Tp R.E. 2 Sec k PONT REMY, 1 Sec to FLIXECOURT. Casualties 1/2 Pioneers RE 1/2 O.R. wounded 2/1 Field Co R.E. O.R. 1 wnd.	RS
"	16.1.17		AMR & 2 Sec 2nd Field Amb to FRUCOURT. S.A. Survey to BAILLEUL, BELLIFONTAINE. Tp on route by road. Casualties 240 Bde R.FA O.R. 1 prisoner.	PL

Army Form C. 2118.

WAR DIARY
or
INTELLIGENCE SUMMARY
(Erase heading not required.)

Instructions regarding War Diaries and Intelligence Summaries are contained in F. S. Regs., Part II. and the Staff Manual respectively. Title Pages will be prepared in manuscript.

Place	Date	Hour	Summary of Events and Information	Remarks and references to Appendices
HALLENCOURT	18.1.17		Casualties 5 5 wounded also 7th Field Coy R.E. O.R. & wounded. Moves N.L.	
do	19.1.17		" D.R.I. "	
do	20.1.17		N.L. Moves N.L.	
	21.1.17		" "	
	22.1.17		H.Q.D.A.C. O.R. wounded. Moves N.L.	
	23.1.17		N.L. Moves N.L.	
	24.1.17			29/30 Jan 17
	25.1.17		Moves. 1st Line Trans. 143 J.y.Bde, No 2 Coy Train. A Sect. 3rd Y Sea Amb. to ARGOEUVRES	Casualties 6.
	26.1.17		" " AUBIGNY.	N.L.
			48th Div Artillery to Fouencamp.	
			1st Line Trans 144 Iy Bde. No 3 Coy Train "B" Sect. 3rd Y Field Amb. to ARGOEUVRES + Pioneer Batt. Tp.) +Divnl Hqrs Tp.)
	27.1.17		1st Line Trans 145 Iy Bde. " A " AUBIGNY	
			" " No 2 " MERICOURT AREA	
			" " No 4 " ARGOEUVRES.	
			Personnel 143 " " " A "	
			" 144 " " " B 2nd Y Field Amb.	
			" 143 " By Tactical Train to MERICOURT AREA.	
			1st 5 M.Field Ambulance from BECOURT to ARGOEUVRES.	
			2nd + 3rd Field Coys R.E. 2nd to MERICOURT. 3rd to CERISY.	
HALLENCOURT	28.1.17		1st Line Trans 144 Iy.Bde No 3 Coy Train A Sect 3rd Y.Fd Amb. + Pioneer Tp. CERISY AREA.	
MERICOURT			" " 145 " No 4 " 2nd Y.Fd Amb.	
			Personnel 144 " + 5th R Sussex (Prs) By Tactical Train to CERISY AREA	
			" Divisional Hdqrs to MERICOURT.	
MERICOURT	29.1.17		1st Line Trans 145 3rd Fd. No 4 Coy Train 2nd Fd Amb. to HAMEL AREA.	
			Personnel 145 " By Tactical Train " do.	
			1st 5 M.Field Ambulance to MERICOURT.	
	28.1.17		N.L.	
	29.1.17		N.L.	
	30.1.17			
	31.1.17		" 143 Bde moved to the reserve area relieving the 152 Bde ment (French Army) Casualties nil	

29/1/17

Vol 23

War Diary.

"A" & "Q" Branch. 48th Divn.,

February 1917.

Volume XXIII.

Army Form C. 2118.

WAR DIARY
or
INTELLIGENCE SUMMARY

(Erase heading not required.)

Instructions regarding War Diaries and Intelligence Summaries are contained in F.S. Regs., Part II. and the Staff Manual respectively. Title Pages will be prepared in manuscript.

Place	Date	Hour	Summary of Events and Information	Remarks and references to Appendices
MERICOURT SUR SOMME	Feb. 1.2.17		On the night of 1/2 143 Bde went into action relieving the 125th French Regiment. Casualties NIL	
"	2.2.17		144 Bde went into the line on the night of 2/3 relieving the 135 French Regiment. Casualties 1 O.R. wounded 145 Bde moved from HAMEL to the CAPPY ECLUSIERS area. O.R. 1 killed 6 wounded	
CAPPY	3.2.17		Div. H.Q. moved to CAPPY. Casualties 1 O.R. killed. 8 O.R. wounded	
"	4.2.17		Casualties 5 O.R. killed, wounded 7.	
"	5.2.17		Casualties 2 officers killed, 1 wounded. 55 O.R. killed. 134 wounded. 15 missing	
"	6.2.17		Casualties O.R. killed 1 wounded 5.	
"	7.2.17		Casualties Officers wounded 1. O.R. killed 6. wounded 13.	
"	8.2.17		Casualties Officers wounded 1. O.R. killed 4 wounded 6.	
"	9.2.17		Casualties O.R. wounded 5. 145 Inf. Bde relieved the 144 Bde in the line on night 9/10	

Army Form C. 2118.

WAR DIARY
or
INTELLIGENCE SUMMARY

(Erase heading not required.)

Instructions regarding War Diaries and Intelligence Summaries are contained in F. S. Regs., Part II. and the Staff Manual respectively. Title Pages will be prepared in manuscript.

Place	Date	Hour	Summary of Events and Information	Remarks and references to Appendices
CAPPY	10.2.17		Casualties. Officer wounded 1, O.R. wounded 5.	
"	11.2.17		Casualties. O.R. wounded 5.	
"	12.2.17		Casualties. Officers wounded 1. O.R. killed 1, wounded 4.	
"	13.2.17		Casualties. Officers wounded 1. O.R. wounded 7.	
"	14.2.17		Casualties. O.R. wounded 5.	
"	15.2.17		Casualties. Officers killed 1. O.R. killed 1, wounded 8.	
"	16.2.17		Casualties. O.R. wounded 4. Divr. H.Q. moved to P.C. OLYMPE (J.32.a.6.8)	
"	17.2.17		Casualties. Nil. 144 Inf Bde. relieved 145 Inf Bde on night 17/18.	
"	18.2.17		Casualties. Officers wounded 1. O.R. wounded 3.	
"	19.2.17		Casualties. O.R. wounded 1.	
"	20.2.17		Casualties. Nil.	
"	21.2.17		Casualties. O.R. killed 1, wounded 2	
"	22.2.17		Casualties. O.R. wounded 1.	
"	23.2.17		Casualties. O.R. killed 3, wounded 6	
"	24.2.17		Casualties. O.R. killed 14, wounded 4.6	
"	25.2.17		Casualties. O.R. wounded 3. 145 Inf Bde. relieved 144 Inf Bde in afternoon	
"	26.2.17		Casualties. Officers wounded 1 (2Lt V.V. GARLICK 1/4 Ox a Bucks, slightly, at duty.) O.R. killed 6 wounded 14 missing 2.	
"	27.2.17		Casualties. Officers. Wounded 2 (2Lt G.H. DRAPER, 1/4 Cheshires attd 1/4 R War Regt.; 2Lt W.H. FLEEMING (Bucks. atd 1/4 R Ox a Bucks) O.R. killed 2 wounded 4. 2 accidentally	

Army Form C. 2118.

WAR DIARY
or
INTELLIGENCE SUMMARY

(Erase heading not required.)

Instructions regarding War Diaries and Intelligence Summaries are contained in F. S. Regs., Part II. and the Staff Manual respectively. Title Pages will be prepared in manuscript.

Place	Date	Hour	Summary of Events and Information	Remarks and references to Appendices
CAPPY	28.2.17		Casualties. Officers, wounded 1 (Capt G.R. CROUCH, 1st Buck. Bn.) O.R. killed 1 wounded 13.	

S White Cope
Major General.
Commanding 48th (S.M.) Division.

Original 24 ~~Vol~~

War Diary.

"A" & "Q" Branch.

48th Divn.,

March 1917.

Volume XXIV.

Army Form C. 2118.

Instructions regarding War Diaries and Intelligence Summaries are contained in F. S. Regs., Part II. and the Staff Manual respectively. Title Pages will be prepared in manuscript.

WAR DIARY
or
INTELLIGENCE SUMMARY
(Erase heading not required.)

Place	Date	Hour	Summary of Events and Information	Remarks and references to Appendices
CAPPY	Mar 1st		Casualties, O.R. killed 3 wounded 5	
"	2nd		Casualties, Officers wounded 1, (Capt. and Adjt. E.E. BRIDGES, 4th Ox. and Bucks LI) missing, believed killed, 1 (Lt G.E. ORTON SMITH, 1/5th R. War. Regt.) O.R. killed 2 wounded 21	HEM
"	3rd		144 Inf. Bde. relieved 143 and 145 Inf. Bdes. 144 Inf. Bde. HQ to Cappy H34d9505. 143 to G15d5040 145 to CAPPY CHATEAU. Casualties O.R. killed 8 wounded 14 (1 slightly - at duty)	HEM
"	4th		Casualties, Officers wounded 1 (2/Lt H.N.E NESS, 4th Worc. Regt.) O.R. wounded 16.	HEM
"	5		Annes-Mid - Casualties 4 Gloucester Regt. 1 OR wounded, 7 Worcester Regt. 1 OR wounded 8 Worcestershire Regt. 2 OR killed, 144 MG Cy 2 OR wounded.	HEM
"	6		Casualties O.R. wounded 3.	
"	7		Casualties O.R. wounded 4. 144th Inf. Bde. was relieved by 145th Inf. Bde. in Right Sector and by 143 Inf. Bde. in Left Sector.	
"	8		Casualties. O.R. killed 4 wounded 1/2.	
"	9		Casualties O.R. killed 7 wounded 31 missing (believed wounded) 2.	
"	10		Casualties Officers killed 3 (Capt. J.D.B. WARWICK, Hants Cyclists att'd 1/1 Bucks Bn.; 2/Lt. S. WISEMAN 4 Essex Rgt. att'd 1/1 Bucks Bn.; 2/Lt. R.B. COOPER-SMITH 6 Essex Rgt. att'd 1/1 Bucks Bn.). O.R. killed 17. Wounded 12.	
"	11		Casualties O.R. killed 4 wounded 5 missing 1	
"	12		Casualties O.R. killed 3 wounded 3	
"	13		Casualties O.R. killed 4 wounded 9. 144 Inf. Bde. relieved 145 Inf. Bde. in Right Sector in the evening.	

INTELLIGENCE SUMMARY

(Erase heading not required.)

-garding War Diaries and Intelligence summaries are contained in F.S. Regs., Part II. and the Staff Manual respectively. Title Pages will be prepared in manuscript.

Place	Date	Hour	Summary of Events and Information	Remarks and references to Appendices
CAPPY	March 14		Casualties. O.R. killed 4 wounded 3.	
	15"		Casualties. Officers Wounded 2 (2/Lieut G. BAILEY & Glowester Regt; 2/Lieut C.R. TAAFFE 7 Manchester Regt att D144 T.M.By.) O.R. wounded 1.	
	16		Casualties. Officers wounded 2 (Capt R.F. GERRARD. 4th R. Scots att /6 Glosters Reg. and 2/Lt J.T. IBBS - 1/8 Worcester Reg.) accidentally wounded O.R. 1. O.R. killed 1. O.R wounded 7.	
	17		Casualties. Officers wounded 4 (2/Lt J. SWAGLAND - 6th Glos. 2/Lt F.S. HILL, 4th Glos. 2/Lt H.R. MARSH, 4th Glos. 2/Lt H.L. HARCOURT, 5th Warwicks). O.R. killed 4, wounded 21.	
	18		Casualties. Officers wounded 1. (2/Lt D.T. Navy 5 E Lancs. Reg. T.F. att 5 R. Warwicks. Reg). O.R. wounded - 3.	
	19		Casualties. OR wounded. Accidentally killed by machine gun fire fault — 2. OR Moved 6 O3B22 143 Inf Bde. to H19a18. 477d Field Coy R.E. moved to G.24d. 5 R W R. G. 21 d 88. 475 Field Coy R.E. moved to G.24d. " H.13d. 477 Field Coy R.E. moved to O.5a.9t. " G.22 Central. 5 R. W R. H.26.C.2.44 " H.8c 91.	
	20		Casualties. OR wounded accidentally, 3. (2 Grenade Trap - 1 by rifle automatic alarm) Moves. 143 Inf Bde. HQ & relinments moves to PERONNE - HALLE, RASEGOURE aden. 478 Field Coy R.E. HALLE 477 " " DOINGT	

WAR DIARY or INTELLIGENCE SUMMARY

Place	Date	Hour	Summary of Events and Information	Remarks and references to Appendices
CAPPY	March 20 (Continued)		Moves. (Cover) 5th R. Sussex moved to CHAPELETTE X + 8 T.M. battery Y 48 " — " Z 48 " — " } moved to R.P.N. - Cappy Herlecourt road V 48 " — " Casualties. Officers. killed 1 (2/Lt H.R. LAMBERT 475 Field Coy. RE) O.R. Wounded 3 Moves. 5th R. War. R. to I19 & H5. 4 5bas. to 63 d 591. Bucks Battn. to I 36. 7th " " 127 & 94. 6 " " Coope 56. 8th " " 621 & 88. 6 " Warc. " H35c 6508. 5th R. Sussex to I 35 b 20 35 " " " " 6 " " H34 d 9506. 240 Bde R.F.A. to CAPPY. 241 Bde. R.F.A. to CHAPELETTE.	
	22.		Casualties - O.R. wounded 6 (includes 2 accidentally). Moves 6th R. War. R. to H56 91.	
	23.		Moves. 143 Bde to PERONNE. Casualties. Nil. 6 R.W.R. " "	
	24.		Casualties - 3rd Corps Mounted Troops - wounded 2 O.R. (includes 1 slightly at Duty) Moves. 143 Inf. Bde to BUSSU. 5 bus. to BOUINCOURT. 5 R.W.R. to Mt St. QUENTIN 4 extras. CARTIGNY. 6 " " to PERONNE 7 " " to BUSSU 8 " " to DRIENCOURT	

WAR DIARY or INTELLIGENCE SUMMARY

(Erase heading not required.)

Instructions regarding War Diaries and Intelligence Summaries are contained in F. S. Regs., Part II. and the Staff Manual respectively. Title Pages will be prepared in manuscript.

Place	Date	Hour	Summary of Events and Information	Remarks and references to Appendices
LA QUINCONCE	25.3.17		Moves. Div. H.Qrs. to LA QUINCONCE. 144 Inf. Bde. to PERONNE. Casualties. 5th R.W.R. to BUSSU. 4 Glos. to CARTIGNY. O.R. killed 1. wounded 6 7th " " to TEMPLEUX LAFOSSE. 6 " " to PERONNE. missing 1. 240 Bde. R.F.A. to AIZECOURT. 7 Worcs " " 1/1 S.M. Field Amb. to PERONNE. D.A.C. " "	
	26.3.17		144 Inf. Bde. to PERONNE. - Casualties. Officers wounded 1 (Lieut. W.B. HATWELL 1/8 R.War.R) O.R. killed 4. wounded 14. Moves -(cont'd) 240 Bde. R.F.A. to COURCELLES. 241 " " " BUSSU.	
	27.3.17		Moves. 8th R.War.R. to J11c95. 8th Worcs. to PERONNE. 145. Inf Bde to TINCOURT 5th Gloue. to CARTIGNY. 4th Oxf. Bucks to TINCOURT. Bucks to HAMEL. 4 R.R Bucks to DOIGNT. 497. Fld. Coy. to TINCOURT. Sussex to TINCOURT. 3rd Fld. Amb. to J13b&bb Sn. Train to ST. DENIS. Casualties. O.R. killed 3 wounded 4 missing 1.	
	28.3.17		Casualties. Officers wounded (Capt. A.J. FIELD) O.R. killed 2. wounded 2. 1/7 R.War.R.	
	29.3.17		Moves. 47th Fld. Coy. to J11a28. 143 Inf. Bde. to TEMPLEUX. 5th R.W.R. to E27a88. 6th R.W.R. to E21a77. Casualties. O.R. killed 1 wounded 5 (2 at duty) 1/7 R.War.R Moves 144 Bde. to TINCOURT. 4 Glos. to MARQUAIX. 6 Glos. to CARTIGNY. 7 & 8 Worcs. to TINCOURT. 5 Glos. to DOIGNT. 4 Oxfords. to MARQUAIX. Bucks to CARTIGNY. 4 Bucks to MARQUAIX.	
	30.3.17		Moves. Div. Qrs. to VILLERS FAUCON. (8 Qrs. LONGAVERNES. 4th Worcs. TINCOURT 5th Glos. DOINGT. 4th Oxfds. Bucks. MARQUAIX. Bucks Batt. CARTIGNY. INDEAUX MARQUAIX	

WAR DIARY
or
INTELLIGENCE SUMMARY

(Erase heading not required.)

Place	Date	Hour	Summary of Events and Information	Remarks and references to Appendices
LA QUINCAN(E	30.3.17	(continued)	CASUALTIES. Officer wounded 1 (2Lt P.T.W. YARRELL) O.R. killed 9 wounded 12. 240 Bde R.F.A.	
TINCOURT	31.3.17		MOVED Div Headquarters to TINCOURT. CASUALTIES Officers wounded 5 (Qothea remaining at LA QUINCONCE) 2/Lt A.J. GARDNER, 2/Lt C.F. HOLLAND, M.C. (Capt F.L. HALL, 2/Lt L.E. WAKEFIELD, 2/Lt H. McCLELLAND 2L 1/4 (North) OR killed 3 wounded 53.	

[signature]
for Major General
Commanding 62 (S.D.) Division.

Vol 25

War Diary.

"A" & "Q" Branch

48th Division.

APRIL 1917.

Volume XXV

Army Form C. 2118.

WAR DIARY
or
INTELLIGENCE SUMMARY
(Erase heading not required.)

Instructions regarding War Diaries and Intelligence Summaries are contained in F.S. Regs., Part II. and the Staff Manual respectively. Title Pages will be prepared in manuscript.

Place	Date	Hour	Summary of Events and Information	Remarks and references to Appendices
TINCOURT	1.4.17		Casualties. Officers killed 2. (2/Lt J.W. BISSEKER 1/6 R War R, and 2/Lt A.S FELLOWS 1/7 Worc R) wounded 1 (2/Lt R.B.W. GORE 1/6 R War R) O.R. killed 18 (10/6 R War R, 8/17 Worc R) wounded 45 (1/4 97 Field Coy R.E., 20 1/6 R War R, 21 1/7 Worc R, 3 1/8 Worc R) Mow. 143 Bde 1-LONGAVESNES, 144 Bde 1- E.22.A.1.3. 1/4 (Oxf & Bucks LT. Inf.) LONGAVESNES, 1/8 Worc R (VILLERS-FAUCON), 1/6 Glo R to VILLERS-FAUCON, 1/7 Worc R to EPEHY.	
"	2.4.17		Casualties. Officer wounded 2 (2/Lt S.E. BOWDEN, and Lt G.H.L. EASTERBROOK 1/6 R War R) O.R. killed 7 (1/1/4th Fd Coy R.E., 5 1/7 Worc R, 1/8 Worc R.) wounded 47 (2 1/6 R War R, 5 1/6 R War R, 25 1/7 Worc R, 7 1/6 Glo R. R, 8 1/6 Worc R, 1 mining 2 (1/6 R War R) Missing. 1/6 Glo R to VILLERS-FAUCON, 1/4 Oxford & Bucks L.I. 3 - LEHAUCOURT. 1/4 R Bucks R to MARQUAIX. D.A.C. to TINCOURT and COURCELLES. A.J. LILLY.	
"	3.4.17		Casualties. Officers wounded 1 (2/Lt ARMSTRONG 1/8 R War R) O.R. killed 5 2. (1/6 R War R) Wounded 10 (1 1/5 R War R, 4 1/6 R War R, 1 1/7 Worc R, 3 1/8 Worc R.) Mow. 1/5 R War R to E.10. 6.2.3. 1/6 R War R to E.21. 6.4.8.	
"	4.4.17		Casualties. Officer wounded 1 (2/Lt V. HOLLAND 1/8 R War R) O.R. killed 3 (3/4 Oxfords) wounded 6 (1 1/5 R War R, 1/7 R War R, 3 1/4 Oxfds. 1/5 Glo R. J. MUNNS J.) Mov. 1/4 Oxfds.) 1/4 Glo R & K CARTIGNY, 26 Glo R to MARQUAIX, 1/7 - 1/6 Worc L. to TINCOURT	

Army Form C. 211b.

WAR DIARY or INTELLIGENCE SUMMARY

(Erase heading not required.)

Instructions regarding War Diaries and Intelligence Summaries are contained in F. S. Regs., Part II. and the Staff Manual respectively. Title Pages will be prepared in manuscript.

Place	Date	Hour	Summary of Events and Information	Remarks and references to Appendices
TINCOURT	5.4.17		Casualties. Officers killed 5 (2/4th H.D. HEPELL, 1/4th T.O. GARSIDE, 2/Lt E.L. BOSTOCK, 2/Lt N.G. HUNT 1/4 R. Berks R. 2/Lt R.F. PAMPHLETT 1/6 Worc R.) Wounded 5: (Capt O.M. JAMES, 2/Lt T. ROGERS 1/4 R. Berks R, Capt E. CONDOR 1/5 Gloster R, 2/Lt W.H. REYNOLDS 1/8 Worc R, 2/Lt F.H. ADSMEADS 1/4 Bde R.F.A.) O.R. Killed 38 (11 1/8 Worc R, 14 1/5 Glo'ster R, 7th 1/4 Oxfords, 6 8/4 R. Berks R.) wounded 132 (3/17 R.War.R, 31 1/8 Worc R, 42 1/4 Glo'ster R, 17 1/4 Oxfords, 7 1/4 TM Bty, 32 1/4 R. Berks R.) missing 6 (3 1/4 R. Berks R, 3 1/4 Oxfords) 1/8 Worc to light outpost line. Moved 5 R. War R to Bois de TINCOURT, 1/4 Glo'ster to K.S. Central, 1/8 Worc to light outpost line	
TINCOURT	6.4.17		Casualties. Officers wounded 1 (2/Lt F.C. LAY 1/4 Oxfords) O.R. killed 2 (1 1/4 TM Bty., 1/4 Oxfords) wounded 7 (1/2 1/5 R.War.R, 4 1/7 R.War.R, 3/8 Worc R 8 1/4 Oxfords) Moves 1/8 R.War.R to W. Bde.	
TINCOURT	7.4.17		Casualties. Officers nil. OR Killed 1 (1/7 R.War.R.), wounded 21 (1 2/4 Bde R.F.A 7 1/2 R.War R 7 1/8 R.War.R 1 1/3 mg. Coy 3 1/4 Bucks Batn.) missing 1 (1/4 R. Berks R.) Moves 1/6 R.War.R to VILLERS-FAUCON, 1/4 Glo'ster to Right outpost line, 1/7 Worc to left output line. 1/5 Glo'ster to HAMLET, 1/5 R.War.R, 1/4 R. Berks R to TINCOURT, 1/6 Gloster output line. 1/8 Worc to VILLERS-FAUCON, 14 5-TB.M 1/9 to HAMLET, 1/4 R. Berks R to MARQUAIX, 1/6 R.Berks R to TINCOURT, 1/4 Oxfords to K.S. Central, Bucks Batn to MARQUAIX, 475 Fd. Coy RE to T.17 D.2.5. 1/4 EMILIE, 474 Fd. Coy RE to J.G.d.85., 475 Fd.Coy RE to T.17 D.2.5.	
TINCOURT	8.4.17		Casualties. Officers wounded 1 (2/Lt R.J. PRING 1/4 R. Berks R) OR killed 1 (1/6 R. Berks R) wounded 9 (2 1/5 Gloster, 2 Bucks Batn, 3 1/4 R. Berks R, 2 2/4 Bde R.F.A.) Moves Hqrs 143 [illegible] DeBarc[?] & Rights Reasbly Re-landed past 1/47 Bns(south to ST EMILIE 1/7 Worc to left outpost line	

143 Bde (S.M) to ST EMILIE. Forms/C.2118/12.

Army Form C. 2118.

WAR DIARY or INTELLIGENCE SUMMARY

(Erase heading not required.)

Place	Date	Hour	Summary of Events and Information	Remarks and references to Appendices
TINCOURT	9.4.17		Casualties. Officers ~~wounded~~ hit [ranks?] Dvr L. Champion 1 OR wounded 1 (3/5 R.War.R), 1/7 Worc.R. 3, 7/K L'n Fus.R. 3, 8/K L'ncs Fus.) Moves. 143 Bde HQ to PERONNE. 1/7 R.War.R to PERONNE. 474 Fd.Coy RE to F22.0.9.4.	
TINCOURT	10.4.17		Casualties. Officers kit wounded 1 (2/Lt. G.A. PEMBERTON 144 M.G.Coy) OR Killed 6 (5/144 M.G.Coy) 1/1/4 (Worc R.) wounded 5 (1/5 K'nown Rgt, 5 L'ncs Fus; 1/240 Bde RFA, 1/24 Hunters R. 1/4 in M.G.Coy) Moves. 1/5 R.War.R to CARTIGNY. 1/8 R.War.R to PERONNE. 1/4 Worc R. to E.29.6. 1/5 Hunter R. to E.13.c.37. 1/7 Worc.R. to V.ULTRES - FALCON. 1/8 Worc R. to F.20.c.4.4. 474 Fd.Coy R.E. 1.3.6.4.8.5.	
TINCOURT	11.4.17		Casualties. Officers wounded 1 (B/Lt F.V. Hemming 1/8 Worc Rgt) OR's wounded 3 (2 Worc Rgt) Moves. 4 Glouc Rgt to F.15.c.37. 6 Glouc Rgt to E.29.B. 7 Worc Rgt to F.25.c.61. 8 Worc Rgt to E.28.B. (approx)	
TINCOURT	12.4.17		Casualties Officers nil. OR's Killed 3 (7 James Fus) wounded 11 (4 Glouc Rgt, 6 Glouc Rgt, 8 Worc Rgt, 7 James Fus) missing nil. Moves nil.	
TINCOURT	13.4.17		Casualties Officers killed 1 (2/Lt A.G. Bradell 1 Glouc Rgt) Killed 10 (6 Bn 4 Glouc Rgt 4, 1 Worc Rgt) Officers wounded 2 (A/B/Lt C.R. Cooke 1 Glouc Rgt, Capt J Saunders 7 James Fus) OR's wounded 56 (26 4 Glouc Rgt 24 7 Worc Rgt 2 7 James Fus, missing 4 (2 4 Glouc Rgt 2 7 James Fus) Moves. 5 R.War.Rgt to F.15 Central. 6 R.War.Rgt to W.30 d 50. 144 M.G. Bde HQ to TINCOURT. 4 Glouc Rgt to HAMEL. 7 War.Rgt to K.5.B. 8 Worc Rgt to TINCOURT. 145 Inf Bde HQ to E 29 61. 5 Glouc Rgt to F.15.c.37. 4 Oxf Bucks LI to F.25.c.61. 6 James Fus to F.15.6. 7 James Fus to E.27. Fus to E 9c.	

2449 Wt. W.14957/M90 750,000 1/16 J.B.C. & A. Forms/C.2118/12.

WAR DIARY
or
INTELLIGENCE SUMMARY

Army Form C. 2118.

(Erase heading not required.)

Place	Date	Hour	Summary of Events and Information	Remarks and references to Appendices
TINCOURT	14.4.17		Casualties. Officers Nil. O.Rs Killed 3 (2. 6th James Fus) Wounded 17 (1. 5th Glouc Regt 5 James Fus 2. 8th James Fus) 1. 45th M.G.Coy 5 James Fus 1. 4th Div Train) Moves 145th Inf Bde HdQrs Ye E22.d.32. 11th Worcester Regt to E22.d.22. 8th R Warwick Regt to E10 & 23. 5th Glouc Regt to F15 a 22. 2nd James Fus to P30 a.	
	15.4.17		Casualties Officers Nil. O.Rs Killed 1. (1/5th Glouc Regt) Wounded Nil. Moves 5th Glouc Regt to E29 & 95. 4th Ox & Bucks to E24.B Bucks Bn to F31 & 05. 125th Inf Bde HdQrs to PERONNE 5 James Fus & 6 James Fus to PERONNE. 7 James Fus to LONGAVESNES 9th James Fus to CARTIGNY.	
	16.4.17		Casualties Officers Nil O.Rs Killed 1 (4th Glouc Regt Previously reported Wounded and missing 14.4.17) Wounded 1 (5 R War Regt) Missing 1 (5 James Fus) Moves 6 Glouc Regt to VILLERS - FAUÇON 7th War Regt to TINCOURT. 5th Glouc Regt to E29 & 95. 4 Ox + Bucks to E 24 + 28 Bucks Bn to F18 & 28. 4 R. Berks to F27 a 28.	
	17.4.17		Casualties. Officers Killed 2 (2nd Lts Irefford 6th War Regt) Wounded 8 (Lieut J H Heys 1/5 R Vaswick Regt 2nd Lt Regt Regge Ellen {Bucks Bn 2/Lt Deatridge 14th M.G. 2/Lt R M Turner 6th R Berks 2/Lt C D Humphreys 4th R Berks Reg (6th War Regt) 2/Lt R M Pump 3/5 R War Regt 26 6 R War Regt 35 7 War Regt 143 & 6 to 5th Glouc Regt 1. Bucks Bn 47 Missing 1 (2nd Lt J Hunter 4 R War Regt) 4th R Bucks 21 Missing Wounded (5 R War Regt 1. 6 R War Regt 12) Wounded 136 (143 & 88 1. Bucks Bn 9) Wounded 1. 4/5 R Berks 1. Bucks Bn 16) O.Rs Killed 59. (5 R Wav Regt 1. 4th R Bucks 12 Missing 29 (5 R Wav Regt 12. 4th R Bucks 12) Moves 5th R War Regt to E22 d 22. 6 R War Regt E 10 d 23. 7 R War Regt to F1C 46. 8 R War Regt W30 d 42. 4 Ox + Bucks to E18 d 50 Bucks Bn to F15 & 97.	

WAR DIARY / INTELLIGENCE SUMMARY

Army Form C. 2118.

Place	Date	Hour	Summary of Events and Information	Remarks and references to Appendices
TINCOURT	18-4-17		Casualties. Officers Killed 6 (T/Capt T.W. Nott, Lieut L. King, 2nd Lt T.V. Nott, Major R.F. Graham) 1/6 Glouc Regt, 2nd Lt E. Harrison (RAMC) att Rev NF Puckle (CF) 1/6 Glouc Regt. Wounded 3 (2/Lt F.L. Wright 7" Worc Regt, 2/Lt C.W.V. Peake 7" Worc Regt, 2/Lt R.F.C. Rutherham Bucks Bn)	Out
			O.R's Killed 3 (2 - 5"R War Regt, 1 - 5"Glouc Regt) Wounded 20 (9 - 5"R War Regt, 2 - 4oth Lt By, 1 - 7"Worc Regt, 2 - 8"Worc Regt, 5 - 5"Glouc Regt, 1 - 241" Bde RFA). Missing nil	
			Move. 5"Glouc Regt to F15 a 94. 4"Ox & Bucks to F21C43 Bucks Bn E29 B62. 4"R Bucks Bn to E29 d 50. 4/5"R.A. Bde to RONSSOY.	
	19-4-17		Casualties. Officers nil O.Rs Killed 3 (7 War Regt) Wounded 2 (1 - 4"Ox & Bucks, 1 - 240 Bde RFA)	
			Move. 143" Inf Bde HQ to E18 c30. 144" Inf Bde to E29 & 77. 7"War Regt to E29. Bucks Bn to VILLERS-FAUCON. 4"R Bucks to K10 c 63. 474 By RG to EPEHY. 145" Inf Bde HQ J24 B67.	
	20-4-17		Casualties. Officers Killed 1 (2/Lt V.S. Wilkins 4"Ox & Bucks LI) Wounded 1 (2/Lt V.S. Wilkins 4"Ox & Bucks LI). O.R's Killed 11 (1-7"R War Regt, 2-7"R War Regt, 3-5"R War Regt, 5-5"Glouc, 4-4"Ox & Bucks LI, 9-4"Ox Bucks LI) Wounded 55 (4-4"Ox & Bucks, 4-5"Glouc, 4-4"Ox & Bucks LI, 4-4"Ox & Bucks LI) Missing 4 (4"Ox & Bucks LI) Missing nil	
			Move. 5"R War Regt to K14 d, 4"Glouc Regt to K15 d, 5"Worc Regt to F15 c 95, 5"Glouc Regt to F21 c 52, 5"Glouc Regt to K5 Central, 6"Glouc Regt to F15 a 70, 6"Glouc Regt to Bucks, 4"Ox & Bucks to TEMPLEUX-LA-FOSSE, 1/6 Bn Were to Vermelles	
			To VILLERS-FAUCON, 10"Hantshirs to LONGAVESNES, 10"VILLERS-FAUCON, 5"LANCS to TEMPLEUX-LA-FOSSE	

WAR DIARY or INTELLIGENCE SUMMARY

Army Form C. 2118.

Place	Date	Hour	Summary of Events and Information	Remarks and references to Appendices
TINCOURT	21-4-17		Casualties. Officers Killed nil Wounded 1 (2/Lt J.J. McKinnel 8th Wor Regt) missing nil. O.R's Killed 1 (8th Wor Regt) Wounded 14 (10. 7th Wor Regt, 1. 8th Wor Regt, 1. 6th Glouc) missing nil.	
			Moves. 6th R Wor Regt to D28d73. 4th E James 18 Fic B. 5th E James 16 E10B23. 5th R Wor Regt 16 E22L22. 5th R War Ry 16 E25B. 10th Manchester ½ right forms. 12674
Kila 79	22-4-17		Casualties. Officers Killed 1 (Capt L.A. Baird RAMC att. 10th Manchester Regt) Wounded + missing nil. O.R's Killed 1 (4th E James Regt) Wounded 2 (2/tc Bde RFA) missing nil.	
			Moves. Divisional HQ Kila79. 145th Bde HQ to E25a95. 4th Glouc Regt to F15c93. 6th Glouc Regt to F13a70. 7th Wor Regt to F21c32. 2nd Wor Regt to E29 G52.
Kila 79	23-4-17		Casualties. Officers nil O.R's Killed 1 (4th Glouc Regt) Wounded 6 (2. 4th E James, 3. 9th Manchester Regt 1. 4th Ox + Bucks L.I.) missing nil	
			Moves. 5th E James to X2bc. 10th Manchesters to SAULCOURT
Kila 79	24-4-17		Casualties. Officers Killed 1 (Major LG Parkinson 4th Glouc Regt) Wounded 2 (2/Lt A.V. Betts 6 R Wor Regt, 2/Lt C.V.A. Freeman 4th E James Regt) missing nil. O.R's Killed nil Wounded 17 (E James 16, 9th Manchesters 2) missing nil	
			Owing to stress of heavy fighting, no casualty report yet received from 144th Inf Bde.
			Moves. 4th Glouc Regt to F13a70 - 6th Glouc Regt to F15c93. 7th Wor Regt to F25a86. 7th Wor Ry to F21c23.
Kila 79	25-4-17		Casualties (corrected list for 24+25-4-17) Officers Killed 7 (2/Lt A Pearce 6th Glouc Ry, 2nd Lt J.F. Brown 6th Glouc Regt, 2/Lt A.M. Davis + 2nd Lt P.P. Edwards 7th Wor Regt, Capt F.W. Hemming + by A Platoshere 8th Wor Regt)	
			2nd Lt N.E. Chatterbuck + 2nd Lt A.R. Shallcross 8th Wor Regt)

WAR DIARY or INTELLIGENCE SUMMARY

Army Form C. 2118.

Place	Date	Hour	Summary of Events and Information	Remarks and references to Appendices
K11a 79	25-4-17		Casualties (contd.) Wounded Officers 14 { 2/7 G H White, 4 Glouc Regt, 2/7 R H Bell, 2/7 J G Sturgeon, 2/7 V M.S. Rose, 2/7 A R Coombs, 2/7 A H Watts, 6th Glouc Regt, Capt G R Watson, 2/7 W R Prescott M.C., 2/7 Dq Tippet M.C., 2/7 H J Campbell, 7 Worc Regt, 2/7 R M Pittard, 2/7 C G Bolton, 2/7 L R Bomford 8 Worc Regt, 2/7 J S Edmonston 14th M.G. Regt } Missing Officers 2 2/7 F G Petrie 2" Worc Regt (wounded). 2/7 A G Richards 8" Worc Regt (believed killed). O.Rs. Killed 25 (4 4" Glouc Rgt, 2 6" Glouc Rgt, 10 7" Worc Rgt, 7 8" Worc Rgt, 2 14" M.G.B.) Wounded 260 (48 4" Glouc Rgt, 70 6 Glouc Rgt, 72 7 Worc Rgt, 62 8" Worc Rgt, 5 14" M.G.B.) Missing 129 (10 4" Glouc Rgt, 13 6 Glouc Rgt, 29 7 Worc Rgt, 77 8 Worc Rgt) Moves. 144" M.G.Bde H.Q. to TINCOURT. 4 Glouc H.Q. F16 c 9 8. 6 Glouc Rgt H.Q. d 94. 7 Worc Rgt Y. K 5 central. 8 Worc Rgt Y. K10 c 4.3. 14.5/T.M. Bdy H.Q. c 10 e 2.9. F.4.1. 5" Glouc Rgt Y. LEMPIRE. 4 Ox. Bucks Y. e 29 f 35. Bucks Bn. to Jr EMILIE 4 R Berks Y. RONSSOY.	
Attempt 79	shapen		Casualties Officers killed 1. (2/7 B8 Green 5" E James Regt) Wounded 2 (2/7 R T Romagon Bhn, 2/7 E.K.P Fudge, 1 Angus at 7 Frankshires) 4th E James. 2/7 E.K.P Fudge, 1" Angus at 7 Frankshires	
K11a 79	26-4-17		O.Rs Killed 5 (2 5" R. Sussex, 2.4" E James, 1 5" Glouc Regt) Wounded 33 (1 4/76 Fd. By, R6. 12 4" E James, 6 5" E James, 9 7 frankshires, 2 5 Glouc Regt, 3 4" R Berks) Missing 12 (9 6" E James, 1 9 Franklshires, 2 10" Franklshires)	

WAR DIARY or INTELLIGENCE SUMMARY

Army Form C. 2118.

Place	Date	Hour	Summary of Events and Information	Remarks and references to Appendices
K11a 7.9	26-4-17		Moves. 5" Glouc Regt to F15a87. 4" Oxf Bucks to F21c Bucks Bn to trenches. 4" R Berks to F23c34. 5" E James to PEIZIERE. 9" trenches to EPEHY. 10" trenches to X26c.	
K11a 7.9	27-4-17		Casualties. Officers Kid. O.Rs. Killed 5 (4 + 5" Glouc Ry.) 1. 4" R Berks). Wounded 35 (3 6" Glouc Regt 1. 1½" A. g. Bn. 5. 4" E James 6. 9" trenches. 1. 21 Bde RFA 5" Glouc Regt. 4. Bucks Bn. 4. 4" R Berks Regt. 6. 1.4.5" Bd. g. Bn.) Missing. 7. (9" trenches.) Moves. 1.4.5" Bd H.Q. to F21a 55. 5" Glouc Regt F15a 85. 5" Sussex Regt to K11a 81. 5" E James K. X26c. 10" trenches Regt to PEIZIERE. 5" trenches Regt to SAVLCOURT. 7" trenches Regt to VILLERS-FAUCON	
K11a 7.9	28-4-17		Casualties. Officers Killed 2 (2Lt Cq Edn 8" Worc Regt) 2Lt AC Walton 5" E James). Wounded 3 (2Lt FW Tompkins 4" Glouc Regy. 2Lt HW Edwards 5" E James. 2Lt R Berks, etc.) Bajt EM Cockshutt 5" E James) O.Rs. Killed 4 (3 4" R Berks 1 4" E James). Wounded 3 (2. 4" R Berks 1. 4" E James) Missing 4 (4" R Berks). Moves. 4" Glouc Regy to J18d94. 6" Glouc Regy to E29a 898. 7" Worc Regy to K15c 43. 8" Worc Regy to K 5" Central. 4" Ox q. Bucks to F23c34. 4" R Berks to F21c 88. 4.74" By RE to Fic 89. 9" trenches to BVIRE 5" trenches to EPEHY. 6" trenches to SAVLCOURT 7" trenches to VILLERS FAUCON	
K11a 7.9	29-4-17		Casualties. Officers Kid. O.Rs. Killed 8 (5" E James Regt) Wounded (33. 5" E James Rgt.) 2. 4" Oxf Bucks 1. 1.4.5" Bde H.Q. 1.45" Bd H.Q. to F21a55. 145" Batarin to HAMEL. 4" Glouc Regy to HAMEL. 6" Glouc Regy to F15a 86. 7" Worc Regy to F21a27. 8" Worc Regy K F22d 75	

WAR DIARY or INTELLIGENCE SUMMARY

Army Form C. 2118.

Place	Date	Hour	Summary of Events and Information	Remarks and references to Appendices
K'ua 79	29-4-17		Armies (continued) 143 Inf Bde HQrs to PERONNE. 5" R. War. Regt. to FLAMICOURT. 6" Bn. 7" & 8" R. War. Regt. to PERONNE. 5" Glouc Regt. to HAMEL. 4" Oxon Bucks to K 5 central. Bucks Bn. to HAMEL. 4" R. Berks. to VILLERS-FAUCON. 126" Bde HQrs to LONGAVESNES. 5" E. James to SAULCOURT. 10" Manchesters to VILLERS-FAUCON. Casualties Officers nil. ORs Killed 4 (3 9" Manchesters. 1 7" Warwicks) Wounded 6 (2 5" E. James. 1 9" Manchesters. 2 Bucks Bn. 1 1/4 S. Staffs) Missing 16 (5" E. James Regt.)	
K'ua 79	30-4-17		Armies 143rd Bde HQrs 15 H 19 a 17. 5" R. War. Regt. G 22 a 72. 6" R. War. Regt. G 15 a 50. 7" R. War. Regt. T 27 & 31. 7" R. War. Regt. to 127 & 31. 145" Bde HQrs to FLAMICOURT. Bucks Bn. to MONS en CHAUSSEE & ESTREES. 5" E. James to SAULCOURT. 10" Manchesters to VILLERS FAUCON. 127 Bde to EIRC. 6" Manchesters to X 26 C 36. 7" Manchesters to EPEHY. 8" Manchesters to PEIZIERE. Honours awarded Received by the Division during the month. April:— See Appendix A. Voyage in Infantry Battalions — See Appendix B.	Attached to Loaned to for Exerc-from Brigade to 4" Division

Appendix A

48th DIVISION.

LIST OF "HONOURS and REWARDS" awarded during April, 1917.

Regtl.No.	Rank and Name.	Regiment.	Award.
	2/Lt.(T.Lt.) F.H. ADSHEAD,	241st Bde, R.F.A.	M.C.
331519.	Gnr. JAMES, A.W.R.	- do -	M.M.

143rd Infantry Bde.

Regtl.No.	Rank and Name.	Regiment.	Award.
240165	Sgt. HUNT J.	1/6th R.Warwick Regt.	M.M.
2001	Pte. RICHMOND C.	1/6th R.Warwick Regt.	D.C.M.
240167	Cpl. BOX S.R.	- do -	M.M.
243115	Sgt. RUBERY J.H.	- do -	M.M.
265013	L/Cl. HICKMAN J.C.	1/7th R.Warwick Regt.	M.M.
265492	Sgt. MITCHELL J.	- do -	M.M.
265162	" SYLVESTER C.H.	- do -	M.M.
265591	L/Cl. HARRIS W.	- do -	M.M.
306824	Pte. COX J.	1/8th R.Warwick Regt.	M.M.

144th Infantry Bde.

Regtl.No.	Rank and Name.	Regiment.	Award.
	Lieut. HOLLAND C.F.	1/4th Gloucester Regt.	Bar to M.C
	Lieut WAKEFIELD L.E.	- do -	M.C.
200651	L/Cl. COOMBS C.	- do -	M.M.
200435	Pte. UNDERHILL W.S.	- do -	M.M.
201136	Cpl. HOPES C.	- do -	M.M.
200197	" CURME W.	- do -	M.M.
200948	Pte. SMITH S.	- do -	M.M.
20237	" LARNER H.C.	- do -	M.M.
265972	Cpl. EDOLLS W.A.	1/6th Gloucester Regt.	M.M.
266435	Pte. TURNER J.	- do -	M.M.
266808	L/Cl. NEEDS J.A.	- do -	D.C.M.
266456	Cpl. ASHMEAD W.J.	- do -	D.C.M.
	2/Lt. SHUTTLETON F.G.	- do -	M.C.
	Lieut PRESCOTT W.R.	1/7th Worcester Regt.	M.C.
	2/Lt. CLARK A.H.B.	- do -	M.C.
201865	Sgt. POSTINS L.	- do -	M.M.
200589	" LANGFORD S.	- do -	M.M.
200806	Pte. TYLER J.	- do -	M.M.
200496	" OAKES J.	- do -	M.M.
200920	Cpl. ASTON F.C.	- do -	M.M.
202038	Pte. DORRIL B.	- do -	M.M.
200505	L/Cl. ROBINSON L.L.	- do -	M.M.
	2/Lt.(T.Capt.) WALLACE G.R.	- do -	Bar to M.C.
3136	Cpl. HARRIS W.A.	1/8th Worcester Regt.	M.M.
240492	Sgt. EDWARDS W.E.	- do -	D.C.M.
240099	Cpl. GISBOURNE H.	- do -	D.C.M.
241339	Pte. WEBB F.	- do -	M.M.
240106	" BRIGGS H.	- do -	M.M.
240150	L/Sgt ADKINS H.	- do -	M.M.
240078	Sgt. COLLINS H.J.	- do -	Bar to M.M
240817	L/Cl. TURNER E.	- do -	M.M.
240264	Sgt. DASH E.W.	- do -	M.M.
240285	L/Cl. TAINTON J.W.	- do -	M.M.
240072	Cpl. BYNG H.	- do -	M.M.
	Lt.(T.Capt.) BATE J.P.,M.C.	- do -	Bar to M.C.
	Lt.(T.Capt.) PAWSEY C.R. M.C.	- do -	Bar to M.C.

Sheet 2.

145th Infantry Brigade.

Regt.No.	Rank and Name.	Regiment.	Award
242487	Pte. (L/Cl) THORNE A.E.	1/5th Gloucester R.	M.M.
240525	Sgt. BARNES H.C.	- do -	M.M.
	2/Lt. HILL F.S.	- do -	M.C.
240289	Sgt. JACKSON A.J.	- do -	M.M.
242501	" HOBBS E.W.	- do -	M.M.
240153	Pte. (L/Cl) E.J. RYDER	- do -	M.M.
240670	Cpl. CHANDLER W.J.	- do -	M.M.
	Lt.(A/Capt) CONDOR E.	- do -	M.C.
1307	Pte. (Drmr) FARMER H.	- do -	D.C.M.
7046	Pte. (L/Cl) PRINGLE F.	- do -	M.M.
1760	Cpl. CAUDLE H.	- do -	M.M.
1599	Pte. (L/Cl) EXELL. W.	- do -	M.M.
240080	Sgt. COOPEY A.	- do -	M.M.
241000	Cpl. BUTT R.	- do -	M.M.
	Lieut.(T.Capt.) GREENWELL G.H.	1/4th Oxf. & Bucks L.I.	M.C.
201049	L/Sgt WIGGINS A.C.H.	- do -	M.M.
200899	L/Cl. UPSTONE T.	- do -	M.M.
201785	L/Cpl. HOBBS W.H.	- do -	M.M.
200793	" BATTS B.	- do -	M.M.
200753	Cpl.(A/Sgt)MUDGE W.H.	- do -	M.M.
200461	L/Cl. WILSON F.G.	- do -	M.M.
200482	Pte. WHITE J.T.	- do -	M.M.
	2/Lt. ALLAN A. (8th Scot.Rifles) attd	- do -	M.C.
200774	Pte.(L/Cl) LEEDS G.J.	- do -	M.M.
201129	" CHAMINGS R.G.	- do -	M.M.
203382	" MAY A.W.	- do -	M.M.
200631	Sgt. HARRIS H.A.	- do -	M.M.
200602	Cpl. KIMBERLY G.	- do -	M.M.
201116	Pte.(L/Cpl) COLLIER R.J.	- do -	M.M.
201472	" AYRES E.	- do -	M.M.
3111	Cpl. WEST J.	1st Bucks Bn. - do -	M.M.
1672	Pte. TWITCHEN G.	- do -	M.M.
265296	" CROSS H.	- do -	M.M.
265405	Sgt. WOODHAM S.T.H.	- do -	M M
266461	Pte HERBERT. A	- do -	M.M.
267533	Pte SEWARD F.G.	- do -	M.M.
	2/Lt. HAMPSHIRE C.D.	1/4th R.Berks Regt.	M.C.
	Lt.(T.Capt) O.B. CHALLENOR.	- do -	M.C.
	2/Lt.(A/Capt) JAMES O.M.	- do -	M.C.
	2/Lt. ROGERS T.	- do -	M.C.
200633	Pte. LAMBDEN R.E.	- do -	M.M.
200426	Sgt. MILLICAN H.	- do -	M.M.
200847	Pte. (L/Cl) De GRUCHY H.	- do -	M.M.
200620	Sgt. MARTIN S.	- do -	M.M.
200661	Pte.(L/Cpl) SLATTER S.G.	- do -	M.M.
201804	" BREADMORE F.	- do -	M.M.
200674	Sgt. SEELEY C.L.	- do -	M.M.
203875	Cpl.(L/Sgt) BAYLIS L.G.	- do -	M.M.

Divisional Signal Coy. R.E.

| 500248 | a/2nd Cpl. COLLINSON C.S.H. | .... | M.M. |

R. A. M. C.

| | Captain. SHERIDAN B.C.O. | (M.O. 1/7th Worc.R.) | M.C. |

Sheet.3.

Regtl.No.	Rank & Name.	Regiment.	Award.

T.M. Batteries.

49715	Gnnr. LIDLOW C.	143rd T.M.Battery.	M.S.M.
39107	Bmdr. ADAMS W.	X/48 T.M. Battery.	M.M.

M.G. Companies.

22902	Pte.(L/Cpl) WILSDON H.	145th Machine Gun Coy.	M.M.
19053	Sgt. HOLMES J.A.	- do -	M.M.
36501	" O'NEILL C.	- do -	D.C.M.

Attached Troops.

946.	Pte.(Interpreter) WEILL P.M.	74me Regt d'Infanterie, attached 240th Bde, R.F.A.	M.M.

Appendix B

RETURN SHEWING WASTAGE IN 48TH DIVISION FROM 31ST MARCH, 1917, TO 30TH APRIL, 1917.

Regiment.	✵ Fighting Strength Mar 31st, 1917.		✵ Fighting Strength April 30 1917.		Casualties.						Decrease from other causes.		Reinforcets.		Total Wastage.	
					Officers.			Other Ranks								
	Off.	O.R.	Off.	O.R.	K.	W.	M.	Total.	K.	W.	M.	Total.	Off.	O.R.	Off.	O.R.	Off.	O.R.
5th R.Warwick Regt.	26.	610.	17.	532.	–	3.	–	3.	8.	44.	3.	53.	10.	68.	4.	43.	9.	78.
6th -do-	25.	597.	15.	440.	–	4.	1.	7.	22.	67.	7.	91.	8.	139.	5.	72.	10.	157.
7th -do-	23.	644.	25.	605.	–	1.	1.	–	6.	29.	–	35.	3.	22.	5.	19.	ẋ 2.	38.
8th -do-	15.	638.	17.	563.	–	1.	1.	2.	1.	15.	2.	16.	4.	71.	10.	12.	ẋ 2.	75.
4th Gloucester Regt.	28.	577.	20.	559.	2.	8.	–	10.	16.	107.	10.	135.	2.	–	4.	100.	ẋ 0.	18.
6th -do-	34.	550.	26.	543.	–	3.	–	11.	2.	88.	11.	103.	–	47.	3.	143.	8ẋ	7.
7th Worcester Regt.	37.	778.	24.	536.	3.	6.	–	9.	25.	165.	9.	219.	8.	68.	4.	95.	13.	192.
8th -do-	30.	703.	20.	604.	7.	3.	1.	11.	55.	121.	11.	207.	3.	11.	4.	119.	10.	99.
5th Gloucester Regt.	24.	732.	25.	638.	1.	1.	1.	1.	21.	63.	1.	84.	2.	15.	5.	5.	ẋ 2.	94.
4th Oxf. & Bks L.I.	25.	722.	22.	663.	1.	2.	–	3.	22.	80.	3.	106.	3.	19.	3.	28.	3.	59.
1/Bucks Battn.	20.	641.	17.	599.	–	5.	–	5.	9.	57.	5.	82.	–	38.	2.	12.	3.	42.
4th R.Berks Regt.	26.	722.	18.	598.	2.	7.	–	9.	12.	66.	9.	94.	–	43.	1.	13.	8.	124.
5th R.Sussex Regt.	28.	861.	33.	896.	1.	–	–	1.	2.	2.	–	4.	1	1	2.	26.	ẋ 5.	ẋ 35.

✵. Does not include Column "B".
ẋ. Except in cases marked thus a decrease is shewn.

Vol 26

War Diary.

"A" & "Q" Branch

48th Divn.

May 1917.

Volume XXVII

Army Form C. 2118.

WAR DIARY
or
INTELLIGENCE SUMMARY

(Erase heading not required.)

Instructions regarding War Diaries and Intelligence Summaries are contained in F. S. Regs., Part II. and the Staff Manual respectively. Title Pages will be prepared in manuscript.

Place	Date	Hour	Summary of Events and Information	Remarks and references to Appendices
K11a79	1-5-17		Bazuelvres Ad. Officers Ad. O.Rs. Killed 3 (1 5E Essex 2 9" Hunts Reg) Wounded 4 (1. 24th Bde RFA 1. 7" Wore Regt 1. 8" Wore Regt 1. 4" R/ves Reg) Horses Kd 5" Glou Regt Yo CARTIGNY. 4" Ox Bucks Yo DOINGT. 4" R. Berks to BUIRE.	
K11a79	2-5-17		Bazuelvres Moves. 14th Bde Yo TINCOURT. M Affairs 6 Glou Regt Yo VILLERS-FAUCON 5" Glou Regt Yo OIYA. 4" R Berks Yo DOINGT. 7" Wore Regt Yo TINCOURT. 4" Ox Bucks Yo TINCOURT AAC Yo 133a b9 240 Bde RFA 241 Bde RFA Yo TINCOURT Bazuelvres.	
FLAMICOURT	3-5-17		Moves. Div HQrs Yo FLAMICOURT. 14 Glou Regt Yo HALLE E from R/VR BUIRE TINCOURT. 143 Bde HQ to PERONNE. 5" 6" Warwicks Yo PERONNE 8"75" Fd Eng RE. Yo PERONNE. 3" Fd Ambulance Bazuelvres. Ad.	
FLAMICOURT	4-5-17		Moves 144- Bde HQrs Yo BUIRE.	
FLAMICOURT	5-5-17		Bazuelvres Ad. Moves Ad. Bazuelvres Ad.	
FLAMICOURT	6-5-17		Moves Ad.	

WAR DIARY
or
INTELLIGENCE SUMMARY

(Erase heading not required.)

Army Form C. 2118.

Instructions regarding War Diaries and Intelligence Summaries are contained in F. S. Regs., Part II. and the Staff Manual respectively. Title Pages will be prepared in manuscript.

Place	Date	Hour	Summary of Events and Information	Remarks and references to Appendices
FLAMICOURT	7·5·17		Casualties Nil	
do			Anores A.A.	
do	8·5·17		Casualties Nil	
do			Anores A.A.	
do	9·5·17		Casualties Nil	
do			Anores A.A.	
do	10·5·17		Casualties A.A.	
			Anores A.A.	
do	11·5·17		Casualties Wounded 2 (1 – 5 R Sussex, 1 – 6" DAC)	
			Anores A.A.	
do	12·5·17		1/Bucks Bn. to FLAMICOURT	
			Anores A.A.	
			S.M. 3rd Cdn Art. moved 143rd (Bde) group consisting of Bde Units from 2 Sectors 1/2 ROEVIGNY – MESNIL Area to 2 Bde group, moved to LE TRANSLOY – S.M.	
			143rd Bde group consisting of Bde units from No 3 4th Corps	
			+ No 4 Bde Tarun, moved to COMBLES area	
			144th 3rd Bde moved to PERONNE	
			5 R Sussex to PERONNE, 4/4 + 4/5 7th Bn RE to PERONNE	
			475 DA 3rd Bde RE moved with 143rd Bde group to S.M. MESNIL.	

Army Form C. 2118.

WAR DIARY
or
INTELLIGENCE SUMMARY

(Erase heading not required.)

Instructions regarding War Diaries and Intelligence Summaries are contained in F.S. Regs., Part II. and the Staff Manual respectively. Title Pages will be prepared in manuscript.

Place	Date	Hour	Summary of Events and Information	Remarks and references to Appendices
FLAMICOURT	19-11-17		Moves. 143rd Bde Group moved to about 125c & d. Ref. map Sheet 57c 1/40,000) & tents for the day & plans for tomorrow to relieve 34th Inf Bde on forward moves: 6" R. War Regt to Right Sector Bn HQrs J.19 d 78. 7" R. War Regt to Centre Sector Bn HQrs J.14 c 81. 8" R. War Regt to Left Sector Bn HQrs D.19 c 50. 5" R. War Regt in Reserve Bn HQrs C.30 d 55. 143rd m.g.c. relieves and from 34th A.G.B. 145 Bde Front to LE TRANSLOY - ROCQUIGNY Area. 144 Bde Front communicating. 1 Bde units Pl Hq 20.13.SM 3rd Ambulance. No 3 Bay train - Corps I.C.C. Bde Sector up to 23 lorries Sectors to COMBLES Area. Casualties. Officers wounded 2/Lt m. A.9am. 1/Lt m.R. Moves. 145 Bde HdQrs to Jaec 67 (the Brigade Relieving over the Right Sector of the 11 Divisional Front.) 4" Royal Berks to Right Sub-sector Bn HdQrs of J.29 & 57. 1/1st Bucks Bn to Left sub-sector Bn HQrs to J.15 d 49. 1/4" Ox Bucks L.I. to Right Reserve Bn HdQrs J.34 & 25. 5" Glouc Regt to Left Reserve Bn HdQrs J.20 c 59. 145" A.G.f. -> TMB to Inur. 144" Inf Bde Move int. Div. Reserve. Bn HdQrs. FREMICOURT. 4" Glouc Regt
FLAMICOURT	14-11-17		to LE BARQUINE. 6" Glouc Regt to FREMICOURT. 7" Wor Regt to MORCHIES. 144 M.G.& TMB take ie up to FREMICOURT. 8" War Regt to VELU.

Army Form C. 2118.

WAR DIARY
or
INTELLIGENCE SUMMARY

(Erase heading not required.)

Instructions regarding War Diaries and Intelligence Summaries are contained in F. S. Regs., Part II. and the Staff Manual respectively. Title Pages will be prepared in manuscript.

Place	Date	Hour	Summary of Events and Information	Remarks and references to Appendices
BEAULENCOURT	15.5.19		Casualties. Officers. Wounded 1 (Capt. J. McGAUSSEN 1/7 R. War Regt.)	
N 11 Central			O.Rs. Killed 2 (1. 1/6 R. War Regt. 1. 4th Div Sig. Coy att. 143rd Bde H.Qrs.) Wounded 2 (1. 6 R War Regt. att. H.Qrs. 143rd Bde. 1. 7 R. War Regt. 2. 8 R. War Regt. att. H.Qrs. 143 Bde 1st Bouzy Trench Bombers att. H.Qrs. 143 Bde.) Missing, nil. Moves. 5 R Sussex Regt., 474 & 477 Fd Coys RE to COMBLES Area. Divisional HQrs to BEAULENCOURT. N 11 Central. D in Train H.Qrs. Yo. M 30 d 43	
N 11 Central	16.5.19		Casualties. O.Rs. Killed 1 (6 R. War Regt.) Wounded 4 (1. 5 R. War Regt. accidental. 3. 5 Glouc Regt.) Moves. 5 R Sussex Regt Yo I 33 d 70. 474 & 477 Fd Coy RE Yo I 27 c 18 4. Stationery. 48 Div. RA HQrs Yo N 11 Central. 240 & 241 Bde RFA and 48 DAC to 'M' Area in neighbourhood of BEAULENCOURT.	
N 11 Central	17.5.19		Casualties. Officers nil. O.R's Killed 1 (Bucks Bm) Wounded 2 (8 R War Regt. 1 Bucks Bn) Moves 6 R War Regt to J 10 a 99.	
N 11 Central	18.5.19		Casualties. Officers. nil. O.R's. Killed nil. Wounded 4 (2. 6 R War Regt. 1. 8 R War Regt. 1. 4 R Berks Regt) Moves. nil.	
N 11 Central	19.5.19		Casualties Officers nil. O.R's Killed 1 (1/2 S.M. Try Amb.) Wounded 4 (1. 7 R War Regt. 1/4 S.M. Try Amb. 2. 1/31 S.M. Fd Amb.)	

WAR DIARY or INTELLIGENCE SUMMARY

Army Form C. 2118.

Place	Date	Hour	Summary of Events and Information	Remarks and references to Appendices
N 11 Central	19.5.17		(cont.) Annex. Nil	
N 11 Central	20.5.17		Battalions. Officers - Nil. O.R.s Killed 2 (6 Glouc Regt) Wounded 4 (2, 6 Glouc Regt. 1, 5 R War Regt. 1, 5 R War R). Annex. Nil.	
N 11 Central	21.5.17		Casualties. Officers Killed Nil Wounded 2 (2/Lt S.G Smith 6 R War Regt 2/Lt C.F Hampshire 4 R Berks Regt) Annex. Nil. O.Rs Killed 3 (1, 5 R War Regt. 2, 4 Oxo Bucks L.I.) Wounded 13 (1, 5 R War Regt. 2, 5 Glouc Regt. 3, 4 Ox & Bucks L.I. Annex 3 (3, 4 Ox & Bucks L.I) Annex. 14/4 Bde relieves 143rd Bde in left sector of Division front. 144 Bde H.Q Qrs Yo. Ille 56. 4 Glouc Regt Yo Right front, 8 War Regt Yo Left front, 7 War Regt to Support. 6 R War Regt Yo FREMICOURT. 6 R War Regt Yo FREMICOURT. 143rd Bde H.Qrs Yo YELU 8 R War Regt Yo C 30 d 56. 7 R War Regt remain at	
N 11 Central	22.5.17		Casualties Officers Nil. O.Rs Wounded 2 (7 War Regt). Annex. 5 R War Regt Yo FREMICOURT. 6 Glouc Regt Yo Suffey (Huy sector) (Bapt No Down. 1 (24 Bde R.F.A). Casualties. Officers Died of Wounds. 1 (Capt Gaskell Operated.) 3 (1. 24 B.R.F.A. 1. 8 War Regt. 1. 4 Ox & Bucks L.I.) O.Rs Killed. Annex. Nil	

WAR DIARY or INTELLIGENCE SUMMARY

Army Form C. 2118.

(Erase heading not required.)

Instructions regarding War Diaries and Intelligence Summaries are contained in F. S. Regs., Part II. and the Staff Manual respectively. Title Pages will be prepared in manuscript.

Place	Date	Hour	Summary of Events and Information	Remarks and references to Appendices
N1 central	24-5-17		Casualties Officers killed, nil. OR wounded nil. OR killed, nil. OR wounded 5 (4 1/5 R War R, 2 1/8 Worcs R, (5 2 R Warx R Pre	
1.3.4.5 Hinden	25.5.17		Casualties. Officers killed nil. Bombardment of Mr Adam 9th dvn. sh. [?] OR killed 10 [?]. (1/7 Worcs R, 1 Oxford Bucks LI (5), 3 3 R Sussex, 1 1/8 2 Warx R.) wounded 19 (5 1/7 Worcs R, 1 1/4 Ox/Bucks LI LI (5), 3 3 R Sussex, 1 1/8 2 Warx R.) Army Div. HQ to 1.3.4.5 a [?]. 143 Bde HQ to HAPLINCOURT	
1.3.4.3.5.26.5.17			Casualties Officers killed and wounded, nil. OR killed 2 (1 1/4/8 T.M.B., 1 × 1/48 T.M.B.) wounded 10 (1 1/7 Worcs R, @ 1 1/4 Glos LR, 1 1/8 Worcs R, 3 1/4 T.M.B., 1 1/6 Glos LR.) ‡ Moves nil	
1.3.4.3.5	27.5.17		Casualties. Officers killed nil. wounded 2 Lieuts: S. CLOSE M.T. ASC. AND 144 M.G. Coy. OR killed nil. Wounded 8 (1 2 1/Bde RFA, 1 1/Bucks Batn, 1 how section 4.9.P. Bgd. Coy, 1, 1/5 Glos R, 4 1/4 R Berks R.) Moves. nil.	
1.3.4.3.5	28.5.17		Casualties. Officers killed nil. wounded 1 (Lt A. SCOFIELD 5th R Sussex R (Lights us Bs 5). OR killed nil. wounded 14 (3 240 Bde RFA, 1 2 1/Bde RFA, 1 1/5 R Warr R, 1/4 Glos R, [?] 1/7 Worcs R 2 1/5 Oxford Batn.) missing 4 (4 1/7 Worcs R.)	

Army Form C. 2118.

WAR DIARY
or
INTELLIGENCE SUMMARY

(Erase heading not required.)

Instructions regarding War Diaries and Intelligence Summaries are contained in F. S. Regs., Part II. and the Staff Manual respectively. Title Pages will be prepared in manuscript.

Place	Date	Hour	Summary of Events and Information	Remarks and references to Appendices
S.34.a.3.5.	29.5.17		Casualties Officers nil. OR wounded 4 (1/8 R.War.R., 2 1/6 Glos.R., 1.145 M.G. Company.) Moves. 143 Bde HQ to J.12.6.43., 1/6 R.War.R to J.10.a.59., 1/7 R.War.R to J.10.a.39., 1/5 R.War.R to d.26.42. 144 Inf Bde to D.3.d.8.t. 1/6 Glos.R to LESBOEUFS, 1/7 Worc.R to K.1.25.b.35., 1/8 Worc.R to VELU.	
34.a.2.5	30.5.17		Casualties nil. Moves. 1/5 R.War.R to C.30.d.55., 1/6 Glos.R. I.11.6.00, 3/1 R.War.R	
S.34.a.3.5	30.5.17		Casualties Officers nil. OR killed nil, wounded 5 (1, 24 Bde RFA, 3/1 R.War.R 1, 143 M.G.Company.) Moves nil.	
			M.O. Return of Intelligence enemy's Movements and amounts for May 1917 attached hereto as Addendum I and Addendum G.	

O.C Whitehead Major
for Hoggweard
Comdt, 143 Bde.

2449 Wt. W14957/M90 750,000 1/16 J.B.C. & A. Forms/C.2118/12.

48th DIVISION.

LIST OF "HONOURS and REWARDS" awarded during ~~April~~ May, 1917.

Regtl.No.	Rank & Name.	Regiment.	Award.
	2/Lt.(T.Cpt) CROSSKEY, J.H.	1/5th R.Warwick Regt.	M.C.
200598.	Pte. COX, L.	- do -	M.M.
240074.	CSM. GOWDIE, H.	1/6th R.Warwick Regt.	M.C.
	Capt.(T.Major) PRYOR, W.M. (2/1st Herts Regt.)	- do -	D.S.O.
	2/Lt.(T.Cpt.) LINFOOT, H.A.	- do -	M.C.
24054.	CSM. EASTHOPE, F.	- do -	D.C.M.
240165.	Sgt. HUNT, J.	- do -	Bar to M.M.
241708.	Pte. JONES, G.O.	- do -	M.M.
241630.	Cpl. TILLEY, L.	- do -	M.M.
241638.	L/C. HEATH, R.S.	- do -	M.M.
	2/Lt. (T.Cpt) FIELD, A.J.	1/7th R.Warwick Regt.	M.C.
	2/Lt. ADAM, M. (3rd R.Scots Fus) attd.	- do -	M.C.
265600.	L/Sgt. METCALF, W.	- do -	D.C.M.
265374.	Cpl. WAGSTAFF, W.	- do -	D.C.M.
	2/Lt. DICK, J.H. (5/R.Sc.Fus)	- do -	M.C.
	Capt. CARROLL, J.D., (R.A.M.C.)	1/8th - do -	M.C.
267721.	Sgt. JARVIS, A.W.	- do -	M.M.
306839.	L/C. GIDDINGS, R.	- do -	M.M.
305057.	Pte. WEBB, A.T.	- do -	Bar to MM
200417.	Sgt. WINTERSON, H.	1/4th Gloucester Regt.	D.C.M.
	2/Lt.(T.Lt.) a/Capt. MERRICK, H.	- do -	M.C.
200477.	Cpl. CROSSMAN, R.E.	- do -	D.C.M.
200478.	Pte. BENNETT, E.	- do -	D.C.M.
200368.	Sgt. KEMP, C.W.	- do -	M.M.
200521.	Cpl. BAILEY, H.A.	- do -	M.M.
200753.	Pte. PRICE, H.E.	- do -	M.M.
200197.	" ASHCROFT, T.	- do -	M.M.
200496.	" OAKES, J.	1/7th Worcester Regt.	D.C.M.
200554.	Cpl. THATCHER, H.	- do -	D.C.M.
200573.	L/C. MARCHANT, W.B.	- do -	D.C.M.
200573.	" " "	- do -	Med.Militaire
	Lieut.PRESCOTT, W.R.	- do -	Bar to MC
201073.	Cpl. GREEN, F.	- do -	M.M.
200711.	Sgt. HANDLEY, H.S.	- do -	M.M.
201596.	Pte. PAYTON, J.	- do -	M.M.
201605.	" BISHOP, A.	- do -	M.M.
200992.	Sgt. DARBY, A.	- do -	M.M.
241572.	Pte. JELFS, W.	1/8th Worcester Regt.	D.C.M.
240504.	L/C. WOODWARD, A.T.	- do -	Croix de gre
242368.	Pte. SMITH, F.	- do -	Bar to MM
242555.	" BEATTY, T.	- do -	M.M.
240793.	" JONES, T.	- do -	M.M.
240198.	Sgt. GRIFFIN, H.	- do -	M.M.
240820.	Pte. SPIRES, A.	- do -	M.M.
	2/Lt. CRUBB, P.N.	1/5th Gloucester Regt.	M.C.
921.	Sgt. CUMMINGS, P.B.	- do -	Med.Militaire
	2/Lt. TIDDY, R.W.L.	- do -	M.C.
	" BENJON, T.N.	- do -	M.C.
	2/Lt.(T.Lt.) FORTESCUE, P.R.	1/4th Ox & Bucks L.I.	M.C.
	Lieut BOWEN, M.	1st Bucks Battalion.	M.C.
265146.	Sgt. SAUNDERS, W.G.	- do -	D.C.M.
265610.	" HOPCROFT, T.	- do -	D.C.M.

(SHEET 2.)

Regtl.No.	Rank & Name.	Regiment.	Award.
	2/Lt. CRUSE, E.W.	1/4th R. Berks R.	M.C.
200682.	Sgt. FULLER, B.H.	- do -	M.M.
200406.	" PADDICK, H.	- do -	M.M.
200846.	" WHITE, H.G.	- do -	M.M.
200373.	Pte. RUSS, E.E.	- do -	M.M.
240395.	Sgt. DALE, W.	1/5th R. Sussex Regt.	M.M.
	Lt.(T.Cpt) FEILD, A.L.	144th Machine Gun Coy.	M.C.
22554.	Sgt. SADLER, J.T.	- do -	M.M.
15530.	A/Cl. CRABTREE, T.	- do -	M.M.
9728.	Pte. JONES, E.G.	- do -	M.M.
22682.	Sgt. WATTS, C.R.	143rd Machine Gun Coy.	M.M.

48th DIVISIONAL ARTILLERY

840058.	Bdr. BOSWORTH, F.A.	D/241 Bde, R.F.A.	Medal Militaire
840058.	" "	- do -	Bar to M.M.
840142.	" AINSLEY, H.R.	- do -	M.M.
	2/Lt. STEPHEN, A.C.	242/ A.F.Arty. Bde.	Croix de Guerre

ROYAL ENGINEERS.

496621.	Cpl. MOSS, A.J.	475th Field Coy, R.E.	Croix de Guerre.
500050.	Sgt. WHITE, H.J.	48th Div. Signal Co.RE	M.M.

R. A. M. C.

	Capt. MOORE, G.	1/3rd S.M.Field Amblce.	M.C.
	Sgt. CANN, E.V.	- do -	M.M.
	Pte. WARD, W.E.	- do -	M.M.
	" RUSSELL, J.S.	- do -	M.M.
	" SAINSBURY, R.W.	- do -	M.M.
	L/Cl. UPTON, J.H.	- do -	M.M.
	Pte. DAVIS, C.L.	- do -	M.M.

ADDENDUM I.

Return showing changes in 4 & 8 Bde
from 30 April to 31 May 1917.

Regiment	Fighting Strength 30 April 1917 Officers	Fighting Strength 30 April 1917 OR	Fighting Strength 31 May 1917 Officers	Fighting Strength 31 May 1917 OR	Casualties Officers K	W	M	Total	Casualties OR K	W	M	Total	Sickness from other causes Officers	OR	Reinforcement Officers	OR	Total wastage Officers	OR
1/5 R War R	17	532	28	591	–	–	–	–	–	4	–	4	–	–	5	66	–	–
1/6 "	15	440	24	582	–	1	–	1	–	4	–	4	–	–	1	94	–	–
1/7 "	25	606	22	631	–	2	–	2	–	8	–	8	1	–	4	55	3	–
1/8 "	17	563	25	602	–	–	–	–	1	13	–	14	–	–	4	61	–	–
1/4 Glouc R	20	557	30	660	–	–	–	–	–	4	–	4	–	–	9	143	–	–
1/6 "	26	543	28	707	–	–	–	–	2	2	–	4	–	–	2	148	1	–
1/7 Worcester R	24	585	23	641	–	–	–	–	1	14	4	19	1	–	5	69	–	–
1/8 "	20	604	20	657	–	–	–	–	–	6	–	6	–	–	3	82	–	–
1/5 Glouc R	26	638	26	654	–	–	–	–	1	15	–	16	–	–	1	21	–	–
1/4 Ox+Bucks L.I.	22	663	25	761	–	–	–	–	4	5	2	11	–	–	1	83	–	–
1st Bucks Bn	17	599	24	647	–	–	–	–	1	3	–	3	–	–	2	54	1	–
1/6 R Berks R	18	598	22	704	1	–	–	1	1	2	–	3	–	–	4	44	–	–
5th R Sussex R	33	856	31	896	–	–	–	–	5	5	–	5	–	–	1	7	2	–
								Total 4				Total 100						

War Diary

48th Division

"A" & "Q" Branch

June 1917

Volume XXVII

WAR DIARY or INTELLIGENCE SUMMARY

Army Form C. 2118.

(Erase heading not required.)

Place	Date	Hour	Summary of Events and Information	Remarks and references to Appendices
T.34.a.3.5.	1.6.17		Casualties. Officers wounded 2 (2/Lt W.E.W. BAMBERGER 1/5 Gloucester R. 2/Lt R.J. CLUTTON 145 M.G. Company, slightly, at duty.) OR Killed 6. (5 1/5 Glost R., 1 1/4 Oxf & Bucks L.I. M.G.) Wounded 4 (1 1/5 R. Warwick R., 3 1/4 Oxf & Bucks L.I. M.G.) Missing nil.	
T.34.a.3.5.	2.6.17		Casualties. Officers nil. OR. wounded 7 (2/5 R. War. R., 1 143 Inf. Company, 4 1/6 Gloucester R.) Missing nil.	
T.34.a.3.5.	3.6.17		Casualties. Officers wounded 1 2/Lt H.B. BARNES 240 Bde R.F.A. OR Killed 4 (1/7 Worc R.) wounded 12 (1 145 Bde R.F.A, 1 1/5 R. Warwick R., 10 1/7 Worc. R.) Missing nil.	
T.34.a.3.5.	4.6.17		Casualties. Officers wounded 2. (2/Lt V.B. BINGHAM - 144th & Capt. W.M. COX 1/2 W. S.M. Field Ambulance) OR nil.	
T.34.a.3.5.	5.6.17		Casualties. Officers nil. OR Killed 2 (1 3/4 R.Berks R.) wounded 7 (2 1/4 Bucks Batt. 2 1/6 R. War R., 2 1/4 R. Berks R., 1 1/4 R. War R.) Missing nil.	
T.34.a.3.5.	6.6.17		Casualties. Officers nil. OR wounded 3 (1 477 Field Coy RE, 1 1/5 War R., 1/7 R. War R.) Moves. 144 Inf. Bde. to S.12 & 43 1143 Inf. Bde. to O.3.d.8.1, 1/5 R. War. R. to T.25.a, 1/7 Warc R to T.25.a, 1/7 Worc R to C.30.d.36	

Army Form C. 2118.

WAR DIARY
or
INTELLIGENCE SUMMARY
(Erase heading not required.)

Instructions regarding War Diaries and Intelligence Summaries are contained in F. S. Regs., Part II. and the Staff Manual respectively. Title Pages will be prepared in manuscript.

Place	Date	Hour	Summary of Events and Information	Remarks and references to Appendices
I.34.a.3.5	7.6.17		Casualties. Officers nil. OR wounded 2 (⁵/5 R.Scots.Fus.—1. ¹/8 H.L.I.—1) Moves. ¹/7 Royal Scots to S.25.B.05. ¹/5 H.L.I. training. ¹/25.a.34.	
I.34.a.3.5	8.6.17		Casualties. Officers nil. OR killed 3. (⁴ Royal Scots Regt.—2. ¹/4.5.T.M.B.—1. (accidental)) OR wounded 10 (Royal Scots Regt—9. ¹/4.5.T.M.B.—1.(accidental)).	
I.34.a.3.5	9.6.17		Casualties. Officers nil. OR killed 1. (¹/8 Royal Scots Reg) OR wounded 3. (245 BDE R.F.A.—1. ¹/4 Gordons—1 accidental. ¹/8 Gordons—1.) Moves. ¹/5 Gordons to J.29.B.57. ¹/4 Gordons J.18.a.44 ¹/4 R.Scots to Q.6.B.99 ¹/7 Royal Scots I.20.c.89	
I.34.a.3.5	10/6/17		Casualties. Officers nil. OR killed (¹/8 Royal Scots Regt—1. ¹/8 Gordons—1.) OR wounded (¹/8 Gordons—3. ¹/4 Gordons—1. ¹/5 Gordons—1. ¹/5 Gordons—1.) Moves. Nil.	
I.34.a.3.5	11/6/17		Casualties. Officers 3. Lieut T.L.Baird ⁷/⁴⁸ T.M.B. Lieut J.P.Winterbottom ¹/5 Gordon Reg. } Slightly wounded at duty. Lieut G.A.Ewing ¹/8 Gordons—accidental. OR wounded 3 { ⁷/⁴⁸ T.M.B.—1 (on duty) ¹/5 Gordons—1 ¹/8 Gordons—1. OR killed 1 (¹/4 Gordons.) Moves Nil.	

WAR DIARY
or
INTELLIGENCE SUMMARY

(Erase heading not required.)

Army Form C. 2118.

Instructions regarding War Diaries and Intelligence Summaries are contained in F. S. Regs., Part II. and the Staff Manual respectively. Title Pages will be prepared in manuscript.

Place	Date	Hour	Summary of Events and Information	Remarks and references to Appendices
			Officers – nil	
I.34.a.35	12/6/17		Casualties. OR wounded 3. (X 1/4.8.Trks – 1. 1/4 Glosrs – 1 (accidental) 1/8 Worc – 1)	
			OR missing 2. (1/4 Glosrs – 2)	
			Moves – nil	
I.34.a.35	13/6/17		Casualties. Officers nil.	
			OR wounded 18. (1/8 R.Warwick. 10 R accidental. 1/7 Worcs – 1 OR. 1/5 Glosrs – 5 OR	
			1/4 Ox/s. 11 OR.)	
I.34.a.35	14/6/17		Casualties. Officers nil.	
			OR wounded – 4 (2/1 1st RFA (Lander), 143 MG Coy 1 OR. 1/4 Glosrs – 1 OR. 1/8 Glosrs 1 OR)	
			OR missing – 3 (1/4 Glosrs [1 wounded & missing] transferred 16/6/17	
			143 M.G.Bn relieves 144 M.G.Bn in left sector.	
I.34.a.35	14/6/17	midnight to 14/6/17	Casualties. Officers nil.	
			OR wounded 2. (5th Aust. Batty artly 2/y. Bde – 1. 1/8 & 50 ars 2/1.1.1.4.5 Regt Coy)	
			Moves.	
I.34.a.35	15/6/17	To midnight	Casualties. Officers nil.	
			OR wounded 10. (1/5 Glosrs – 1 accident. 1/4 Oxfs – 1. 1/4 Bcrks – 1. 1/4 Bcrks – 5. 143 MG Coy – 1.	
			1/48 Warks – 1)	
			OR – killed. 1. (1/4 R.Berks).	
			Moves.	

WAR DIARY
or
INTELLIGENCE SUMMARY

(Erase heading not required.)

Army Form C. 2118.

Instructions regarding War Diaries and Intelligence Summaries are contained in F.S. Regs., Part II. and the Staff Manual respectively. Title Pages will be prepared in manuscript.

Place	Date	Hour	Summary of Events and Information	Remarks and references to Appendices
I 34 a 35	14/6/17		Casualties. Officers nil. O.R. wounded accidental – 2. (1/6 Warwicks.)	
	15/6/17 midnight		Shores. 17 twos E. I 24 B 8.3	
	16/6/17 noon		Casualties. OR killed – 1. (1/8 Warwicks.)	
	18/6/17		Casualties. OR wounded – 1 (accidental – 1/4 Bucks).	
	19/6/17		Casualties. Officers wounded 3 (Capt G. Linfoot. 2/Lt A.J.S. Green. 2/Lt R.F. Dowsett, all 1/6 R&BR.). O.R. wounded 36 (1/6 R&BR. 33. 1/7 wbm I. accidental. 1/6 Warwicks – 1. 2nd Bn. RFA. 2.) O.R. missing 11 (all of R&BR. believed killed). (+ 2 OR reported wounded 21/6/17) Shores. 1/6 R&BR to J 29, 65.7. 1/8 Warwicks I 25 a 00. 1/6 Warwicks. I 31. a 36.	
	20/6/17		Casualties. Officers – nil. OR wounded – 7. (1/6 Bucks – 3. 1/7 Warwicks – 2. 1/5 Warwicks – 2.) OR killed – (1/7 R&BR.). Shores. 1/5 Warwicks E. J 29, 65.7. 1/4 Oxfs. K J 18 D 49. 1/6 Warwicks K O 6 b 99. 1/4 R.Bucks to J 20. C. 89	
	21/6/17		Casualties. Officers nil. OR wounded – 6. (1/6 R&WR – 1. 1/4 Oxfs – 1. 1/4 R.Bucks 2. 2nd Bn RFA – 2). Shores.	

2449 Wt. W14957/M90 750,000 1/16 J.B.C. & A. Forms/C.2118/12.

WAR DIARY
or
INTELLIGENCE SUMMARY

Army Form C. 2118.

(Erase heading not required.)

Place	Date	Hour	Summary of Events and Information	Remarks and references to Appendices
	22/6/17		Moves. 144 Inf Bde relieving 143 Inf Bde in left Sector.	
			Casualties. Officers killed 2/Lt V.T. Cooper (died of wounds). 1/8 R.W.R.	
			O.R. killed 1. (1/8 R.W.R.)	
			O.R. wounded 13. (1/7 R.W.R. – 11, 1/8 R.W.R. – 1, 1/4 R.W.R. – 1).	
	23/6/17		Casualties. Officers wounded Lieut G. Hawkins (accid.) 1/5 Glos. (appd).	
			O.R. wounded 1. (appd).	
I 34 a 3 5 24/6/17 →			Casualties. Nil	
I 34 a 3 5	25.6.17		Casualties. O.R. killed 1.	
			" wounded 11. (1/7 Warwicks 1. 1/8 Warwicks 1 – 1/8 Warwicks 2 – 1/5 Glos. 6 (slightly at duty), accidents 1/4 Ox+Bucks 1 – 1/4 Berks 1.)	
I 34 a 3 5	26.6.17		Casualties. O.R. wounded 1. (1/4 Ox+Bucks L.G.)	
			" missing 1. (1/4 Gloucesters) – since reported killed body found.	
I 34 a 3 5	27.6.17		Casualties. O.R. killed 1. 1/5 Gloucesters.	
			" wounded 4. (slightly at duty) (2 1/4 Ox+Bucks L.G. – 1 1/4 Berks 1 1/5 Gloucesters)	
			Moves. H.Q. 1/4 R Berks relieved 4/R Ox+B L.G.	
I 34 a 3 5	28.6.17		Casualties. Officers killed 1 – 2/Lt Dodson H.D. 1/6 Gloucesters (2 instant.)	
			O.R. killed 2 – 1/4.5 Hrs. Coyb. 1/5 Glos. 1.	
			" wounded 6 – 2/Lt Bn. R.F.A. 1. 1/4 Wounded 2. 1/4 Warwicks 2, 1/4 Berks L.G. 1.	

WAR DIARY or INTELLIGENCE SUMMARY

Army Form C. 2118.

Place	Date	Hour	Summary of Events and Information	Remarks and references to Appendices
T34a35	29.6.17		Casualties Officers Nil O.R. Killed 1 Wounded 1 Missing 1 (all 1/4 Bucks)	
"	30.6.17		Casualties O.R. Wounded 2 – 10 R. 1/4 Bucks. 1 O.R. 143 M.G. Coy. 1 O.R. Missing 29/6/17 now reported killed 10.R. 143 Bde to Gomiecourt and relieved by 6th Bde. 5th Gloucs relieve Bucks in 4th Ox + Bucks 4th Berks. 144 M.G. Coy + 144 T.M.B. relieved by 5th M.G. Coy + 5th T.M.B. T.M.B and moved back to Hupdrincourt	

M M M Capt
for Major/General
Comdg 48 Divn

LIST OF HONOURS AND REWARDS AWARDED TO OFFICERS, N.C.Os.
AND MEN OF 48TH DIVISION,

Month of June, 1917.

Rank and Name.	Unit.	Award.
Capt. COTTON, W.E.L.	(S.Capt. 144 Inf: Bde).	M.C.
" R.D. KITSON,	(B.Major 145 Inf: Bde).	M.C.
Lt.(T.Capt). HILL, J.B.	1st Bucks Bn. Oxf & Bucks L.I.	M.C.
Major.(T.Lt.Col) LORD WYNFORD, P.G.	H.Q. 240/Bde, R.F.A.	D.S.O.
2nd.Lt. MORGAN, D.P.	240th Bde, R.F.A.	M.C.
851241. Gnr. COWSELL, F.A.	D/241 Bde, R.F.A.	M.M.
2nd.Lt. MACLENNAN,	477 Field Coy, R.E.	M.C.
Lt.(T.Capt.) WATSON, W.A.P.	1/5th R. Warwick Regt.	M.C.
Lt.(T.Capt.) MELLOR, J.L.	1/6th R. Warwick Regt.	M.C.
242695. Cpl. NICKLESS, R.H.	1/6th R. Warwick Regt.	M.M.
Lt.(T.Capt.) HOSKINS, H.R.	1/7th R. Warwick Regt.	M.C.
Lieut. SHERWOOD, H.P.	1/7th R. Warwick Regt.	M.C.
Lt.(T.Capt.) TEAGUE, J.	1/8th R. Warwick Regt.	M.C.
Captain. FISHER, W.E.	1/4th Gloucester Regt.	M.C.
Captain. GERRARD, R.F.	4/R.Scots (attd 1/6 Glos.R.) k in action.	M.C.
1235. C.S.M. MOULE, W.L.	1/7th Worcester Regt.	M.C.
A/Lt.Col. TOMKINSON, F.M.	1/7th Worcester Regt.	Bar to D.S.O.
Lt.(T.Capt.) WATSON, G.G.	1/7th Worcester Regt.	M.C.
2/LT(T/Lt.) LLOYD, A.O.	1/7th Worcester Regt.	M.C.
2/Lt.(T.Lt) CASSELLS, W.C.	1/7th Worcester Regt.	M.C.
2/Lt.(T.Lt.) MELHUISH, J.W.D.	1/7th Worcester Regt.	M.C.
200671. L/Cl.SNEYD, G.	1/7th Worcester Regt.	M.M.
201564. Pte. BREEZE, A.	1/7th Worcester Regt.	M.M.
200980. L/C. WILLIAMS, J.T.	1/7th Worcester Regt.	M.M.
2nd.Lt. WILKES, S.H.	1/8th Worcester Regt.	M.C.
2nd.Lt. PITTARD, R.M.	1/8th Worcester Regt.	M.C.
2nd.Lt. JONES, G.H.	1/8th Worcester Regt.	M.C.
240457. Sgt. PITT, W.	1/8th Worcester Regt.	D.C.M.
240504. L/C. WOODWARD, A.T.	1/8th Worcester Regt.	D.C.M.
240877. Cpl. TOLLEY, P.G.	1/5th Gloucester Regt.	M.M.
611. C.S.M. WATTS, H.	1/1st Bucks Battalion.	M.C.
265472. Pte. BALDOCK, W.C.	1/1st Bucks Battalion.	M.M.
266857. CPL.(L.Sgt) ROGERS, F.G.	1st Bucks Battalion.	M.M.
2/Lt.(T.Capt) WARD, D.J.	1/4th Royal Berks Regt.	M.C.
200150.Sgt. GARRETT, E.J.	1/4th Royal Berks Regt.	M.M.
2/Lt.(T.Capt) STEELE, E.	6 Mnchr attd 143 T.M.Bty.	M.C.
Lieut. GELDARD, S.H.	3rd S.W.B., attd 145 M.G.Coy.	M.C.
Capt.(A/Major). KNOX, W.J.	50th Aust. Fld Bty, 13th A.F.Arty Bde.	M.C.
Lieut. McMULLIN, W.J.	" " "	M.C.

Vol 28

WAR DIARY.

'A' & 'Q' BRANCH. 48th DIVN.

JULY 1917

VOLUME XXVII

WAR DIARY or INTELLIGENCE SUMMARY

Army Form C. 2118

(Erase heading not required.)

Instructions regarding War Diaries and Intelligence Summaries are contained in F. S. Regs., Part II. and the Staff Manual respectively. Title Pages will be prepared in manuscript.

Place	Date	Hour	Summary of Events and Information	Remarks references to Appx
I 34 a 3.5	1/7/17		**Casualties** O.R. 1 wounded (1/7 Wore.)	
			Moves. 144 M.G. Coy. & 4 M.B. to Achiet-le-Petit area 1/7 Wore & 1/4 Glouc. from front system to Hapincourt. 145 M.G. Coy & Y.M.B. to Hapincourt	
I 34 a 3.5	2/7/17		**Casualties** O.R. wounded 4 (5th Glouc. 2, 4th Ox & Bucks 1, 2/4 Bde R.H.4. 1)	
			Moves H.Q. & 1/5 Wore & 1/6 Glouc. to Reserve area 1/4 Wore & 1/4 Glouc to Achiet-le-Petit area 2 Bns 145 Bde (4th Bucks & 5th Glouc) from front system to trenches at I.21 L.T. 5th R. Sussex Regt to Bihucourt area	
I 34 a 35	3/7/17		**Casualties** O.R. 1 wounded (1/5 Glouc.)	
			Moves HQ. 144 Bde 1/5 Wore & 1/5 Glouc. To Achiet-le-Petit area 1/4 Bucks 1/5 Glouc } to Bihucourt area 146 M.G. Coy & T.M.B 145 Bde, Bucks Br & 1/4 Ox & Bucks to Bihucourt area HQ 145 Bde (halting at I.21 L.T area after breakfast).	

2449 Wt. W14957/M90 750,000 1/16 J.B.C. & A. Forms/C.2118/12.

WAR DIARY
or
INTELLIGENCE SUMMARY

(Erase heading not required.)

Army —

Instructions regarding War Diaries and Intelligence Summaries are contained in F. S. Regs., Part II. and the Staff Manual respectively. Title Pages will be prepared in manuscript.

Place	Date	Hour	Summary of Events and Information	Remarks references to Appendices
T34a 2.5.	3.7.17 (cont.)		143 Bde Groups from Gomiecourt to Pommier area. (HQ, 6th War, at Pommier – 5th Hospital at Berles-au-Bois – 7th war, M.G. Coy + T.M.B at Bienvillers – 1/7 London, 1/4 London, 144 MG + T.M. to BLAIRVILLE. Casualties – Nil.	
ADINFER WOOD X26a (Sheet 51c)	4.7.17		MOVES D.H.Q. from T 34a.2.3.5 to Adinfer 6th London to HENDECOURT 8th War. MONCHY 4th Berks + 5th Glouc to Bavincourt (Bellacourt) 145 MG Coy to Bavincourt area Casualties – Nil.	
	5.7.17		MOVES 4th Ox & Bucks – Gouy-en-Artois to B accoutrement, 145 T.M.B. to Bavincourt. 5th R Sussex to Bailleulmont D.A Company to 18th Corps R.E. area. Artillery dispond remounts by units reorganis TM Bs. Casualties Nil.	
	6.7.17		Casualties V.R. Nil	
	7.7.17		Casualties V.R. killed 6 wounded 15	
	8.7.17		Casualties Nil	
	9.7.17		Moves All M.G. Coys to XVIII Corps area	

Army Form C. 2118

WAR DIARY
or
INTELLIGENCE SUMMARY
(Erase heading not required.)

Instructions regarding War Diaries and Intelligence Summaries are contained in F. S. Regs., Part II. and the Staff Manual respectively. Title Pages will be prepared in manuscript.

Place	Date	Hour	Summary of Events and Information	Remarks references to Appendices
ADINFER WOOD X 26 a.	10.7.17		Casualties Officers 2 wounded (Capt J.E.H MOSTYN and 2/Lt A/Capt F.P.TWINE - 1/5 R Sussex)	
do	11.7.17		Casualties nil	
do	12.7.17		Casualties nil	
do	13.7.17		Casualties Officers 1 wounded (T/Lieut E.A. SAINSBURY H.Q. R.E.) H.Q. R.E. 3 wounded	
do	14.7.17		Casualties O.R. 3 wounded	
do	15.7.17		Casualties: O.R = 5 wounded (4/4 Rcd Cy 1 - 477 Rcd Cy 2) Y 48 T.M.B.- 1 - V 48 T.M.B - 1)	

2449 Wt. W14957/M90 750,000 1/16 J.B.C. & A. Forms/C.2118/12.

WAR DIARY or INTELLIGENCE SUMMARY

Army Form C. 21

Place	Date	Hour	Summary of Events and Information	Remarks
ADINFER WOOD X.26.a. (SHEET. 51c)	16.7.17	—	CASUALTIES — Officers, wounded — 1 (2nd Lieut W.H. Millard, 1/4th Oxford & Bucks L.I., Attached 145 T.M. By.) (accidentally) O.R. wounded — 1	
	17.7.17	—	CASUALTIES — Officers, killed — 1 (2nd Lieut J. Hunter, 474 Field Coy, R.E.) (accidentally) O.R. killed — 1 wounded — 6. (1/99 Field Coy, R.E.)	
	18.7.17	—	CASUALTIES — O.R. killed — 1 (R.F.A.) wounded 6 (4 R.E., 2 R.F.A. at duty) " (gassed) 17 (R.E.)	
	19.7.17	—	CASUALTIES — O.R. killed — 1 (R.E.) wounded 12 (R.E.-3 (at duty 1) / R.F.A. 9 (" " 3)) missing — 1 (275 MGn Rg) gassed 25 (R.E. 9 (Man 18 wnd) / R.F.A. 16 (Man 18 wnd))	
	20.7.17	—	MOVES — 143 Brigade (less 143 M.G. Coy) from POMMIER AREA to HALLOY area and 2nd Coy 3rd Field Ambulance and No 2 Coy Divisional Train " " 144 Brigade (less 144 M.G.Coy and 1/8 190 cook Rgt) from BLAIRVILLE area to POMMIER area 144 Coy and CASUALTIES — Officers, gassed — 1 (2nd Lieut G.F.H. MATTHEWS — R.A.) O.R. killed — 1 (R.F.A.) — wounded — 3 (R.F.A.) — gassed — 3 (R.F.A.)	
	21.7.17	—	CASUALTIES — O.R. killed — 1 (R.F.A.) — wounded 17 (R.F.A. 8 (at duty) / S.R. Wanks A. 4) gassed 18 wnd 3 (J.R. ?) R.E. 5 / 17	

2449 Wt. W14957/M90 750,000 1/16 J.B.C. & A. Forms/C.2118/12.

WAR DIARY or INTELLIGENCE SUMMARY

Army Form C. 21

Place	Date	Hour	Summary of Events and Information	Remarks references to Appendices
BANKER WOOD T26.a (Sheet 27)	21/22 7/17		NOTES — 143 Brigade Relieved 2nd C.(North Stafford Bg) from MALLOY area (returning AUTHEUX) & ST JEAN-ter-BIEZEN area (detraining at GODERWAERSVELDE) & No 3 Sn Fd Amb. 2nd Fd Ambulance & No 2 Cy Train RCC (ditto) ——— 144 Brigade (less M.G.C.) from POPERINGHE area (entraining SAULZY-LABRET) & POPERINGHE area (detraining HOPOUTRE) H.Q. & No 3 Coy Train, A.S.C. from ADINKER WOOD and BLANYKE areas respectively & ST JAN DER BIEZEN and POPERINGHE areas (entrain SAULZY-LABRET) (detrain HOPOUTRE) 145 Brigade (less 1st M.G.C.) 1/2nd Gt. 2nd Aux. and No 1 Cy Train M.C. from RASSEUX area (entraining MONDICOURT) & HOUTKERQUE area (detrain HOOGENHOUE) 144 and 145 M.G.C. from JERQUES area & Camp A.30. M.S. (POPERINGHE) DIVISIONAL H.Q. from ADINKER WOOD (entraining SAULZY-LABRET) & BORDER CAMP. A.30.b. Jul.28. (detraining HOPOUTRE)	
BORDER CAMP A.30.b (Sheet 28)	23.7.17		CASUALTIES — Officers gassed 2. (Capt N A Nowells 2/KRRC Gomt. RFA) O.R. Killed 1 (RFA) — wounded 15 { RFA 2, Trinity 2 (incl 1 accid) Soosex 4 (incl 2 actdly), R.E. 7 (., 1. ,,) } gassed 10 { RFA 2, R.E. 8 } CASUALTIES — Officers - wounded 1 (2nd Lieut. J. H. Hoyle, 1/5 R Lincs Regt - at duty) O.R. — Killed 2 (1 RFA; 1 6th Glos. S.I) wounded 6 { 4 - 1/5 R. Lincs Regt. at duty, 1 RFA, 1 Glos (,, at duty) }

2449 Wt. W1957/M90 750,000 1/16 J.B.C. & A. Forms/C.2118/12.

Army Form C. 21

WAR DIARY
or
INTELLIGENCE SUMMARY
(Erase heading not required.)

Instructions regarding War Diaries and Intelligence Summaries are contained in F. S. Regs., Part II. and the Staff Manual respectively. Title Pages will be prepared in manuscript.

Place	Date	Hour	Summary of Events and Information	Remarks references to Appendices
BORDER CAMP A 30 (Central) Sheet 28	24.7.17		CASUALTIES — Officers, wounded — 2 (Lt R. HAMILTON - RFA and 2nd Lt B.C. EARLE - DAC) (at duty)	
	25.7.17		O.R. wounded — 5 (RFA-3; RE-2) — gassed 8 (RFA-2; RE-6)	
			O.R. killed — 5 (RFA-2; ASC Gallipoli 28 Amb 3) — wounded — 14 (RFA 4 / RE 5 / 1/5 Pl Invrs 3 / ASC & 1/5 Inf T.F. 2) gassed — 15 (RB ill - 1/5 Pl Amchr Rgt - 4)	3 (1 am / 3 (3
	26.7.17		CASUALTIES — Officers wounded — 1 (2nd Lieut W.R.M. ISAACS - RFA - at duty)	
			O.R. wounded — 2 (RFA) — gassed 7 (RB.)	
	27.7.17		CASUALTIES — Officers gassed — 1 (2nd Lieut A.J. LOWE - RFA)	
			O.R. wounded — 2 (RFA) — gassed 35 (RE)	
	28.7.17		CASUALTIES — Officers wounded — 3 (2nd Lieut W.R.N. ISAACS - RFA / Lieut V.R. FOX-SMITH — " / 2nd Lieut R.G. FOSTER - Border Rgt attd M.G.C.)	
			O.R. killed — 1 (SAT (N RFA) — wounded 18 (8 RFA / 8 RE)	8 RFA - at duty 1 / 3 RE at duty R=4 / 2 RFA # / 3
			gassed 10 (2 RFA / 8 RE)	
			missing 3 (2 RFA / 1 MM MGC)	
	29.7.17		CASUALTIES — Officers wounded 2 (Maj C.P. NICKALLS - RFA / Lieut A.T. MATHIESON - RFA)	
			O.R. killed 3 (2 M.G.C. attd dtg / 1 RFA) — wounded 5 (3 at M.G.C. attached 1 / 2 RFA & Rgt T : 1)	

WAR DIARY or INTELLIGENCE SUMMARY

Army Form C. 2

Place	Date	Hour	Summary of Events and Information	Remarks references to Appendices
BORDAGE CAMP & 30 October (SHEET 28)	30.7.17		CASUALTIES. Officers wounded, 1 Lt T.I. BOND 4/48 T.M.Bty. O.R. killed 3, wounded 11, gassed 27, missing 1. 3 Field Coys R.E. from A21.c.7. to H.10.c.08.	K. 3. 4/48 T.M.Bty W. 4/RFA 2, 7th Worcs 3, 5 Sussex 1, 8th x 1, HSMG 4 M. 1. 8 – Note standard summary for Camp in A. Bde group
	31.7.17		143 Brigade (less MG Coy) from Camp > K&L STJAN-TER-BIEZEN to Camp from A Bde group area (BRAKE CAMP). 144 Brigade (less MG Coy) from STJAN-TER-BIEZEN (HQ 12Bn) and POPERINGHE (Pioneers) to Camps in C Bde Group Area (ROODKANT CAMP). 145 Brigade (less MG Coy) from HOUTKERQUE to Camps vacated by 143 Bde in STJAN-TER-BIEZEN. 5th R. Sussex from A.15.c.73. to Camp at H.4 & 9.0. HQ. No.2 1st Cav Farm A.S.C. transferred to EIKHOEK area, top by 4th Pontoons. CASUALTIES. Officers wounded, 3 Lt S. ALEXANDER 145 MG Coy (slight at duty) Lt F.W. MAFFER, 5th Sussex. Lt A.B. EDWARDS, RFA missing 1 Lt D.L. CRAIG, RFA (believed killed) O.R. killed 2, wounded 37. RFA 13 R.E. 4 4/5MG 4 2 WS " 12 5th Sussex, 5.W. 1 gassed	

2449 Wt. W14957/M90 750,000 1/16 J.B.C. & A. Forms/C.2118/12.

HONOURS AND AWARDS JULY 1917.

THE MILITARY CROSS.

2/Lieut. (T./Capt.) G. LINFOOT,
    7th Bn. Chesire Regt.
        attd. 1/6th Bn. R. Warwick Regt.

THE DISTINGUISHED CONDUCT MEDAL.

No. 240311 C.S.M. W. JONES,
    1/6th R. Warwick Regt.

THE MILITARY MEDAL.

No. 825534 Cpl. J. T. LUSH.
    V/48 H.T.M. Battery R.F.A. (T).

No. 851241 Gunner F. A. GOWSELL.
    D/241 S.M.Bde. R.F.A.

WAR DIARY

Vol 29

48th Divn.   A & Q Branch

1st Aug. to 31st Aug.

Vol. XXXI

Army Form C. 2118.

WAR DIARY
or
INTELLIGENCE SUMMARY

(Erase heading not required.)

Instructions regarding War Diaries and Intelligence Summaries are contained in F.S. Regs., Part II. and the Staff Manual respectively. Title Pages will be prepared in manuscript.

Place	Date	Hour	Summary of Events and Information	Remarks and references to Appendices
BORDER CAMP. A 30 central Sheet 28 1/40,000	1.8.17		MOVES. NIL. CASUALTIES Officers wounded, 4 2/Lt A WASHINGTON R.B. " " Lt Col C RETALLACK 15th Nav, slightly at duty " " 2/Lt E C BATCHELOR RFA " " " Lt J C FORSYTH RFA gassed O.R., wounded 23 R.F.A. 7 (incl 3 at duty) D.A.C. 1 accidental R.E. 4 145th FA 8 (incl 2 at duty) 5th Suan. 3 (incl 1 at duty).	
	2.8.17		MOVES NIL. CASUALTIES. Officers wounded 1, Capt J H PYKE RFA gassed on 31.7.17 8th Warwicks, died of wounds 1, 5th Suan 2. O.R. killed 3, R.F.A. wounded 15, RFA 6, R.E. 3, 5th S x 2, 145th FA. 3 (incl 1 gassed), 145th 4 2y 1 (previously reported), missing 1, RFA.	
	3.8.17		MOVES NIL. CASUALTIES. O.R. killed 1, RFA wounded 5 {RFA 3 wilfully 1, 9 road D.A.C. 2 (1 S.I.W. 1 accidental)	

WAR DIARY
or
INTELLIGENCE SUMMARY

Army Form C. 2118.

(Erase heading not required.)

Place	Date	Hour	Summary of Events and Information	Remarks and references to Appendices
BOROJR CAMP	4/8/17		MOVES. 145 Inf Bde from SCHOOL CAMP, ST JAN TER BIEZEN to DAMBRE CAMP and CANAL BANK. Corps M.G.Coy Rest CASUALTIES. OR wounded 14, RFA 3; DAC 1; TMBty 1; 5th Sussex 7; 1/1 SMPA 2. (accident)	
	5/8/17		MOVES. 145 Inf Bde from DAMBRE CAMP, CANAL BANK to FRONT LINE. CASUALTIES. Officer, wounded 1. Lt.Col.H.W.CURLEY, RFA (slightly at duty) OR wounded 5. R.F.A. 2 (incl 1 slightly at duty); R.E.1; 5th Sussex 1; 1/5 SMPA 1.	
	6/8/17		MOVES. 144 Inf Bde from ROOBART CAMP to DAMBRE CAMP. CASUALTIES. Officers. Killed 2, 2/Lt R.N. WHITE 25 (County of London) Cyclist Bn attd 1/4th Oxfords 2/Lt T.G. MAY, 143 M.G. Coy Wounded 6, Capt. E. CONDER, 1/5th Glosters. 2/Lt N.H. ENOCH, 1/4th Oxfords 2/Lt T.D. DIPPLE, 1/1 Bucks Bn 2/Lt H.C.F. MASON " " 4/Lt G.A. JOHNSTON " attd from 6th Bn Essex (slightly at duty) Lt A.A. AUSTEN-LEIGH 1/1 Bucks Bn O.R. Killed 5, 145TM Bty 2; 143 M.G. Coy 2; 1/6 R.War R. 1 (self-inflicted) Wounded 65. 1/5 Glos 20; 1/4 Oxfords 11; 1/4 R Berks 14; 145 M.G Coy 2; 145 TM Bty 3; 1/5 Sussex 3; R.E.1; 1/3 SMPA 2; A.S.C. 1; 39 TM Bty 3 (incl 2 slightly at duty); 2/4 Bdr RFA 1; 155 Bde AFFA (attd) 5. Missing 1. 143 M.G Coy.	

Army Form C. 2118.

WAR DIARY
or
INTELLIGENCE SUMMARY
(Erase heading not required.)

Instructions regarding War Diaries and Intelligence Summaries are contained in F.S. Regs., Part II. and the Staff Manual respectively. Title Pages will be prepared in manuscript.

Place	Date	Hour	Summary of Events and Information	Remarks and references to Appendices
BRAKE CAMP. G6.a.2.8 Sheet 28	7.8.17	10 a.m.	MOVES. Dvl HQ moved from BORDER CAMP to BRAKE CAMP	
			CASUALTIES. Officers, wounded 2, At T.P. Nintzerbotham 1/5 Glosters. Lt. FS NAGLAND. O.R. Killed 24, 1/6 Warwicks 1; 1/4 3 M.G. Coy. 1; 1/5 Glosters 11; 1/4 Oxfords 5; 1/3 Londo 2; (4 Central) wounded 38, RFA 2 (Hellowden) RFA 3; 1/6 Warw 1; 143 M.G. Coy 1; 1/5 Glosters 9; 1/4 Oxfords 10; 1/5 nocks 9 (incl. 2 orderly); 1/4 R.Berks 5; 1/5 nocks 9 (incl. 2 orderly); 1/4 R.Berks 5; missing 1, 1/4 Oxfords. 143 M.G. Coy 1 O.R. reported missing 6.8.17 now reported returned to duty.	
			MOVES. 48th Dvl SALVAGE COY to REIGERSBURG CAMP. 2 Bns 143 INF BDE } to FORWARD AREA relieving 145 INF BDE. 2 " 144 " " 145 BDE H.Q. " 2 Bns 144 INF BDE } from DAMBRE CAMP to BRAKE CAMP. H.Q. 144 " " 145 INF BDE from FORWARD AREA to DAMBRE CAMP. H.Q. Nos 2.3.4. Corps Tram A.S.C. to PEESELHOEK AREA from LIJKHOEK AREA	
	8.8.17		CASUALTIES Officers, killed 1, 2/Lt H.E. GIBSON, 1/4 Oxfords (on 7th inst) wounded 4, 2/Lt N GULLICK, 1/5 Glosters. 2/Lt JAS MACLEAN 1/4 Oxfords. Lt. F W SPENCER, 448 TM Bty. Lt. Col R. STEPHENS, 1/4 Oxfords.	

2449 Wt. W14957/M90 750,000 1/16 J.B.C. & A. Forms/C.2118/12.

WAR DIARY
or
INTELLIGENCE SUMMARY
(Erase heading not required.)

Army Form C. 2118.

Place	Date	Hour	Summary of Events and Information	Remarks and references to Appendices
BRAKE CAMP	8.8.17 (Cont'd)		CASUALTIES O.R. Killed 15; 1/5 Glos 3; 1/4 Oxfords 10; 3rd Sussex 2). wounded 77, RFA 3; DAC 1; RFA 2; 1/5 Warw 1; 17 Warw 1 (slightly at duty); 144 MG Coy 1; 1/5 Glos 20; 1/4 Oxfords 33; 1/4 R (Berks) 2; 145 MG Coy 1; 145 TM By 3; 1/2 SMFA 6; 1/3 SMFA 1; ASC 2. Missing 5; 1/5 Glos 1; 1/4 Oxfords 4.	
	9.8.17		CASUALTIES Officers, Killed 1. Major C.N. TODD, R.F.A. wounded 3. Lt W.B. FULLERTON R.F.A.; Lt F.S. GEDYE R.F.A.; 2/Lt G.C. WOODBRIDGE 1/6 Sussex O.R. Killed 13. 1/5 R Warw 2; 1/42 MG Coy 1; 1/5 Glos 1; 1/4 Oxfords 4; 1/4 R (Berks) 4; 1/6 Sussex 1; 145 TM By 1; 1/2 SMFA 1; 1/3 SMFA 1. wounded 94. RFA 1; RE 3; 1/5 R Warw 5; 142 MG Coy 8; 1/4 Glos 5; 1/6 Glos 19; 144 MG Coy 1; 1/4 Oxfords 10; 1/4 (Berks) 29; 145 MG Coy 2; 145 TM By 1; 1/5 Sussex 2; 1/2 SMFA 3; 1/3 SMFA 5. Missing 3. 144 MG Coy 1; 1/6 Berks 1; 1/4 Oxfords 1 (believed killed)	
			MOVES 7th R. Warwicks relieved 5th R. Warwicks in front line. 6th Glosters from O.G.1 relieved 4th Glos in front line. 4th Glos to CANAL BANK.	
	10.8.17		CASUALTIES O.R. Killed 11. 4th Glos 2; 6th Glos 3; 4 R Berks 6. wounded 44. RFA 1; 1/5 R Warw 10; 142 MG Coy 2; 1/4 Glos 3; 1/6 Glos 9; 144 MG Coy 7; 1/6 Glos alld 144 MG Coy 7; 1/4 R Berks 5.	

WAR DIARY or INTELLIGENCE SUMMARY

Army Form C. 2118.

Place	Date	Hour	Summary of Events and Information	Remarks and references to Appendices
BRAKE CAMP	11.8.17		MOVES NIL CASUALTIES Officers, wounded, 5. 2/Lt F.COULSON 1/5 R.War 2/Lt J.B.FLORANCE " slightly at duty 2/Lt D.R.MARSHALL & 2/Lt G.S.CHYNOWETH 1/7 R.War (but at duty) 2/Lt H.T.WILLIAMS 1/7 Worcestors. O.R. killed 21. 1/5 R.War 11; 1/7 R.War 2; 1/4 S.T.M.B+y 2; 1/4 Glos 3; 1/6 Glos 2; 1/4/5 T.M.B+y 1. wounded - 72. D.A.C. 1; R.E 2; 1/5 R.War 26; 1/7 R.War 10; 1/4 S.T.M.Y. G+y 2; 1/4/5 T.M.B+y 6; 1/4 Glos 10; 1/6 Glos 7; 1/5 Glos 1; 1/5 R.Sussex 4; 1/1 S.M.F.A. 2; 1/3 S.M.F.A. 1. 144 Inf. Bde H.Q. relieved 143 Inf. Bde H.Q. in Forward Area, latter returning to BRAKE CAMP	A wd. 2 at duty 1 ac dt B " 2 at duty C " 3 " " D " 1 " " E " 4 at duty F " 2 at duty
	12.8.17		MOVES 4. CASUALTIES Officers, wounded. 2/Lt (M.Capt) J.T.H.DICK, 1/5 R.War.R. 2/Lt G. STEPHENS, 1/6 Glos (D.w. 11.12.17) 2/Lt H.A.PAYNE. 1/5 R.Sussex Capt C.R. LANGHAM " slightly at duty O.R. killed 7. 1/7 R.War 6, RFA 1. wounded, 50. RFA 1; R.E 2; 1/5 R.War 6; 1/7 R.War 22. 1/4 S.M.G. G+y 5; 1/4/5 T.M.B+y 2; 1/6 Glos 11; 1/5 R.Sussex 11; 1/1 S.M.F.A. 1	

WAR DIARY or INTELLIGENCE SUMMARY

Army Form C. 2118.

Place	Date	Hour	Summary of Events and Information	Remarks and references to Appendices
BRAKE CAMP	13/8/17		MOVES. 145 T.M.G. Coy from ROOBART CAMP to DAMBRE CAMP.	
			CASUALTIES. Officers, wounded 2, Lt T.D. SEARLE. A.S.C. 2/Lt F. PERKINS. A.S.C.	
			O.R. killed, 4. 1/4 Glos 1; 1/6 Glos 2; A.S.C. 1.	
			wounded, 47. RFA 3; R.E. 6; 1/4 Glos 6 (incl. 2 accdnty); 1/6 Glos 7; 1/7 R.War 14; × accidental	
			1/4 Oxf 1; 1/5 Glos 1; A.S.C. 2; M.M.P. 1. × see 14/8	
			Missing, 1. 1/7 R.War 1 (behind reported killed). ×	
	14/8/17		MOVES NIL	
			CASUALTIES. Officers, wounded 3. Capt F.D. ANDREWS 1/4 Glos. 1; 2/Lt W. SPINK 1/5 M.G. Coy; 2/Lt N.L.E. MACHON 1/6 Glos. N.H. GREEN admitted hospital sick 2 VIII 17, now reported wounded. 145 M.G. Coy. Lt N.H. GREEN	
			O.R. killed, 7. RFA 1; 143 M.G. Coy. 1; 1/7 R.War 1; 144 M.G. Coy 1; 1/6 Glos field 144 TM Coy 1; 1/4 R Berks 2.	
			wounded, 106. RFA 12; DAC 1; RE 1; 1/5 R.War 5; 143 M.G. Coy. 2; 1/7 R.War 24; 1/6 Glos 45; 1/8 Wore 1; 144 M.G. Coy. 3; 1/7 Wore 2/4 M.MTM Bty 2; 1/4 R Berks 6; 1/5 R. Sussex 1; 1/5 M.M.F.A. 1; 1/2 S.M.F.A. 1; 1/3 S.M.F.A. 1; M.M.P. 2.	
			Missing 1. 143 TM Bty. believed killed. × 1/7 R.War 1 reported "missing believed killed" now reported "wounded".	

Army Form C. 2118.

WAR DIARY
or
INTELLIGENCE SUMMARY

(Erase heading not required.)

Instructions regarding War Diaries and Intelligence Summaries are contained in F. S. Regs., Part II. and the Staff Manual respectively. Title Pages will be prepared in manuscript.

Place	Date	Hour	Summary of Events and Information	Remarks and references to Appendices
BRAKE CAMP & CANAL BANK YPRES.	15.8.17		MOVES. Advanced Bde HQ opened at CANAL BANK FORWARD AREA 145 Inf Bde from DAMBRE CAMP to FORWARD AREA 241 Bde R.F.A.	
			CASUALTIES Officers; killed 1. Lt K. TURPIN 2/4 R.F.A. wounded 2. 2/Lt R.P. Quenby 69 Bn.; 2/Lt G. EVILVERTING 69 Bn. O.R. Remitted 4, 1 R.F.A, 2 R.E, 1 A.S.C. wounded 26, 10 R.F.A, 9 R.E, 3 5th Suecos, 2 R.A.M.C., 2 A.S.C.	Appendix 1.
	16.8.17		MOVES. 143 Bde from BRAKE CAMP to FORWARD AREA.	
			CASUALTIES Officers, O.R. As in annexed Casualty hist attached.	Appendix 2.
	17.8.17		MOVES. 145 Bde from FORWARD AREA to DAMBRE CAMP.	
			CASUALTIES. As in annexed Casualty hist attached.	Appendix 3.
	18.8.17		MOVES. NIL.	
			CASUALTIES. As in annexed Casualty hist attached.	
	19.8.17		MOVES. NIL.	
			CASUALTIES Officers, killed 2, 2/Lt A.E. WOOLDRIDGE 1/6 R.War.; 2/Lt J. GUILDING 1/8 Worc. wounded 4. 2/Lt N.J.F. KOMER (shghty shaw); Capt A.O. LLOYD 3/4 R.P. THOMPSON, 1/7 Worc. wounded 4. 2/Lt G. MACKAY 144 M.G. Coy (on 16.8).	

WAR DIARY or INTELLIGENCE SUMMARY

Army Form C. 2118.

Place	Date	Hour	Summary of Events and Information	Remarks and references to Appendices
BRAKE CAMP & CANAL BANK.	19.6.17 (contd)		CASUALTIES (Cont'd) OR killed 33, RFA 3; RE 1; 1/6 R.War 1; 1/4 Glos 4; 1/7 Wore 18; 1/8 Wore 3; 144 MG Coy 3; wounded 183, RFA 6; RE 3; 1/3 SMFA 2; ASC 2 (not at duty); 1/6 R.War 1; 1/6 R.War 20; 1/8 R.War 9; 1/6 Glos 5; 1/7 Wore 107 (incl 13 at duty); 1/7 Wore att'd 144 MGCoy 5; 1/8 Wore 11 (incl 1 at duty); 1/8 Wore att'd 144 MG Coy 2; 144 MG Coy 10; 1/8 Wore att'd 144 MG Coy 1. Missing 24, 1/8 R.War 3 (believed wounded); 1/7 Wore 20; 1/8 Wore att'd 144 MG Coy 1.	
	20.6.17		MOVES NIL	
			CASUALTIES Officers killed 1, 1/8 Worcesters 2/Lt N.M. JOTCHAM (on 19th) wounded 3, 1/6 R.War CAPT. W.A. CHOVIL, 1/8 R.War 2/Lt C.M. HOLMES, 2/Lt ET SCALE (action 17th) O.R. killed 21, 1/5 R.War 1, 1/6 R.War 8, 1/6 Glos 1, 1/7 Wore 1; 1/8 Wore 4; 144 MG Coy 6, 1/3 SMFA 1. wounded 70(?), 1/5 R.War 3, 1/6 R.War 9, 1/8 R.War 6 (seriously reported missing. 1 OR formerly reported missing, now reported hospital wounded), 1/6 Glos 4, RAMC att'd 1/6 Glos 2; ASC att'd 1/6 Glos 1; 1/7 Wore 8 (incl 2 at duty), 1/8 Wore 19; 144 MG Coy 8; 1/5 R.Sussex 1; 1/1 SMFA 1; RFA 2 (incl 1 Belgian civilian); 1/5 R.Sussex 1; 1/4 Glos 1. Missing 4 - 1/5 R.War 3 (incl 2 missing believed killed) 1/4 Glos 1.	64
	21.6.17		MOVES. NIL	
			CASUALTIES Officers wounded 3, RE 2/Lt L.BRIGGS (at duty), 2/Lt A.N. DAVIES 1/5 Sussex (at duty), ASC 2/Lt DE BUCHNEY. O.R. killed 12, RE 7; 1/7 R.War 4, 3rd SMFA 1. wounded 34, RFA 2, RE 11; 5th R.War 2; 6th R.War 9; 7th R.War 4; 1/4 R.Berks 1; 5th Sussex 1. Missing 1, 7th R.War 1.	+ incl 5 at duty × " 1 " " ⊗ " 1 " "

Army Form C. 2118.

WAR DIARY
or
INTELLIGENCE SUMMARY

(Erase heading not required.)

Instructions regarding War Diaries and Intelligence Summaries are contained in F. S. Regs., Part II. and the Staff Manual respectively. Title Pages will be prepared in manuscript.

Place	Date	Hour	Summary of Events and Information	Remarks and references to Appendices
BRAKE CAMP & CANAL BANK.	22.8.17		MOVES NIL CASUALTIES. Officers killed 1. 2/Lt R.CRICHTON, 1/5R Now. wounded 7. 2/Lt G GASCOYNE RFA, 1/5R Now, H Col C RETALLACK 2/Lt H.L.WOSTENHOLM (attached) 2/Lt LT O HANLON (attached) 1/6 R Now. CAPT R.S. PARTRIDGE, CAPT J BONATER (attached), 143 MG Coy. 2/Lt A H HAYES OR Killed 16. RFA 2; 1/5R Now 8; 1/6R Now 1; 143 MG Coy 1; 1/6 Glos R 4; wounded 9B. RFA 23; 1/5R Now 38; 1/6R Now 4; 145 MG Coy 4; 1/6 Glos R 12; 1/5R S Now 9. NOTE Net Casualty Report of 1/5 " mot of 20 O.R. 1/4 W N C R previously reported minery on 6 have now appeared and 5 traced to hospital wounded " making a total of 11 O.R. " missing"	Kind 8 ards × × 1 assist ⊗ × 2 K.M.102 ⊗ " 9 W. " Appendix 4.
	23.8.17.		MOVES NIL CASUALTIES from 23rd to 30th August-chart shown in amended Casualty lists attached.	
	24.5.17		MOVES N.I.L	
	25.8.17		MOVES. 6th Gloster from CANAL BANK to REIGERSBURG CAMP 7th Worcestos - REIGERSBURG CAMP to CANAL BANK REIGERSBURG CAMP	
	26.8.17.		MOVES 5th R.W. aumilies from hur to REIGERSBURG CAMP 7th " " CANAL BANK 4th Gloster " " " 5th Gloster " DAMBRE CAMP 1/Bucks " 1/4th Oxfords " 1/4th R. Berks CANAL BANK 145 T.M. B+y "	

Army Form C. 2118.

WAR DIARY
or
INTELLIGENCE SUMMARY
(Erase heading not required.)

Instructions regarding War Diaries and Intelligence Summaries are contained in F. S. Regs., Part II. and the Staff Manual respectively. Title Pages will be prepared in manuscript.

Place	Date	Hour	Summary of Events and Information	Remarks and references to Appendices
BRAKE CAMP and CANAL BANK	26/8/17 (contd)		MOVES (Contd) 6th R Warwicks from REIGERSBURG CAMP to hine 6th Glosters " " " 144 T.M.Bty " " " 8th Worcesters " " "	
	27/8/17		MOVES. 143 Bde HQ from hine to REIGERSBURG CAMP 5th R Warwicks from " to BROWN CAMP A 23 a. Sheet 28/40,000 7th " " " " " 4th Glosters " " " " 6th R Warwicks " " hine " 8th " " " " " 143 M G Coy " " " " 143 " " " " " 144 Bde HQ leaves HQ + 4th Glosters from hine to DAMBRÉ CAMP 5th Glosters from REIGERSBURG CAMP to hine 1/Bucks " " " "	
	28/8/17		MOVES. 48th Divl Recn HQ from BRAKE CAMP to WORMHOUDT 143 Bde HQ from REIGERSBURG CAMP to POPERINGHE 143 M G Coy " " " " 143 T.M.Bty " " " " 6th R Warwicks from " " BROWN CAMP 8th " " " " " 144 Bde HQ from CANAL BANK to DAMBRÉ CAMP	

Army Form C. 2118.

WAR DIARY
or
INTELLIGENCE SUMMARY
(Erase heading not required.)

Instructions regarding War Diaries and Intelligence Summaries are contained in F.S. Regs., Part II. and the Staff Manual respectively. Title Pages will be prepared in manuscript.

Place	Date	Hour	Summary of Events and Information	Remarks and references to Appendices
WORMHOUDT	29.8.17		MOVES. 48th Divl Adv HQ from CANAL BANK to WORMHOUDT. A25c17 HQ RE from CANAL BANK to OOSTHOEK A24a57 474 Fld Coy - line to DROOGENTALIFARM 474 " " - to VLAMERTINGHE – YPRES Road 475 " " - CANAL BANK to BRAKE CAMP 477 " " - " 143 Bde from POPERINGHE & BROWN CAMP to TUNNELLING CAMP ST JAN TER BIEZEN 144 " " DAMBRE & BROWN CAMPS. SCHOOL " 145 " " LINE to DAMBRE CAMP 5th R Sussex from CANAL BANK to GWENT FARM near POPERINGHE. 1/1 SMFA - GWENT FARM to L'ABBÉ FARM, EIKHOEK 1/2 SMFA - OOSTHOEK to ST JAN TER BIEZEN 1/3 SMFA - OOSTHOEK area to EIKHOEK area H/d TRAIN ASC. from OOSTHOEK area to ROADCAMP, ST JAN TER BIEZEN. - 3 Coys (a.3. +4)	
	30.8.17		MOVES. 145 Bde from DAMBRE CAMP to ROADCAMP, ST JAN TER BIEZEN.	
	31.8.17		MOVES NIL CASUALTIES. O.R. wounded	

A.W. Gibson Capt
for Major Commdt
for Commdr. RE

Appendix 1

Casualties to noon 16th August.

Unit.	Officers.				Other Ranks.				
	K.	W.	M.	K.	W.	M.			
240 Brigade R.F.A.	-	3	-	-	6	-	Wounded:-	2/Lt.F.W.Burridge; Lt.E.H.Edwards;2/Lt. A.A.Leslie.	
241 Do.	-	1	-	1	5	-	Wounded:-	Lieut.R.N.S.Withers.	
48th D.A.C.	-	-	-	-	5	-			
48th Div.Signal Coy,R.E.	-	-	-	-	6	-			
474 Field Coy R.E.	-	-	-	-	8	-			
475 Do.	-	-	-	1	2	-			
477 Do.	-	-	-	-	2	-			
1/5th R. Sussex Regt.	1	-	-	-	-	-	Killed:-	Capt.C.R.Langham.	
1/1st S.M.Field Ambulance.	-	-	-	-	2	-			
1/3rd S.M.Field Ambulance.	-	-	-	-	2	-			
M.M.P.	-	-	-	-	1	-			
1/5th Gloucester Regt.	-	7	-	-	-	-	Wounded:-	Lt.J.E.Hollington; 2/Lieut.W.E.Bamberger; 2/Lieut.M.Steel; 2/Lieut.W.P.Grubb;Lieut. E.J.Cornish; 2/Lieut.F.J.Bretherton; 2/Lieut.F.F.La Trobe.	

Casualties to noon 16th August (Contd)

Unit.	Officers				Other Ranks				
	K.	W.	M.		K.	W.	M.		
1/4th Oxford & Bucks L.I.	1	5	-		-	-	-	Killed:-	2/Lieut.A.S.Wotherspoon.
								Wounded:-	2/Lieut.A.E.Crew; 2/Lieut.D.F.Cochrane; 2/Lieut H.Jefferson; 2/Lieut.F.E.Jones(Slightly at duty); 2/Lieut.E.C.H.Wincer (Slightly at duty)
1/Bucks Battalion.	-	6	-		-	-	-	Wounded:-	2/Lieut.G.A.Johnston; 2/Lieut.E.C.H.Feve'tt; 2/Lieut.F.G.Marshall; 2/Lieut.R.E.Norman; Capt.G.R.F.Knight; Capt.M.S.Reid.
1/4th Royal Berks Regt.	1	4	-		-	-	-	Killed:-	Lieut.H.Tripp.
								Wounded:-	Capt.F.Winsloe; Lieut.B.F.Holmes; 2/Lieut.G.A. Brooke; 2/Lieut.D.Wood.
145 M.G.Company.	1	3	-		-	-	-	Killed:-	2/Lieut.C.H.Inwood.
								Wounded:-	2/Lieut.R.H.Clutton; 2/Lieut.J.S.Selbie; 2/Lieut.H.R.Taunton.
	14	29			3	39			

Note:- 1/5th Glouc.Regt;- 2/Lieut.N.Steel afterwards reported killed. 2/Lieut.W.E.Bamberger afterwards reported Missing.

Appendix 2

Casualties to noon 17th August.

Unit.	Officers K.	W.	M.	Other Ranks K.	W.	M.	
240 Brigade R.F.A.	-	-	-	-	3	-	
241 " "	-	-	-	-	2	-	
474 Field Company R.E.	-	-	-	1	2	-	
475 " " "	-	-	-	1	10	-	
477 " " "	-	-	-	-	2	-	
1/5th R.Sussex Regt.	1	1	-	3	32	-	Killed:- 2/Lieut.H.W.Green. Wounded:- 2/Lieut.H.J.Holdsworth.
1/1st S.M.Field Ambulance.	-	-	-	-	2	-	
1/2nd S.M.Field Ambulance.	-	-	-	-	1	-	
48th Div.Signal Coy.	-	-	-	-	1	-	
48th Div.Train.	-	-	-	-	1	-	
					56		

Appendix 3

Casualties to noon 18th August.

Unit.	Officers K.	Officers W.	Officers M.	Other Ranks K.	Other Ranks W.	Other Ranks M.	
241 Brigade R.F.A.	-	-	-	3	1	-	
R.A.M.C. att. 240 Brigade R.F.A.	-	-	-	-	1	-	
48th D.A.C.	-	-	-	-	1	-	
48th Div. Train.	-	-	-	-	1	-	
1/1 S.M. Field Ambulance.	-	-	-	-	1	-	
1/3 S.M. Field Ambulance.	-	-	-	-	1	-	
A.S.C. att. 1/3 S.M.Fd.Amb.	-	-	-	-	1	-	
1/5th R. Sussex Regt.	-	-	-	1ˣ	2	-	ˣ Previously reported missing on 17th
474 Field Company R.E.	-	-	-	-	1	-	
475 Field Company R.E.	-	-	-	-	1	-	
145 M.G. Company.	-	-	-	3	16	3	1 Believed killed, 2 believed wounded.
1/5th Gloucester Regt.	-	2	-	-	-	-	Wounded:- 2/Lieut.E.J.Cornish; 2/Lieut.W.Lake.
1/4th Oxfords.	1	3	-	-	-	-	Killed:- 2/Lieut.C.H.Bowman. Wounded:- 2/Lieut.J.Swatbridge; 2/Lieut.J.H.Early; 2/Lieut. A.F.Salmon.
1/Bucks Battalion.	-	2	-	-	-	-	Wounded:- 2/Lieut.F.M.Passmore; 2/Lieut.F.D.Ollard.

Casualties to noon 18th August (Contd)

Unit.	Officers K.	Officers W.	Officers M.	Other Ranks K.	Other Ranks W.	Other Ranks M.	
1/4th Royal Berks Regt.	-	1	-	-	-	-	Wounded:- 2/Lieut.J.H.Oldridge.
145 T.M.Battery.	-	-	-	4	4	-	
1/5th R.Warwick Regt.	-	-	-	-	1	-	
1/6th R.Warwick Regt.	-	1	-	1	17	-	Wounded:- 2/Lieut.J.Rhodes.
1/7th R.Warwick Regt.	-	-	-	1	3	1	
1/8th R.Warwick Regt.	-	3	-	18	44	-	Wounded:- Capt.S.Hanstey; Lieut.S.Hoskins; 2/Lieut.F. Radcliffe.
143 M.G.Company.	-	1	-	-	3	-	Wounded:- 2/Lieut.A.J.Waye.
1/6th Gloucester Regt.	-	1	-	-	-	-	Wounded:- Capt.J.K.Fullerton.(Since died of wounds)
1/7th Worcester Regt.	-	5	-	-	-	-	Wounded:- Capt.A.B.Montgomery; Capt.WN.S.Brown; Lieut. H.B.Rate; 2/Lieut.G.H.Hazlewood; 2/Lieut.R.S. Leake.
1/8th Worcester Regt.	-	-	-	3	11	-	
144 M.G.Company.	-	-	-	1	1	-	

Appendix 4.

CASUALTIES to Noon 22nd August.

Unit.	Officers			Other Ranks.			Remarks.
	K.	W.	M.	K.	W.	M.	
R.F.A.	-	1	-	2	23	-	2/Lt.G.Gascoyne.
1/5th R.Warwick Regt.	1	3	-	8	38	-	Killed:- 2/Lt.R.Crichton. Wounded:- Lt.Col.C.Retallack. 2/Lt.H.L.Wostenholm.) At 2/Lt.L.T.O'Hanlon) duty
1/6th R.Warwick Regt.	-	2	-	1	4	-	Capt.R.S.Partridge)Slightly at Capt.J.Bowater.) duty.
143 M.G.Company.	-	1	-	1	4	-	2/Lt.A.H.Haynes.
1/6th Gloucester Regt.	-	-	-	6	15	-	
1/5th R.Sussex Regt.	-	-	-	-	9	-	
					93		

Casualties to noon 23rd August.

Unit.	Officers K.	Officers W.	Officers M.	Other Ranks K.	Other Ranks W.	Other Ranks M.	
1/5th R.Warwick Regt.	1	-	1	2	25	-	2/Lieut.T.C.Magness.
1/7th R.Warwick Regt.	1	1	-	10	20	-	Killed:- Capt.V.R.C.Caley. Wounded:- 2/Lieut.R.H.North.
Do.	-	1	-	5	20	-	Wounded:- 2/Lt.W.A.Inber (Slightly at duty)
1/8th R.Warwick Regt.	-	-	-	2	1	-	
143 M.G.Company.	-	-	-	1	3	3	
143 Bde. H.Q.	-	1	-	-	-	-	Wounded:- Capt.C.K.Steward,M.C.
1/4th Gloucester Regt.	-	-	-	-	16	-	
1/6th Gloucester Regt.	-	1	-	4	30	1	Wounded:- Capt.A.P.Coombs.
144 M.G.Company.	-	-	-	-	3	-	
5th R.Sussex Regt.	-	-	1	-	1	-	
48th Div.Signal Coy.	-	-	-	-	-	-	Missing:- 2/Lieut.C.K.Mathew.
A.S.C. att. Div.H.Q.	-	-	-	-	1	-	
R.E.	-	1	-	-	3	-	Wounded:- 2/Lieut.A.J.Skinner.
R.A.M.C.	-	-	-	-	7	-	
R.F.A.	-	1	-	-	5	-	Wounded:- 2/Lieut.G.F.Pustard.

Casualties to noon 24th August.

Unit.	Officers			Other Ranks.		
	K.	W.	M.	K.	W.	M.
1/5th R.Warwick Regt.	-	-	-	5	15	-
1/6th R.Warwick Regt.	-	-	-	2	4	-
1/7th R.Warwick Regt.	-	-	-	1	10	-
1/4th Gloucester Regt.	-	-	-	-	6	-
5th R.Sussex Regt.	-	-	-	1	4	-
R.A.M.C.	-	-	-	-	4	-
R.E.	-	-	-	-	3	-
R.F.A.	-	-	-	4	-	-

Casualties to noon 25th August.

Unit.	Officers				Other Ranks.			
	K.	W.	M.	K.	W.	M.		
1/5th R.Warwick Regt.	-	1	-	3	5	-	Wounded:- 2/Lieut.S.F.Snape.	
1/7th R.Warwick Regt.	-	-	-	-	6	1		
143 T.M.Battery	-	-	-	-	1	-		
1/4th Gloucester Regt.	-	1	-	-	6	-	Wounded:- 2/Lieut.G.Best.	
1/4th Royal Berks Regt.	-	-	-	-	2	-		
145 M.G.Company.	-	-	-	-	7	-	Includes 5 at duty.	
R.F.A.	-	-	-	-	1	-		
R.E.	-	-	-	1	1	-		
R.A.M.C.	-	-	-	-	2	-		

Casualties to noon 26th August.

Unit.	Officers K.	Officers W.	Officers M.	Other Ranks K.	Other Ranks W.	Other Ranks M.	
1/7th R.Warwick Regt.	-	-	-	1	3	-	
1/8th R.Warwick Regt.	-	-	-	-	7	-	
143 M.G.Company.	-	-	-	1	1	-	
143 T.M.Battery.	-	-	-	3	4	-	
1/4th Gloucester Regt.	-	-	-	-	20	-	
1/7th Worcester Regt.	-	-	-	-	11	-	
144 M.G.Company.	-	1	-	1	31	-	2/Lieut.O.M.Tacker.
5th R.Sussex Regt.	-	1	-	-	18	-	2/Lieut.J.J.Farmer.
R.E.	-	1	-	-	5	-	Major H.Clissold.
R.F.A.	-	-	-	1	3	-	

103

-66-

Casualties to noon 27th August.

Unit.	Officers			Other Ranks.			
	K.	W.	M.	K.	W.	M.	
1/6th R.Warwick Regt.	-	-	-	1	5	6	
143 M.G.Company.	-	-	-	-	1	-	
1/7th Worcester Regt.	-	-	-	17	21	-	
1/8th Worcester Regt.	-	1	-	1	2	-	Wounded:- 2/Lieut.J.T.Hill.
144 M.G.Company.	-	-	-	-	1	-	
5th R.Sussex Regt.	-	1	-	1	1	-	Wounded:- Capt.J.L.Perry.
R.F.A.	-	-	-	1	5	-	
R.A.M.C.	-	-	-	-	1	-	

Casualties to noon 28th August.

Unit.	Officers K.	Officers W.	Officers M.	Other Ranks K.	Other Ranks W.	Other Ranks M.	
1/5th R.Warwick Regt.	-	1	-	20	72	26	
1/6th R.Warwick Regt.	3	3	-	27	129	8	Killed:- Capt.W.M.E.Baxter; 2/Lieut.E.Austin; 2/Lieut.R.J.Ferrington. Wounded:-Capt.R.S.Partridge; 2/Lieut.F.B.Williams; 2/Lieut.E.Spencer.
1/7th R.Warwick Regt.	1	2	-	2	73	22	Killed:- 2/Lieut.W.H.Imber. Wounded:-2/Lieut.H.D.Twine; Capt.W.N.Bushill (at duty).
1/8th R.Warwick Regt.	-	1	1	25	118	44	Wounded:- 2/Lieut.G.M.Ewing. Missing(believed killed):- 2/Lieut.(A/Capt) S.W.Pepper.
1/7th Worcester Regt.	1	5	-	10	45	3	Killed:- Capt.C.R.Wallace,M.C. Wounded:- Capt.A.H.Butcher(atduty); Capt.P. Carter,M.C.; Capt.R.P.Thompson; 2/Lieut.W.S.Figgs-Walker. Capt. H.O.Lloyd
1/8th Worcester Regt.	3	-	-	49	88	3	Killed:- Capt.P.H.Tullidge; 2/Lieut.R.N.Horsley; 2/Lieut.J.C.Hemming. Wounded:-2/Lieut.H.T.Mynill; 2/Lieut.S.H.Williams; 2/Lieut.H.R.Ryan-Pell.2/Lt. J.H.Clark
1/5th Gloucester Regt.	-	1	-	4	25	2	Wounded:- Capt. R.F.McDowall.
1/Bucks Battalion.	-	2	-	9	45	-	Wounded:- 2/Lieut.P.A.Coates;2/Lt.W.H.Fleeming.
1/4th Oxfords.	-	-	-	7	17	-	
1/4th Royal Berks	1	1	-	1	3	-	Killed:- Capt.W.Norrish. Wounded:- Capt.C.C.Shew.

43   613   108

Casualties to noon 28th August (Cont'd)

Unit.	Officers			Other Ranks.			
	K.	W.	M.	K.	W.	M.	
R.E.	-	-	-	-	3	-	
5th R.Sussex Regt.	-	-	-	-	1	-	
144 M.G.Company.	1	-	-	2	-	-	Killed:- 2/Lieut.C.D.Heaton.

Casualties to noon 29th August.

Unit.	Officers.			Other Ranks.		
	K.	W.	M.	K.	W.	M.
1/5th Gloucester Regt.	-	-	-	-	1	-
1/4th Oxfords.	-	-	-	1	3	-
1/Bucks Battalion.	-	-	-	-	3	-
1/4th Royal Berks.	-	-	-	1	2	-
R.A.M.C.	-	-	-	-	1	-
A.S.C. attd. R.A.M.C.	-	-	-	-	1	-

Casualties to noon 30th August.

Unit.	Officers.				Other Ranks.			
	K.	W.	M.		K.	W.	M.	
R.A.M.C.	-	-	-		-	3	-	

Casualties to noon 31st August.

R.F.A.	-	1	-		-	1	-	Lt.Col.J.H.Curley (Admitted to Hospital as result of wound reported on 5.8.17.)

1/5th Royal Warwickshire Regiment.

Bar to the Military Medal.

200983 Sgt. F.Oreton.

Military Medal.

200235	Pte	J.Sorrell.
200139	"	E.H.Burrows.
200455	"	W.Webster.
242278	"	R.Eggington.
201797	"	J.Riley.
203036	"	A.Johnson.

1/6th Royal Warwickshire Regiment.

Distinguished Conduct Medal.

Military Medal.

242542 Pte H.Dean.
242638 " W.Jones.
240432 L/c C.A.Oreson.
240098 Corpl (A/Sgt) E.Jones.
240456 Pte J.Sutton.

1/7th Royal Warwickshire Regiment.
Military Medal.

268513 Pte A.Hare.
265095 Sgt. W.J.Lyons.
268519 L/c A.George.
265468 A/L/Sgt.A.Parkinson.

1/8th Royal Warwickshire Regiment.

Distinguished Conduct Medal.

307552 L/c J.W.Barriman.

Military Medal.

305199 L/c S.Williamson.
306452 Pte F.Baylis.
307597 " A.Roden.
307788 " F.Wootton.

143 Machine Gun Company.

Military Medal.

24401 Sgt. F.H.Gardner.

1/4th Gloucester Regiment.

Military Medal.

11321/9 L/Sgt. F.Bearcroft.

1/6th Gloucester Regiment.

Military Cross.

2/Lieut. D.G.Stewart.

Military Medal.

267319 Pte H.Powell.
265774 Sgt. J.Osgood.
265687 Pte J.H.Griffiths.

1/7th Worcester Regiment.

Dist. Conduct Medal. 200684 Sgt. G.Cooper.

Military Cross.

2/Lieut. H.B.Bate.
200445 C.S.M. W.Shakespeare.

Military Medal.

201073 Corpl. F.Green.
200423 Pte T.Smith.
200692 " E.G.Kelley.
200488 " G.T.Bell.
200671 Corpl. G.Sneyd.
41349 Pte B. Novis.
200268 " A.Protherow.

Bar to Military Medal.

201504 Pte A.Breeze.

Bar to Military Cross.

Lieut. (A/Capt) A.O.Lloyd, M.C.

1/8th Worcester Regiment.

Bar to Military Cross.

2/Lieut. S.H.Wilkes.

Distinguished Conduct Medal.

240414 Pte F.Taylor.

Military Medal.

241191 Sgt. R.H.Warren.
242349 L/Sgt. F.Birch.
240811 Corpl. H. Rorledge.
241268 Pte C.A.Clay.
241790 " C.F.Rice.
240194 " R.Whiley.
240618 Corpl. A.N.Turner.
240244 Pte A.Corbett.
241318 L/c A.T.Smith.
241661 Pte W.Williams.

1/5th Gloucester Regiment.

Military Cross.

2/Lieut. K.A. Robertson.
Lieut. G.E. Ratcliff.
Lieut. (A/Capt) E. Conder.

Distinguished Conduct Medal.

240276 Pte P.J. Millichap.
240038 C.S.M. V.G. Smith.

Military Medal.

203244 Corpl. E. Pullan.
203706 " J.T. Hodges.
21973 L/c C.A. Streake.
240750 " C. Cooke.
203696 Pte W. Clee.

1/4th Oxford & Bucks L.I.

Bar to Military Medal.

201785 Corpl. W.N. Hobbs.

Military Medal.

200677 L/c C.G. Gray.
200072 Corpl (A/Sgt) F. Haley.
201728 Pte J. Finch.
200749 " H.S. Pearce.

1/Bucks Battalion.

Bar to the D.S.O.

Major (Temp. Lieut. Col) L.L.C. Reynolds, D.S.O.

Military Cross.

2/Lieut. G.A. Johnston.

Distinguished Conduct Medal.

266100 Sgt. E. Bridges.
266477 L/c W. Buckland.
265094 Sgt Golding

Bar to Military Medal.

267533 L/c F.G. Seaward.

Military Medal.

265923 Sgt. S.G. Rogers.
265583 Corpl. W. Hines.
265473 Pte F.T. Cripps.
265046 Sgt. G. Richardson.
266733 L/c S.G. Stone.
265036 Sgt. A.J. Hart.
285074 Pte F. Moore.
265292 L/c G.W. Wallington.

1/4th Royal Berks Regiment.

Military Cross.

Lieut.(A/Capt) B.F.Holmes.
201108 C.S.M. W.H.Heath.

Distinguished Conduct Medal.

203794 Sgt. F.Gilding.

Military Medal.

203771 L/c W.W.Stratton.
379397 "   S.Rogers.
203809 "   W.Ranscombe.
200485 Corpl. F.W.Child.

145 Machine Gun Company.

Military Medal.

21119 Sgt. N.G.Waite.
21113 Pte H.J.Grear.

48th Div. Signal Company, R.E.

Military Medal.

500091 Sgt. J.C.Williams.
500069 Sapper W.Phillips.
31695   "   A.W.Middleton.
74425   "   W.E.Rowley.

No. 2 Section, 48th Div. Signal Coy.

Military Medal.

500205 Sgt. F.Beckett.
500206 Corpl. J.Knight.

No. 3 Section, 48th Div. Signal Coy.

Military Medal.

500239 L/c H.L.Feltham.

No. 4 Section, 48th Div. Signal Coy.

Military Cross.

Lieut. J.D.J.Saner.

Bar to Military Medal.

500447 Sapper C.E.Beard.
500248 Corpl. G.S.Collison.

Military Medal.

500432 Sapper F.D.Reid.
500247 2/Cpl. F.R.P.Procter.

5th R.Sussex Regiment.

Military Medal.

240665 Corpl. R.Bryant.
~~210210~~
210130 Pte G.Arnold.

240 Brigade S.M. R.F.A.

Military Cross.

Lieut. G.P.Brooke-Taylor.
2/Lieut. G.F.Bustard.
2/Lieut. D.L.L.Craig.

Military Medal.

840333 Corpl. G.W.Pache.
74248 Gunner J.Riley.
184452   "   A.Morton.

241 Brigade, S.M.R.F.A.

Bar to Military Cross.

Lieut. N.L.Nichols.   (Signal Service, attached).

Military Cross.

Lieut. R.N.S.Withers.
Lieut. J.H.Brindley.
Lieut. C.James.

Distinguished Conduct Medal.

840150 Batt. S.M. G.Hopewell.

Military Medal.

830055 Sgt. A.H.Duggins.
830478 Gunner C.F.Bradley.
830291   "   (A/Bombardier) J.W.Berry.
580836   "   A.Squires.
831495   "   S.l'Tessier.
830039 Sgt. G.Boulton.
159653 Gunner W.P.Roberts.
840029 Bombardier W.Vearss

48th D.A.C.

Military Medal.

830029 Bombardier F.E.Preece.
845256   "   S.Houlme.

X/48th T.M.Battery.

Military Cross.

Lieut. V.R.F.Smith, 1/8th Worcester Regt. attached.

477 Field Company R.E.

Military Medal.

294298 L/c F.A.White.
292491 L/c F.J.Jones.

48th Divisional Train.

Military Medal.

T/4/248048 Sgt. W.Green.

1/1st S.M.Field Ambulance.

Military Medal.

435075 Pte C.Allan.
435334 Pte J.Cox.

1/2nd S.M.Field Ambulance.

Military Cross.

Capt. A.E.P.McConnell.

Military Medal.

437308 Pte F.Rolands.
437002 "   W.Bennett.
437086 "   A.Lakin.
437184 L/c N.Valentine.
437098 "   H.Rowe.

1/3rd S.M.Field Ambulance.

Military Medal.

439244 Corpl. L.Weeks.
439226 Pte. H.G.Bird.

Vol 30

WAR DIARY

48th DIVISION   A & Q BRANCH

1st SEPTr to 30th SEPTR

Vol. XXXII

Army Form C. 2118.

WAR DIARY
or
INTELLIGENCE SUMMARY
(Erase heading not required.)

Instructions regarding War Diaries and Intelligence Summaries are contained in F. S. Regs., Part II. and the Staff Manual respectively. Title Pages will be prepared in manuscript.

Place	Date	Hour	Summary of Events and Information	Remarks and references to Appendices
NORMHOUDT	Sept 1st	—	MOVES. NIL	
	2nd		CASUALTIES. NIL	
	3rd		O.R. wounded 1. ½ S.M.F.A	Appendix 1.
	4th		" " 4. RFA 2, R.E 2 (slightly at duty)	
	4.45		" " 1. RFA	
	6.30		" " 1. REA (slightly at duty)	
	7th		" " 1. United (Wesl. Chaplain Rev. J.M. Ash attached 48th Div.C	
	8th		Officers. Killed 1. Capt. R.R.S. wounded "Q" Not during recent Operations.	
			wounded 7. Lt Col (Bgd) A.F. HOPKINS, Lt-Col G.B. HUISTON-BROWNE, Capt F. MOTTRAM — shell splinter	
			Capt. T. MARKHAM (at duty), Major C. FOWLER, Lt C.F. STEDMAN — all RFA	
			Capt A. MORRIS R.A.M.C attached R.F.A.	
			Capt A. MORRIS R.A.M.C attached R.S.A.W. 3	
	9th		O.R. wounded 15. RFA 11 (3 at duty), R.E. 1, 5th R.Sussex. 3	
			O.R. drowned 1. ½ R. War. Rgt. accidental	
			" wounded 1. RFA	
	10th		O.R. Killed 1. R.E.	
			" wounded 4. RFA 3, 5th R.Sussex 1.	
	11th		O.R. Killed 8. RFA (gassed)	
			" wounded 14. RFA. 12 (incl 5 gassed "5" at duty) 5th R. Sussex 2.	
	12th		O.R. wounded 6. RFA. 4, 148th Labour Coy attd 48th Divl S.W Coy. 2.	

Army Form C. 2118.

WAR DIARY
or
INTELLIGENCE SUMMARY
(Erase heading not required.)

Place	Date	Hour	Summary of Events and Information	Remarks and references to Appendices
NORMHOUDT	13th		CASUALTIES. O.R. killed 4, RFA 3, 3rd Lst Bn attd 14 S.R/Bde. 1 (accidental) wounded 25, RFA 25.	
	14th		" O.R. wounded 4, 5th R. Sussex.	
	15th		MOVES. Move of Division (less Artillery) Pioneer Bn, 2 Fld Coys and 2 Sections R.E.) to new area in neighbourhood of RECQUES commenced in accordance with Movement Tables attached Appendix A	Appendix A
	16th		CASUALTIES. O.R. killed 5 5th R. Sussex. wounded 16. 15, R.E. 1	
			MOVES Move of Division to new area Continued	
	17th		CASUALTIES. O.R. killed 1, R.F.A. wounded 14, R.F.A 11 (incl 1 at duty), 5th R Sussex 3 (incl 2 at duty).	
CROQUE CHATEAU RECQUES.	17th		MOVES. Move of Division to new area concluded. Location of Units as per Location Table attached. Appendix B	Appendix B
	18th		CASUALTIES. Officers wounded 1. 17. F.O. CROSSLING R.F.A. O.R. killed 3 R.F.A. wounded 3 R.F.A.	
	19th		CASUALTIES O.R. wounded 3 R.F.A (incl 1 at duty)	
	20th		CASUALTIES. O.R. wounded 4 R.F.A	

Army Form C. 2118.

WAR DIARY
or
INTELLIGENCE SUMMARY

(Erase heading not required.)

Instructions regarding War Diaries and Intelligence Summaries are contained in F.S. Regs., Part II. and the Staff Manual respectively. Title Pages will be prepared in manuscript.

Place	Date	Hour	Summary of Events and Information	Remarks and references to Appendices
CHATEAU COCOVE RECQUES	21st		CASUALTIES. O.R. wounded. 1, RFA	
"	22nd		CASUALTIES. O.R. killed. 5, 6⁄R Sussex. wounded. 25. 5⁄R Sussex 19, RFA. 4.	
"	23rd		CASUALTIES. Casualties from Sept 2nd to 30th inclusive as in list appended marked Appendix 'C'.	Appendix 'C'
"	24th		MOVES. Move of Division (less Artillery Pioneer Bn, 2 Fld Coys, 2 Secs R.E.) to the line N. of YPRES in relief of 55th Division (Command) in accordance with Orders Movement Tables attached Appendix 'D.E.F.'	Appendix D " E " F
BRAKE CAMP POPERINGHE	28th		MOVES. Div. H.Q. moved from COCOVE CHATEAU, RECQUES to BRAKE CAMP POPERINGHE	
"	30th		MOVES. Move of Division from RECQUES area to line N. of YPRES completed. Dispositions as follows:— Divl Artillery. NORDPEENE Area. R.E. H.Q. BRAKE CAMP. 1/1 S.M.F.A. CANAL BANK. 474, 475 Fld Coys. ⁄ in line 477 " DROOGENTAN FARM 300yds NNE of POPERINGHE 1/2 " GHENT FARM 2000 yds NE of POPERINGHE 1/3 " OOST HOEK. Mob Vet Sectn. HAM HOEK. 143 Inf Bde. DAMBRE CAMP less 8th R Warw at REIGERSBURG CAMP. 144 " BRAKE CAMP 145 " Moving into the line. 5th R Sussex H.Q. DuTram. PESELHOEK. No 1 Cy Tram. NOORDPEENE Area 2 " " PESELHOEK. 3 " " PESELHOEK.	

War Diary. Appendix. 1.

48th Division Q.T.1224.

"Q" NOTES DURING RECENT OPERATIONS.

1. TRANSPORT.

The organisation and drilling of a Pack Transport Train is absolutely essential.

The organisation adopted by this Division is shewn on attached appendix "A" and was found to work well during operations.

A great deal of drill and practice is necessary before the pack train becomes really handy especially in teaching the men to adjust their loads quickly and in the dark.

It is necessary to have Pack Transport ready for use because occasions will always arise during the modern offensive when it is the only possible method of getting supplies and material to the troops in the battle area.

Care must however, be taken to see that "Pack" is only used when other means are impossible.

First Line Transport Officers are apt to go "Pack" Mad and to forget that any form of wheeled transport is more economical and preferable in every way if it can be used.

The principle to follow is that wheel transport should be used as far forward as practicable and thereafter Pack or Man haulage according to the distance of the carry.

It was found that pack transport could usually get right forward with comparative immunity within a few hours of Zero.

An experienced Officer should be in charge, if possible in direct communication with his Brigade H/Q. He must take advantage of the situation and push his convoy through as opportunity offers.

This method worked successfully on several occasions and only failed once when a convoy was pushed forward into direct Machine Gun fire, owing to information being received that certain strong posts had been taken by us when in reality they were still held by the enemy.

The total casualties to horses during 3 weeks operation were; Killed 94, Wounded 102. Of these about half were incurred in camps and standings by Bombs from Enemy Aircraft or Shells from H.V. Guns.

2. WATER.

Petrol tins on pack or wheel seems to be the most satisfactory way of getting water to the troops.

Each Battalion should keep 80 petrol tins for this purpose.

The tins get lost, hit, and left about in the front line. It is necessary therefore to rigidly enforce on battalions the necessity for collecting empty tins and sending them back to meet the transport each day. Otherwise the supply of tins soon melts away.

Each battalion transport should keep up a reserve of 200 wooden stoppers for tins as the brass stoppers get lost in large numbers.

An advanced water point was established for this Division about 3000 yards behind the front line, consisting of:-

        Two   120 Gallon Barrels.
        600   Petrol Tins.
        200   Waterbottles.

This was kept supplied by the Divisional Train which delivered a supply of full petrol tins and waterbottles and took away an equal number of empties, and water to fill the barrels from a Water Cart.

The Guard in charge of the water point had orders to give out a full tin or waterbottle in exchange for an empty one to any Infantry or Artillery who asked for it.

This point worked well, although in area heavily shelled at times, and always maintained a reserve supply.

3. **HOT FOOD AND SPECIAL RATIONS.**

Hot Food Containers were not used. They are too bulky and heavy for troops to carry over bad ground.

Solidified Alcohol was in great demand and is undoubtedly the very best way of ensuring troops in the most exposed positions getting a hot drink or meal.

4 oz tins are better than 8 oz as they can be more widely distributed. It often happens that the 1 or 2 men carrying 8 oz tins for a platoon get knocked out and consequently the platoon goes without. 2 oz tins would be better still.

A certain number of tins of Auto Bouillante bought specially from Paris were issued. These weigh about 1½ lbs each and contain an excellent tinned ration. - By boring a hole in the lid and poring water in, a chemical action is produced which boils the contents in about 20 minutes.

There is no doubt that they are of great value, but they are very bulky and the expense (2.50 Fcs each) precludes an issue on a very large scale.

Battalions about to go into action were issued with an extra ration of cheese and biscuit which was popular and of great value.

Spare waterbottles filled with cold tea and rum were also used for attacking troops and were either dumped forward or sent up by special carrying parties.

Precautions against Trench Feet must be taken even at this time of year and Whale Oil must be applied before a battalion goes into action.

4. **COMMUNICATIONS.**

Trench Board tracks must be provided and must be laid immediately after an advance. At least 2 tracks are necessary on each Divisional front, and these should be doubled as material and labour become available.

A permanent maintainance party of about 6 men per mile is required to repair breaks.

A track for wheel transport and another for pack transport should also be made and clearly marked with posts. These, in Flanders, can probably only be used in fine weather, but they save the roads and give the men working on the roads more chance of working.

5. **DUMPS.**

R.E. material is best dumped as far forward as wheels can get it with comparitive safety. 15 G.S. wagons of the Divl Train were used daily for supplying the forward R.E. Dump, these wagons being replaced by 6 lorries supplied by Corps.

Two Divl Grenade and Ammunition Dumps were formed, one about 3000 yards from the line, the other about 2,500 yards further back. Brigades drew what they wanted from the forward dump.

The following approximate amounts were kept:-

	Advanced Dump.	Rear Dump.
S.A.A.	800,000	700,000
Grenades.	4,000	3,000
Rifle Grenades.	2,000	2,000
Very Lights.	1,000	1,000
Flares.	1,000	1,000
P. Bombs.	200	200
Smoke Candles.	2,000	2,000
Stokes Amn. complete.	1,250	1,500

besides various small quantities of special stores.

It is best to scatter a dump over an area about 150 yards square making small heaps of S.A.A., Grenades, etc., each 10 to 15 yards apart.

If possible a wire fence should be put round and notice boards erected to prevent Tanks and vehicles from drivi

6. SALVAGE.

There is never sufficient personnel in a Salvage Coy. It would result in a great saving to the Country if at least 200 labour personnel could be attached to each Salvage Coy.

It was found useful to erect small bins or cages at every 200 yards along the trench board tracks marked "SALVAGE". Into these were put anything picked up by individuals and the bins were cleared by the Salvage Coy daily.

A special party should be detailed for Artillery Salvage. There were an enormous quantity of 18 pdr. and 4.5 rounds dropped about and of course quantities of empty cases.

7. BURIALS.

The personnel of 1 Officer and 9 trained O.R. assisted by a labour detachment of 40 was found to be sufficient. Over 300 bodies were buried during 3 weeks. The best system is to work from the rear forwards, systematically clearing an area up to a certain line before moving on to another area.

8. EVACUATION OF WOUNDED.

Each Battalion had 16 additional Stretcher bearers, and 200 extra men from a Reserve Brigade were told off for work under the A.D.M.S. prior to each attack.

These men were distributed between the A.D.S., D.C.P., Relay Posts and Regimental Aid Posts.

Owing to the state of the roads the "carry" was a very long one. In some cases over 5000 yards.

The above personnel however successfully accomplished the evacuation of about 850 wounded in one period of 24 hours and there was never any serious congestion.

Only perfectly fit and strong men should be employed on stretcher bearing duties as it is extremely exhausting.

9. PROVOST DUTIES.

These worked smoothly - Stragglers Posts were posted on each Bridge over the Canal and any stragglers found were collected and sent straight back to their Brigades.

In addition a patrol of M.M.P. were detailed to move about in the Artillery area and watch for any unauthorised men coming back.

Traffic control worked well and blocks only occurred as the result of roads being holed by crumps. It is necessary to have a small repair party of pioneers in proximity to any road likely to be shelled who can effect immediate repairs.

In bad weather 2 Caterpillars should also be kept handy to pull out any lorries which get stuck. First Aid lorries are useless for getting out a badly ditched lorry.

Lieut-Colonel.,
A.A. & Q.M.G., 48th Division.

6th.September.1917.

APPENDIX "A".

COMPOSITION OF PACK TRANSPORT COLUMN.

Company.	Unit.	Drivers, Animals & Pack Saddles.	Remarks.
No.1 Coy.	143 Bde.	90	Organised in 5 Sections, each of 18 animals. 1 from each Battalion and the M.gun. Coy.
No.2 Coy.	144 Bde.	90	-----ditto-----
No.3 Coy.	145 Bde.	90	-----ditto-----
No.4 Coy.	R.E.	80	Organised in 4 sections, each og 20 animals. 1 from each Field Coy, and 1 from Pioneer Battalion.
No.5 Coy. (Divl Reserve)	D.A.C. & Divl Train.	80	Organised in 4 Sections, each of 20 animals. Three from the D.A.C. and One from Divl Train.

Each Coy commanded by an Officer and each Section by an Officer or N.C.O. not below rank of Sergt.

The following loads were found practicable:-.

S.A.A.	2 Boxes.
Lewis Gun Drums.	4 Tin Boxes each containing 8 drums
Grenades.No.5 or No.23.	6 Boxes.
" No.20 or 24.	5 Boxes.
P. Bombs.	5 Boxes.
Smoke Candles.	2 Boxes.
Very Lights.	3 Boxes.
Flares.	2 Boxes.
Stokes.	4 Boxes.
Water.	6 Tins. (8 is possible where going is very good.).
Biscuits.	165 Rations.
Preserved Meat.	192 "
Tools.	22 Shovels and 6 picks.
Wire.	4 Rolls.
Sand bags.	300.

SECRET.   Copy No. 15D.

48th DIVISION ORDER No. 217.

14.9.1917.

Ref.Maps:
   HAZEBROUCK 5A.) 1/100,000.
   CALAIS 13.   )

1. The 48th Division (less Artillery, Pioneer Bn., 2 Fd. Cos. and 2 Secs. R.E.) will move by rail and route march to XIX Corps Area (RECQUES area) on 15th, 16th and 17th inst.

2. The following (less Transport) will move by rail:-

On 16th inst.:   145 Inf.Bde.
                 2nd Field Ambulance.

On 17th inst.:   Div. HdQurs.
                 143 Inf.Bde.
                 144 Inf.Bde.
                 1st and 3rd Field Ambulances.
                 2 Secs. R.E.

   Entrainment orders will be issued later by 48th Div. "Q".

3. (a) Entraining Station APEELE.
   ~~(b)~~ Detraining Station AUDRUICQ.

   (b) Units will be accommodated in RECQUES Area as under:-

         143 Inf.Bde. in NORDAUSQUES Bde. Area.
         144 Inf.Bde. in NIELLES Bde. Area.
         145 Inf.Bde. in LICQUES Bde. Area.

4. Units will march to Entraining Stations and from Detraining Stations to Billeting Areas by the most direct route.
   A distance of 500 yards between Battalions and 200 yards between Companies will be maintained.

5. Transport will move in accordance with attached Table. Times of starting will be notified later.
   200 yards distance will be maintained between Groups of wagons, which will move in Groups of not more than ten.

6. 48th Div. Supply Column will move to RECQUES on 17th inst. Billets from Area Comdt. RECQUES.

   Route: STEENVORDE - CASSEL - St.OMER - NORDAUSQUES. To be clear of St. OMER by 12 noon.

7. Accommodation tables are attached.
      Advanced parties will report at Area Commandant, RECQUES, on arrival. Transport will be arranged by 48th Div. "Q".

8. Div. HdQrs. will move to CHATEAU COCOVE, near RECQUES, on 17th inst.

                x   x   x

                              (Sgd) T.J.LEAHY, Major,
                                 for Lieut.Colonel,
                                    General Staff.

Transport Movement Table - To accompany 48th Div. Order No. 217 d/- 14.9.17.

Serial No.	Date	Unit.	From	To	Route	Remarks.
1	15th Sept.	Transport of 145 Inf.Bde.,2nd.Fd. Amb., & 1 Co.Div. Train.	XVIII Corps Area.	ZEGGERS CAPPEL.	WATOU - HOUTKERQUE & WORMHOUDT.	Billets from Area Commandant, ZEGGERS CAPPEL.
2	16th Sept.	do.	ZEGGERS CAPPEL.	RECQUES AREA.	BOLLEZEELE - MERCKEGHEM - WATTEN - thence most direct route.	
3	16th Sept.	Transport of 48th Divn.(less Arty., Pioneer Bn., 2 Fd. Amb Cos., & 2 Secs R.E., Serial Nos. 1 & 4 & Div.Hdqrs.	XVIII. Corps Area.	ZEGGERS CAPPEL.	As for Serial No. 1.	Billets from Area Commandant ZEGGERS CAPPEL.
4	16th Sept.	Transport of 144th Inf.Bde. & 3rd Fd. Ambulance.	XVIII Corps Area.	ZEGGERS CAPPEL.	As for Serial No. 1.	To follow Serial No. 3. Billets from Area Commandant, ZEGGERS CAPPEL.
5.	17th Sept.	Serial No. 3	ZEGGERS CAPPEL.	RECQUES AREA.	BOLLEZEELE - MERCKEGHEM - WATTEN - thence most direct route.	
	"	Div.H.Q.Transport	"	"	"	
6.	17th Sept.	do.	"	"	"	To follow Serial No. 5.

Appendix B

48th DIVISION.

DISPOSITIONS (RECQUES AREA).   18.9.17.

48th Divl H.Q.	"G" and "A & Q" CHATEAU COCOVE. & (near RECQUES).
	Other Offices – ZUTKERQUE.
48th Div R.A., H.Q.	LANLRETHUN.
H.Q., 143 Inf Bde.	NORDAUSQUES.
5th R. Warwick Regt.	"
6th -do-	LOUCHES.
7th -do-	LA PANNE.
8th -do-	ZOUAFQUES.
143 M.G. Coy.	AUTINGUES.
143 T.M. Bty.	"
H.Q., 144 Inf Bde.	NIELLES.
4th Gloster Regt.	"
6th -do-	ZUTKERQUE.
7th Worcester Regt.	"
8th -do-	RECQUES.
144 M.G. Coy.	BERTHAM.
144 T.M. Bty.	NIELLES.
H.Q., 145 Inf Bde.	LICQUES.
5th Gloster Regt.	ALEMBON, SANGHEM AND VENTU d'ALEMBON
4th Oxfords & Bucks L.I.	BONNINGUES.
1st Bucks Bn.	LICQUES (H.Q.), CAHEN, HERBINGHEM,)
	LE BREUIL, CANCHY.)
4th R. Berks Regt.	AUDENFORT.
145 M.G. Coy.	CLERQUES (H.Q.), and HAMEL.
145 T.M. Bty.	LICQUES.
1/1st S.M. Field Ambulance.	GRAS PAYELLE.
1/2nd S.M. Field Ambulance.	LICQUES.
1/3rd S.M. Field Ambulance.	BLANC PIGNON.
H.Q., Divl Train.	NORTHKERQUE.
No.2 Company Train.	ZOUAFQUES.
No.3 Company Train.	LA RECOUSSE.
No.4 Company Train.	LICQUES, and HERICAL.
D.A.D.O.S.	ZUTKERQUE. (Billet No 79)
48th Divl Supply Column.	RECQUES.
2 Sections R.E.	LA RECOUSSE.

Appendix "C"

Casualties from 23rd to 30th Sept.

Unit.	Officers K	Officers W	Officers M	O.R. K	O.R. W	O.R. M	
	\multicolumn{6}{c	}{To noon 24th Septr.}	
240 Bde.R.F.A.	-	-	-	-	-	-	
B/241 Bde.R.F.A.	-	1	-	-	1	-	2/Lieut.J.S.Lycett, on 23rd.
C/241 Bde.R.F.A.	-	-	-	-	1	-	
D/241 Bde.R.F.A.	-	-	-	-	2	-	
	\multicolumn{6}{c	}{To noon 25th Septr.}	
C/241 Bde.R.F.A.	-	-	-	1	1	-	
48th D.A.C.	-	-	-	-	1	-	
	\multicolumn{6}{c	}{To noon 26th Septr.}	
240 Bde.R.F.A.	-	-	-	-	1	-	
A/241 Bde.R.F.A.	-	1	-	-	-	-	2/Lieut.J.Summersgill, on 26th.
C/241 Bde.R.F.A.	-	-	-	-	1	-	
5th R.Sussex Regt.	-	-	-	-	2	-	Includes 1 O.R. slightly at duty.
	\multicolumn{6}{c	}{To noon 28th Septr.}	
1/5th Gloucester Regt.	-	4	-	-	-	-	Capt.G.Hawkins; 2/Lt.E.G.Townsend; 2/Lieut. S.H.A.Moore; 2/Lt.C.W.E.Rawlings, (all gassed on 28.9.1917)
1/4th Oxford & Bucks L.I.	-	1	-	-	-	-	Capt.L.W.Birt, on 28.9.1917 (shell)
1/4th Royal Berks Regt.	-	-	-	-	2	-	Includes 1 O.R. S.I.W. 37981 Pte Golding,W.
5th R.Sussex Regt.	-	-	-	-	4	-	Includes 3 O.R.at duty.
474 Field Coy, R.E.	1	-	-	2	13	-	Major H.Clissold on 28.9.1917. Includes 1 O.R. at duty.
B/240 Bde.R.F.A.	-	-	-	1	4	-	

Unit.	Officers			Other Ranks.			
	K	W	M	K	W	M	
				To noon 29th Septr.			
1/5th Gloucester Regt.	-	4	-	1	17	1	Lieut.Col.W.Adam; Capt.L.R.C.Sumner) 2/Lieut.F.S.Clifton; 2/Lieut.H.W.Cruickshank. (All gassed on 29.9.17) Includes 7 O.R. gassed, 4 shell-shock.
1/4th Oxford & Bucks L.I.	-	-	-	3	2	-	Slightly at-duty.gassed.
1/4th Royal Berks Regt.	-	2	-	-	1	-	2/Lt.C.E.Clothier, 6thE.Kents attd. 2/Lieut.C.B.Ellwood (Both gassed on 29.9.17)
1/Bucks Battalion.	-	-	-	-	-	-	Slightly at duty.
145 M.G.Company.	-	-	-	2	1	-	
474 Field Coy, R.E.	-	-	-	-	-	-	
				To noon 30th Septr.			
1/5th Gloucester Regt.	-	-	-	5	35	5	Includes 25 O.R. gassed.
1/4th Oxford & Bucks L.I.	-	-	-	1	2	-	
1/Bucks Battalion.	-	-	-	-	12	-	Includes 8 O.R. gassed.
1/4th Royal Berks Regt.	-	-	-	-	6	-	Includes 3 O.R. gassed.
145 M.G.Company.	-	-	-	-	1	-	
475 Field Coy, R.E.	-	2	-	-	2	-	
5th R.Sussex Regt.	-	-	-	2	1	-	

Appendix "D"

SECRET.

48th DIVISION ORDER No. 218.   24.9.17.

1. The 48th Division will relieve the 58th Division from CLIFTON HOUSE (exclusive) to D.1.b.43 and the 11th Division from D.1.b.43 to V.25.d.37 in the Right Sector of XVIII Corps front on 27/28th instant.

2. 145th Inf.Bde. will take over the front line of Div. sector on 27/28th inst. and will move from present area as follows:-

(a) By train on 25th inst. 2 Battns and 1 Sect. M.G.Co. to BRIELEN thence to REIGERSBURG where they will come under orders of G.O.C. 58th Division.

(b) By Car and Lorry on 26th inst. Headquarters 145 Inf. Bde. and Advanced Parties as desired by G.O.C. 145 Inf.Bde.

(c) By train on 27th inst. Remainder of 145 Inf.Bde.

3. H.Qrs 145 Inf.Bde. will be established in the CANAL BANK on 26th inst.

4. Detailed orders for the above moves, and for that of the Transport of 145 Inf.Bde. will be issued by D.A. & Q.M.G. 48th Division.

5. Acknowledge.

Issued at 7 a.m.   (Sgd) H.C.L.Howard,Lieut.Col.,
                                              General Staff.

SECRET.

ADDENDUM No. 1 to 48th Div. Order 218.

25.9.17.

1. Further moves of 48th Divn. to the forward area will be carried out in accordance with attached movement table.
Detailed orders for these movements will be issued by A.A. & Q.M.G., 48th Div.

2. Arrangements for taking over the front line of the Div. Sector by 145 Inf.Bde. will be made between Brigadiers concerned.

3. On completion of movements Inf.Bdes. will be disposed as under:-

   143 Inf.Bde.   DAMPRE CAMP.
   144 Inf.Bde.   BRAKE CAMP.
   145 Inf.Bde.   Line.

4. Orders for the moves, accommodation, and work of Field Cos. R.E. and Pioneers are being issued by C.E. XVIII Corps.

5. (a) Div.H.Q. will close at COCOVE CHATEAU, RECQUES at 10 a.m. on 28th inst. and will open at same hour at BRAKE CAMP, (A.30.c) at which hour G.O.C. 48th Div. takes over command of the sector from G.O.C. 58th Div.

(b) At the same hour on 28th inst. C.R.A. 48th Div. will take over command of the Field Artillery covering the Div. sector from C.R.A. 58th Div.

(c) Brig.Gen. DONE, D.S.O. Commanding 144 Inf.Bde. will command the troops of 48th Div. remaining in the RECQUES Area from 10 a.m. 28th inst. until they move to the forward area.

6. Acknowledge.

Issued at 9.30 p.m.

(Sgd) H.C.L.HOWARD, Lieut.Col.
General Staff.

MARCH TABLE - To accompany Addendum No. 1 to 48th Division Order 218.

Serial No.	Unit.	Date.	From	To.	March or Train.	Remarks.
9.A.	H.Q. 48th Div.	Sept 28	RECQUES Area	BRAKE CAMP (A.30.c)	-	-
10.	Transport of 48th Div. (less Arty., R.E., Pioneers Bn., 145 Inf. Bde. and 2 Fd.Amb) not proceeding by rail.	Sept. 29	RECQUES Area	WORMHOUDT Area	March	Orders from A.A.&Q.M.G. 48th Div.
12.	Serial No. 10.	Sept. 30.	WORMHOUDT Area	XVIII Corps Area	March.	Position of Transport Lines from A.A. & Q.M.G. 48th Division.
14.	48th Div. (less Div.H.Q., Arty., R.E. and Pioneers, 145 Inf.Bde. and 2 Fd.Ambulances)	Sept.30.	RECQUES Area	XVIII Corps Area	Tactical trains with two omnibus trains for each tactical set	Entrain AUDRUICQ Detrain (personnel) VLAMERTINGHE, (transport) PESELHOEK.

SCERET.

ADDENDUM No. 2 to 48th Division Order No. 218.
----

1. Ref. para. 1 of 48th Div.Order No. 218 dated 24.9.17.
That part of the line held by 11th Division will/be (not)
taken over by 145th Inf.Bde. until the night 28/29th inst.

Issued at 11 a.m. 26.9.17.   (Sgd) H.C.L.HOWARD, Lieut.Col.,
                                              General Staff.

Appendix "E"

48th Division.
No. S/303.

Orders for Move of 1/2nd and 1/3rd S.M.Field Ambulances.
----

1. Personnel of 1/2nd and 1/3rd S.M.Field Ambulances will move by rail on 27th instant from AUDRUICQ.
   Detraining Station BRIE LEN.
   Time of train will be wired to A.D.M.S. as soon as known.
   Captain YOUNG, Headquarters, 145th Inf. Bde., will allot accommodation for 10 Officers and 400 O.R. on the train.

2. The transport of these 2 Ambulances under command of Captain SUTER, R.A.M.C. will move on 26th instant to ESQUELBECQUES.
   Route - NORDAUSQUES - EPERLECQUES - WATTEN - MERCKEGHEM.
   Advance Party to report to Town Commandant, ESQUELBECQUES for billets 2 hours before arrival of column.

3. The march will be continued on the 27th instant to XVIII Corps Area. Route - HOUTKERQUE - ST JAN TER RIEZEN.

4. The destination on 27th instant will be -

   1/2nd S.M.Field Ambulance.   A.23.c.2.8.
   1/3rd   -do-   GWENT FARM.

5. ACKNOWLEDGE.

H. Crawshay Major
D.A.Q.M.G.
                                      for Lieut-Colonel,
25-9-17.   A.A.& Q.M.G. 48th Division.

Distribution.

   Copy 1. XIX Corps.
    "   2. XVIII Corps.
    "   3. "G".
    "   4. A.D.M.S.
    "   5. 58th Division.
    "   6. 145th Inf. Bde.,
    "   7. O.C. 48th Div. Train.
    "   8. Retained.
    "   9.   "

Appendix "F"

Copy No........

SECRET.

48th Division
S/305. 26/9/1917.

ORDERS for move of Division in connection
with Addendum No. 1 to 48th Division Order No. 218.

Order of March.
143 Bde Train
      Waggons
144 "   "
No. 2 Coy Div.
      Train.
No. 3 "   "
1st Field Amb.

1. The transport of 1st Field Ambulance, No. 2 and 3 Companies, Divisional Train and that portion of 143 and 144 Brigades transport which cannot be taken by train (see para 4), (the whole under Command of Lieut.Col. Crosskey, A.S.C) will march on 29th instant to WORMHOUDT area - Route - NORDAUSQUES - OUEST MONT - WATTEN - LES CLITRES - MERKEGHEM Starting point - road junction 400 yards N.E. of MONNECOVE on NORDAUSQUES - TILQUES road. Head of column to pass at 9 a.m.

Each formation will send an officer to report to Lieut. Col. Crosskey at the starting point at 8.45 a.m.

2. Billets for night 29/30th will be obtained from Area Commandant, WORMHOUDT to whom advanced parties will report 3 hours before arrival of Column.

3. The March will be continued on 30th instant into 18th Corps area under the orders of Lieut.Col. Crosskey.
Route - HOUTKERQUE - ST. JAN TER BIEZEN. Final destinations will be notified to Lieut.Col. Crosskey.

4. Personnel of (and part 1st line transport) 143 and 144 Brigades, and personnel 1st Field Ambulance move by rail from AUDRUICQ on 30th instant.
Detraining stations - VLAMERTINGHE for personnel - PESELHOEK for transport.
Each Brigade group will have two tactical and two Omnibus trains. The 1st Field Ambulance will travel with 143 Brigade group.
For composition of Tactical and Omnibus Trains see S.S. 200, page 11.12.
All transport not shown in tables B and C page 11.12 S.S. 200 as being taken in the Omnibus Trains will proceed by road on the 29th instant (see para. 1).

5. Times of departure of trains will be wired to Brigades as soon as known. Personnel must be at the station 1 hour and transport 3 hours before departure of train.
Each Brigade group will detail a fatigue party of 100 men under an officer for loading at entraining station and another party of 100 for unloading at PESELHOEK.

6. All troops proceeding by rail on 30th instant will take rations for consumption 30th and 31st. O.C. Train will arrange to deliver these by evening of 29th.

7. From 8 a.m. on 28th Brigadier-General DONE, D.S.O., Commanding 144 Inf.Bde. will be in command of troops in rear area. He will issue necessary instructions to 143 Brigade and 1st Field Ambulance as to times of trains and march to AUDRUICQ.
He will also detail an officer as assistant to the R.T.O. at both entraining and detraining stations.

P.T.O.

Capt. Gibson will remain at CHATEAU COCOVE until 30th instant and will act as liaison officer between Traffic, HAZEBROUCK - 19th Corps and Brigadier-General DONE, informing the latter of any orders received re trains and movements. He will also deal with any demands for extra lorries.

8. Acknowledge.

Issued at   p.m.   *[signature]*
                                          Lieut.Colonel,
                                   A.A. & Q.M.G., 48th Division.

```
Copy No.  1.   19th Corps
  "   "   2.   18th Corps
  "   "   3.   Brig-Genl.Done,D.S.O.
  "   "   4.   144 Bde.
  "   "   5.   143  "
  "   "   6.   1st Fd. Amb.
  "   "   7.   Div. Train.
  "   "   8.   Lt.Col.Crosskey.
  "   "   9.   "G"
  "   "  10.   58th Division.
  "   "  11.)
  "   "  12.)  Retained.
  "   "  13.)
```

To accompany War Diary for September, 1917

LIST OF HONOURS AND REWARDS AWARDED TO OFFICERS, N.C.Os. AND MEN OF THE 48th DIVISION.

Month of September, 1917.

Regtl No.	Rank.	Name.	Unit.	Award.
840162.	Cpl.	J. Lord.	D/240th Bde., R.F.A.	M.M.
--	2/Lt.	G.G. Bowerman.	1/8th R.War.R.	M.C.
--	"	R.L. Hugman.	145th M.G. Company.	M.C.
--	Capt.	A.E.P. McConnell.	1/2nd S.M. Field Amb.	M.C.
240414.	Pte.	F. Taylor.	1/8th Worc.R.	D.C.M.
201785.	Cpl.	W.N. Hobbs.	1/4th Ox & Bks L.I.	Bar to M.M.
845256.	Bdr.	S. Hulme.	48th Div. Ammn. Col.	M.M.
240618.	Cpl.	A.N. Turner.	1/8th Worc.R.	M.M.
240244.	Pte.	A. Corbett.	-do-	M.M.
241318.	L/Cpl.	A.T. Smith.	-do-	M.M.
241661.	Pte.	W. Williams.	-do-	M.M.
265473.	"	F.T. Cripps.	1/Bucks Bn.,	M.M.
37937.	L/Cpl.	S. Rogers.	1/4th R.Berks R.	M.M.
242278.	Pte.	R. Eggington.	1/5th R.War.R.	M.M.
201797.	"	J. Riley.	-do-	M.M.
203036.	"	A. Johnson.	-do-	M.M.
240098.	Cpl.(a/Sgt)	E. Jones.	1/6th R.War.R.	M.M.
240456.	Pte.	J. Sutton.	-do-	M.M.
268513.	"	A. Hare.	1/7th R.War.R.	M.M.
265095.	Sgt.	W.J. Lyons.	-do-	M.M.
307597.	Pte.	A. Roden.	1/8th R.War.R.	M.M.
24401.	Sgt.	F.H. Gardner.	143rd M.G. Company.	M.M.
500205.	"	F. Beckett.	(48th Sig.Coy.Attd.	M.M.
500206.	Cpl.	J. Knight.	(143rd Inf.Bde.,	M.M.
240750.	L/Cpl.	C. Cook.	1/5th Glouc.R.	M.M.
203696.	Pte.	W. Clee.	-do-	M.M.
201728.	"	H.J. Finch.	1/4th Ox & Bucks L.I.	M.M.
285074.	"	F. Moore.	1/Bucks Bn.,	M.M.
265292.	L/Cpl.	G.W. Wallington.	-do-	M.M.
266733.	"	S.G. Stone.	-do-	M.M.
265036.	Sgt.	A.J. Hart.	-do-	M.M.
265046.	"	G. Richardson.	-do-	M.M.
200485.	Cpl.	F.W. Child.	1/4th R.Berks R.	M.M.
203809.	L/Cpl.	W. Ranscombe.	-do-	M.M.
21119.	Sgt.	N.G. Waite.	145th M.G. Company.	M.M.
21113.	Pte.	H.J. Gear.	-do-	M.M.
307788.	"	F. Wootton.	1/8th R.War.R.	M.M.
--	Lieut.(a/Capt.)	A.O. Lloyd, M.C.,	1/7th Worc.R.	Second Bar to MC.
200445.	C.S.M.	W. Shakespeare.	-do-	M.C.
200684.	Sgt.	G. Cooper.	-do-	D.C.M.
11329.	L/Sgt.	F. Bearcroft.	1/4th Glouc.R.	M.M.
268519.	L/Cpl.	A. George.	1/7th R.War.R.	M.M.
265468.	Cpl.(a/L/Sgt)	A. Parkinson.	-do-	M.M.
--	Major.(T.Lt.Col.)	L.L.C. Reynolds, D.S.O.	1/Bucks Bn.,	Bar to D.S.O.
--	Lt.(a/Capt)	B.F. Holmes.	4th Norfolk Regt. Attd.1/4th R.Berks R.	M.C.
--	2/Lt.	G.A. Johnston.	1/6th Essex Regt. Attd.1/4th Ox & Bks L.I.	M.C.
--	Lt.	G.E. Ratcliff.	1/5th Glouc.R.	M.C.
--	Lt.	C. James.	D/241st S.M.Bde.R.F.A.	M.C.
201108.	C.S.M.	W.H. Heath.	1/4th R.Berks R.	M.C.
--	2/Lt.	D.G. Stewart.	7th Royal Scots. Attd. 1/6th Glouc.R.	M.C.
--	2/Lt.	S.H. Wilkes, M.C.,	1/8th Worc.R.	Bar to M.C.
240276.	Pte.	P.S. Millichap.	1/5th Glouc.R.	D.C.M.
240038.	C.S.M.	V.G. Smith.	-do-	D.C.M.
265094.	Sgt.	T. Golding.	1/Bucks Bn.,	D.C.M.
266100.	"	E. Bridger.	-do-	D.C.M.
266477.	L/Cpl.	W. Buckland.	-do-	D.C.M.
23951.	Cpl.	L. Malpass.	145th M.G. Company.	D.C.M.
307552.	L/Cpl.	J.W. Berriman.	1/8th R.War.R.	D.C.M.
203794.	Sgt.	F. Gilding.	1/4th R.Berks R.	D.C.M.

Regtl No.	Rank.	Name.	Unit.	Award.
201073.	Cpl.	F. Green.	1/7th Worc. R.	M.M.
41349.	Pte.	D. Novis.	-do-	M.M.
200268.	"	A. Protheroe.	-do-	M.M.
200671.	Cpl.	G. Sneyd.	-do-	Bar to M.M.
241191.	Sgt.	R.W. Warren.	1/8th Worc. R.	M.M.
242349.	L/Sgt.	F. Birch.	-do-	M.M.
240811.	Cpl.	H. Norledge.	-do-	M.M.
241268.	Pte.	Clay, C.	-do-	M.M.
241790.	"	Rice, C.F.	-do-	M.M.
240194.	"	Whiley, R.	-do-	M.M.
267319.	"	Dowell, H.	1/6th Glouc. R.	M.M.
265774.	"	Osgood, J.	-do-	M.M.
210130.	"	Arnold, G.	1/5th R. Sussex R.	M.M.
240665.	Cpl.	Bryant, R.	-do-	M.M.
265687.	Pte.	Griffiths, J.H.	1/6th Glouc. R.	M.M.
435075.	"	Allen, C.	1/1st S.M. Field Amb.	M.M.
435334.	"	Cox, J.	-do-	M.M.
437308.	"	Rowlands, F.	1/2nd -do-	M.M.
437002.	"	Bennett, W.	-do-	M.M.
437086.	"	Lakin, A.	-do-	M.M.
437184.	L/Cpl.	Valentine, H.	-do-	M.M.
437098.	"	Rowe, H.	-do-	M.M.
--	Lieut.	A.O. Lloyd, M.C.,	1/7th Worc. R.	Bar to M.C.
--	2/Lt.	K.A. Robertson.	1/5th Glouc. R. Attd. H.Q., 145th Inf. Bde.,	M.C.
--	Lt.	J.D.J. Saner.	48th Sig. Coy. R.E., Attd. 145th Inf. Bde.,	M.C.
206983.	Sgt.	F. Oreton.	1/5th R. War. R.	M.M.

WAR DIARY

48ᵀᴴ DIVISION

"A" & "Q" BRANCH

OCTOBER 1917

VOLUME XXXIII

Army Form C. 2118.

WAR DIARY
or
INTELLIGENCE SUMMARY
(Erase heading not required.)

Instructions regarding War Diaries and Intelligence Summaries are contained in F. S. Regs., Part II. and the Staff Manual respectively. Title Pages will be prepared in manuscript.

Place	Date	Hour	Summary of Events and Information	Remarks and references to Appendices
BRAKE CAMP (A.3.c.) Sheet 28	1 Oct 1917		CASUALTIES — TOTALS 1 & 12th October — nil extra tender Oct 12th nil	
			MOVES — 144 Bde (less 2 Battns) from NIELLES area to BRAKE CAMP	
	2		MOVES — 2 Battns 144 Bde " " "	
CANAL BANK (C.25.C.2.3) Sheet 28	3	10 am	143 Bde took over divisional front line from 145 Bde	
			144 M.G. Coy from BRAKE CAMP to front line	
			144 Adv (less 144 M.G. Coy) from BRAKE CAMP to DAMBRE and REIGERSBURG camps	
	4		143 Bde from line to CANAL BANK and REIGERSBURG Camp	
			2 Battns 145 Bde from CANAL BANK to CALIFORNIA TRENCH in support to 143 Bde	
			48th Divl R.A. to WATOU Arty area	
			No 1 Coy Train ASC " "	
			144 M.G. Coy to REIGERSBURG Camp	
			2 Battns 144 Bde to CANAL BANK	
			2 Battns 144 Bde from CAMP to DAMBRE Camp	
	5		MOVES — 144 Bde to IRISH FARM SHELTERS and REIGERSBURG Camp	
	6		MOVES — 143 Adv to DAMBRE and REIGERSBURG Camps	
	7		MOVES — 48th Divl Arty from WATOU ARTY area to 2nd ANZAC CORPS area	
			No 1 Coy Train A.S.C. " " "	
			145 Inf Bde relieved 143 Bde in front line	

WAR DIARY or INTELLIGENCE SUMMARY

(Erase heading not required.)

Army Form C. 2118.

Instructions regarding War Diaries and Intelligence Summaries are contained in F.S. Regs., Part II. and the Staff Manual respectively. Title Pages will be prepared in manuscript.

Place	Date Oct 1917	Hour	Summary of Events and Information	Remarks and references to Appendices
CANAL BANK (C.21.c.2.3) Sheet 28	7		MOVES (CONTD) – 144th Bde from IRISH FARM SHELTERS and REGERSBURG Camp to CANAL BANK and DAMPARE Camp	
			143 Bde from line to IRISH FARM SHELTERS	
	8		MOVES – 143 Bde from IRISH FARM SHELTERS to DAMPARE camp	
			144 Bde (Holding 143 Bde in front line)	
			143 Bde (less 2 Battns) moved to DAMPARE camp	
			2 Battns 143 Bde moved to CANAL BANK	
			2 Battns 143 Bde from CANAL BANK to CALIFORNIA DRIVE	
	9		MOVES – 143 Bde moved from DAMPARE CAMP to POPERINGHE	
			143 Bde relieved in front line by 26th Bde. 9th Division	
	10		MOVES – proceeded to SIEGE Camp	
			2 Battns 145 Bde moved from CALIFORNIA TRENCH to DAMPIRE CAMP	
			3 & 7 Sussex Rgt (Pioneers) moved to SIEGE Camp	
			HQ. 48 Div moved from CANAL BANK to X CAMP	
X CAMP (A.16.c.5.9 Sheet 28)	11	10 am	MOVES – 48 Divl R.E. moved to X and BROWNE Camps	
			1/1st S.M. Fuel Coy moved to SCHOOL CAMP	
			1/2 " " " GWENT FARM	
			1/3 " " " L'ERAE FARM	

Army Form C. 2118.

WAR DIARY
or
INTELLIGENCE SUMMARY

(Erase heading not required.)

Instructions regarding War Diaries and Intelligence Summaries are contained in F. S. Regs., Part II. and the Staff Manual respectively. Title Pages will be prepared in manuscript.

Place	Date	Hour	Summary of Events and Information	Remarks and references to Appendices
X CAMP (A.16.c.80) Sheet 28	12 Oct 16		MOVES — 11/A Inf Bn moved from SIEGE Camp to SCHOOL CAMP	1ST JAN — 7TH BUSSEN
			" " " " DAMPIERRE " ROAD CAMP	
			17gust I.M. 70 Cans moved from GWENT Fm to TUNNELLING CAMP	
			13th S.M. " " " " L'EBBE — GWENT Fm	
			CASUALTIES — for period from 1st to 12th October 1917 inclusive — See Appendix A attached	
PERNES (Sheet 11)	13		MOVES — Divisional HQ moved from X Camp to PERNES	
			CASUALTIES Officers — wounded — Nil	
			O.R. killed — 4 (11th R. Sussex Rgt)	
			wounded — 18 (11th R. Sussex Rgt)	
	14/10		MOVES 143 Bde moved from POPERINGHE to BARLY Area (North du ALEUX)	
			entraining at RESEGHEM and detraining at MARGERIVE	
			HQ 118 Div RA moved from X camp to MORBECQUE, forming artillery	
			Brigade (Fire.)	
			R.E. (HQ all four Coys) moved from X + BROWNE Camps to First Army Area	
			(ACQ) entraining RESEGHEM and detraining at MARGEVIL	
			11th R. Sussex Rgt moved from SIEGE Camp to First Army Area (ACQ)	
			entraining PESEGHEM detraining at MARGEVIL	
			HQ and No 2 Coy Train K.S.C. moved to MONT ST ELOY	
			3rd S.M. Fd Amb. — do —	
			MGC Vet. Officer — do —	

Army Form C. 2118.

WAR DIARY
or
INTELLIGENCE SUMMARY

(Erase heading not required.)

Instructions regarding War Diaries and Intelligence Summaries are contained in F. S. Regs., Part II. and the Staff Manual respectively. Title Pages will be prepared in manuscript.

Place	Date (Oct 1917)	Hour	Summary of Events and Information	Remarks and references to Appendices
PERNES (SHEET 16SE 10)	13/15		MOVES (contd) - 144 Bde moved to VILLERS-AU-BOIS (5th Army Area) ent HOUDITRE det. LIGNY ST FLOCHEL	
			113 Coy Train A.S.C.	do-
			114 S.M. to Canl.	do-
			145 Bde moved to CAMBLIGNEUL-CAMBLAIN L'ABBÉ area	do-
			No 4 Coy Train A.S.C.	do-
			115 S.M. to Canl.	do-
	14		CASUALTIES - Nil	
	15		CASUALTIES - Nil	
	16		MOVES. 143 Bde relieved 8th Can Inf Bde in front line, right subsector MERICOURT sector	
			114 M.G.Coy relieved M.G.Coy of 1st Can Inf Bde in left subsector MERICOURT sector	
			CASUALTIES - Nil	
	17		MOVES - 144 Bde (less M.G.Coy) relieved 6th Can Inf Bde in front line, left subsector, MERICOURT sector	
			64th Bde moved from CAMBLIGNEUL-CAMBLAIN L'ABBÉ area to VILLERS-AU-BOIS area	
			H.Q. Division (tny) PERNES to VILLERS-CHATELET (8th Rutlandshire Regt)	
			CASUALTIES - Officers 1 (2nd Lieut R. DINSDALE 1/6 Warwick Regt)	
			Wounded (gas) O.R. 1 (1/8 R. Warwick Regt)	
CHATEAU D'ACQ (VILLERS AU BOIS) V.30.c.5.3 Sheet 36	18	10 a.m	MOVES - Divisional H.Q. moved from VILLERS-CHATELET to CHATEAU D'ACQ, VILLERS-AU-BOIS, relieving 2nd Canadian Division	

WAR DIARY or INTELLIGENCE SUMMARY

Army Form C. 2118.

(Erase heading not required.)

Instructions regarding War Diaries and Intelligence Summaries are contained in F. S. Regs., Part II. and the Staff Manual respectively. Title Pages will be prepared in manuscript.

Place	Date Oct 1916	Hour	Summary of Events and Information	Remarks and references to Appendices
CHATEAU D'ACQ (VILLERS-AU-BOIS)	18		CASUALTIES — O.R. wounded 1 (15th Worcestershire Regt — slightly, at duty)	
W30.L.S-3 Sheet 36	19		MOVES —	
			11th D.M. to Camb. to FRESNICOURT	
			2nd S.M. to Camb. to MONT ST ELOI	
			13rd S.M. Fd Amb. CHATEAU DE LA HAIE	
			48 Bde Train A.S.C. LA TARGETTE	
			46 Hvy Bty R.A. from MORBECQUE area to FORT GEORGE	
			4° R.G.A. to FORT GEORGE	
			15th R Sussex Regt A.A. to Fd P.2	
	20		CASUALTIES — O.R. wounded 1 (1/5th R Warwick Regt — gas)	
			NOTES NIL	
			CASUALTIES — O.R. killed 3 } (2nd Bde RFA — 11 O.R (horses) wounded 13 } to Sin Brigade	
			MOVES 2nd Adv. R.F.A from FORT GEORGE to MACHINE GUN FORT. S.27 central.	
	21		CASUALTIES NIL	
	22		MOVES 46 Hvy Bty moved from ZOLLERN HOUSE, PETIT VIMY to MACHINE GUN FORT, S.27 central	
			CASUALTIES — O.R. wounded 2 (1/4th Gloucester Regt — 1)	

Army Form C. 2118.

WAR DIARY
or
INTELLIGENCE SUMMARY
(Erase heading not required.)

Instructions regarding War Diaries and Intelligence Summaries are contained in F. S. Regs., Part II. and the Staff Manual respectively. Title Pages will be prepared in manuscript.

Place	Date	Hour	Summary of Events and Information	Remarks and references to Appendices
CHATEAU D'ACQ (VILLERS AU BOIS) W 30.6.C.3 Dec 31	(1917) Dec 23		MOVES — HQ. 48 Div. RA from FORT GEORGE to CHATEAU D'ACQ. CASUALTIES — OR wounded 2 1 (1/75 Worcestershire Rgt)	
	24		MOVES — NIL CASUALTIES — O.R. killed 1 (1/8 R Warwick Rgt) wounded 4 (1/7 R Warwick Rgt - 2) (1/8 Gloucestershire Rgt - 2)	
	25		MOVES — NIL CASUALTIES — O.R. wounded 3 (1/5 + 1/6 Gl RE - 2 (not duty)) (1/5 R Warwicks 1)	
	26		MOVES — NIL CASUALTIES — O.R. killed 1 (1/8 R Warwick Rgt) wounded 4 (240 Bde R.F.A. 2) (1/8 R Warwick Rgt 2 - (on duty))	
	27		MOVES — NIL CASUALTIES — Officers wounded 1 (Capt P. CARTER - 1/7 Worcestershire Rgt) OR wounded 6 (1/7 Worcesters Rgt)	
	28		MOVES — NIL CASUALTIES — OR wounded 1 (143 M.G. Cy)	

2449 Wt. W14957/M90 750,000 1/16 J.B.C. & A. Forms/C.2118/12.

Army Form C. 2118.

WAR DIARY
or
INTELLIGENCE SUMMARY.
(Erase heading not required.)

Instructions regarding War Diaries and Intelligence Summaries are contained in F. S. Regs., Part II. and the Staff Manual respectively. Title pages will be prepared in manuscript.

Place	Date	Hour	Summary of Events and Information	Remarks and references to Appendices
CHATEAU DAQ (VILLERS AU BOIS) Sh 36c S.3	29		MOVES — NIL	
			CASUALTIES — O.R. killed — 1 (1/5th R. Warwick Regt)	
			wounded 1 (1/5th R. Warwick Regt)	
	30		MOVES — NIL	
			CASUALTIES — O.R. wounded 2 (1/5th R. Warwick Regt)	
			Att. 2 Section 143 M.G. Coy relieves 2 Section 143 M.G. Coy in right front	
			B.H.Q. 143 M.G. Coy relieves H.Q. 143 M.G. Coy	
	31		1/5 M.G. Coy 1 (2nd Lieut R. W. STEVENS 1/8th Worcesters — on 30th)	
			Officers — killed 1 (2nd Lieut A. WHISTON)	
			wounded 9 { 1/5th R. Warwick Regt — 4	
			1/7th R. Warwick Regt — 2	
			1/8 R. Warwick Regt — 1	
			143 M.G. Coy — 1	
			1/8 Worcesters — 1	
			List of Honours & Rewards awarded during October 1917 — Appendix B. attached	

[Signature] Lieut Col
for Maj General Comdg
[illegible]

APPENDIX A

Casualties to noon 1st October.

Unit.	Officers			Other Ranks.			
	K	W	M	K	W	M	
1/5th Gloucester Regt.	-	-	-	4	13	-	
1/4th Oxford & Bucks L.I.	-	-	-	3	2	-	
1/Bucks Battalion	-	1	-	3	5	-	2/Lt.C.W.Phinn on 30.9.17.
1/4th Royal Berks.	-	-	-	-	7	-	
145 T.M.Battery.	-	-	-	-	1	-	
475 Field Coy, R.E.	-	-	-	-	1	-	
1/3 Field Ambulance.	-	-	-	1	3	-	

Casualties to noon 2.10.17.

Unit.	Officers			Other Ranks		
	K	W	M	K	W	M
1/5th R.Warwick Regt.	-	-	-	-	1	-
143 M.G.Company	-	-	-	-	1	-
1/4th Gloucester Regt.	-	-	-	1	-	-
1/4th Oxfords & Bucks L.I.	-	-	-	1	1	-
1/Bucks Battalion	-	-	-	1	3	-
1/4th Royal Berks	-	-	-	-	8	-
5th R.Sussex Regt.	-	-	-	-	1	-
13th Labour Coy attd 242 Employment Coy.	-	-	-	-	1	-
148 Labour Coy attd 242 Employment Coy.	-	-	-	1	5	-
242 Employment Coy.	-	-	-	1	11	-

Casualties to noon 3.10.17.

Unit.	Officers			Other Ranks.			
	K	W	M	K	W	M	
1/5th R.Warwick Regt.	-	1	-	-	-	-	2/Lt.G.L.Gordon on 2nd.
1/6th R.Warwick Regt.	-	3	-	-	4	-	2/Lt.O.W.Gassett; 2/Lt.W.G.Box; 2/Lt.A.G.Green, on 2nd
1/7th R.Warwick Regt.	-	-	-	-	4	-	
1/8th R.Warwick Regt.	-	-	-	-	1	-	
1/4th Gloucester Regt.	-	-	-	8	11	2	
1/7th Worcester Regt.	-	-	-	-	2	-	
1/5th Gloucester Regt.	-	-	-	1	1	-	
1/4th Oxford & Bucks L.I.	-	1	-	-	-	-	Capt.M.Bowen on 2nd.
1/4th R.Berks Regt.	-	-	-	4	5	-	
5th R.Sussex Regt.	-	-	-	1	3	-	
475 Field Coy,R.E.	-	-	-	-	12	-	
477 Field Coy,R.E.	-	-	-	-	1	-	

Casualties to noon 4th Oct. 1917.

Unit.	Officers			Other Ranks.			
	K	W	M	K	W	M	
1/5th R.Warwick Regt.	1	7	-	47	134	-	Killed:- Capt.R.S.Turner. Wounded:- Capt.E.Holt; 2/Lt.S.G.Mincher; 2/Lt.J.H.Lade; 2/Lt. A.G.Foster-Sutton;2/Lt.G.A.Palmer; 2/Lt.W.Shadbolt; 2/Lt. F.O. Pickering - all on 4th.
1/6th R.Warwick Regt.	-	3	-	8	121	-	2/Lt.T.H.Collins; Capt.B.Musgrave; Capt.H.S.Powell - on 4th.
1/7th R.Warwick Regt.	-	2	-	13	70	-	Lt.G.F.Bennett; 2/Lt.N.L.Hearne - on 4th.
143 M.G.Company.	-	2	-	-	-	-	2/Lt.G.Norrish; 2/Lt.G.E.Brown on 4th.
1/8th Worcester Regt.	-	-	-	-	1	-	
144 M.G.Company.	-	-	-	-	5	-	
1/5th Gloucester Regt.	-	-	-	-	1	-	
1/Bucks Battalion	-	-	-	2	14	-	
1/4th Royal Berks Regt.	-	-	-	4	15	-	
145 M.G.Company.	-	1	-	1	4	-	2/Lt.P.D.Cherry on 4th.
145 T.M.Battery.	-	1	-	1	4	-	2/Lt.R.Mallett 1/4th R.Berks Regt. attd. - on 4th.
5th R.Sussex Regt.	-	-	-	1	4	-	

Casualties to noon 5th Oct. 1917.

Unit	Officers K	Officers W	Officers M	Other Ranks K	Other Ranks W	Other Ranks M	
1/5th R.Warwick Regt.	2	-	-	7	15	-	2/Lt.C.W.White; 2/Lt.R.C.Brett – on 4th.
1/6th R.Warwick Regt.	4	2	1	10	20	40	Killed:- 2/Lt.A.V.Bisseker; 2/Lt.H.Hallam; 2/Lt.J.Poynton; 2/Lt.F.Hussey. Wounded:-2/Lt.A.G.Thurman; 2/Lt.A.L.Trickett. Missing:-2/Lt.W.H.A.Fisher.
1/7th R.Warwick Regt.	1	1	-	10	82	10	Capt.J.J.Croall, killed on 4th; 2/Lt.R.J.W.Brant wounded 4th.
1/8th R.Warwick Regt.	2	3	1	5	70	10	Killed:- 2/Lt.C.V.Sanders; 2/Lt.R.R.Cheshire. Wounded:-Capt.G.W.Arnell; 2/Lt.T.Hard; 2/Lt.E.Pigg. Missing:-2/Lt.E.C.Bastin.
143 M.G.Company.	-	2	-	6	25	5	Wounded:- 2/Lt.G.W.Hayward; 2/Lt.P.E.Turner.
143 T.M.Battery.	-	-	-	-	4	-	
7th Worcester Regt.	-	-	-	1	5	-	
8th Worcester Regt.	-	-	-	1	10	-	
1/Bucks Battalion.	-	-	-	3	2	-	
1/4th Royal Berks Regt.	-	3	-	-	3	-	2/Lt.J.W.Cawley; 2/Lt.F.Wallis; 2/Lt.K.Jones.
5th R.Sussex Regt.	-	1	-	2	9	-	2/Lt.W.I.Grantham.
1/5th Gloucester Regt.	2	4	-	14	83	7	Killed:- 2/Lt.H.Till; 2/Lt.R.Twelvetrees. Wounded: Capt.E.F.T.Fowler; 2/Lt.K.A.Robertson; 2/Lt.M.R.Browne; 2/Lt.Q.V.Davies; – on 4th.
1/4th Oxford & Bucks L.I.	-	-	-	-	7	-	
145 M.G.Company.	-	-	-	-	3	-	
475 Field Coy,R.E.	-	-	-	-	1	-	
477 Field Coy,R.E.	-	-	-	1	1	-	
1st Field Ambulance.	-	-	-	-	1	-	

Casualties to noon 6th Oct.1917.

Unit.	Officers			Other Ranks.			
	K	W	M	K	W	M	
1/5th R.Warwick Regt.	-	-	-	5	10	8	
1/6th R.Warwick Regt.	-	-	-	5	5	-	
1/7th R.Warwick Regt.	1	-	-	2	3	-	2/Lt.H.F.Rogers on 5th.
1/8th R.Warwick Regt.	-	1	-	22	22	-	2/Lt.L.M.Chadwick on 5th.
1/4th Gloucester Regt.	-	-	-	-	1	1	
144 M.C.Company.	-	-	-	2	-	-	
1/5th Gloucester Regt.	-	-	-	-	4	2	
1/4th Oxford & Bucks L.I.	-	-	-	-	2	-	
145 T.M.Battery.	-	-	-	-	3	-	
1/5th R.Sussex Regt.	-	-	-	-	4	-	

Casualties to noon 7th Oct. 1917.

Unit.	Officers			Other Ranks.		
	K	W	M	K	W	M
1/5th R.Warwick Regt.	-	-	-	-	35	5
1/6th R.Warwick Regt.	-	-	-	-	5	-
1/7th R.Warwick Regt.	-	-	-	-	10	-
1/8th R.Warwick Regt.	-	-	-	-	6	-
143 T.M.Battery.	-	-	-	-	1	-
1/4th Oxford & Bucks L.I.	-	-	-	-	1	-
1/4th Royal Berks Regt.	-	-	-	-	2	3
475 Field Coy, R.E.	-	-	-	-	2	-
48th Div.Train.	-	-	-	1	3	-
242 Employment Coy	-	-	-	-	2	-
A.S.C. attd. 1st Fd.Ambce	-	-	-	-	6	-

Casualties to noon 9th Oct.1917.

Unit.	Officers			Other Ranks.		
	K	W	M	K	W	M
1/4th Oxford & Bucks L.I.	-	-	-	1	4	-
1/4th Royal Berks Regt.	-	-	-	-	5	-
145 M.G.Company.	-	-	-	-	1	-

Casualties to noon 9th Oct.1917.

Unit.	Officers K	W	M	Other Ranks K	W	M		
1/4th Gloucester Regt.	4	5	1	49	156	13	Killed:-	Capt.F.W.Ward; 2/Lt.H.N.Ferris; 2/Lt.W.F.Burns; 2/Lt.C.I.McDonnell.
							Wounded:-	Lt.Col.J.H.Crosskey;2/Lt.H.W.Merrell; 2/Lt.EE. Shephard; 2/Lt.F.Sanders; 2/Lt.P.L.Morse.
							Missing:-	2/Lt.H.C.Organ.
1/6th Gloucester Regt.	1	5	-	48	151	43	Killed:-	2/Lt.A.S.Hill.
							Wounded:-	2/Lt.C.L.Morris;2/Lt.A.G.Poole; 2/Lt.E.D.Warren; 2/Lt.W.C.Townsend; Capt.R.G.Titley (died of wounds on 13th Oct)
1/7th Worcester Regt.	5	5	-	57	124	20	Killed:-	Capt.R.W.Hoare; 2/Lt.F.W.Gould; 2/Lt.D.S.E. Milligan (R.A.M.C. attd); Lt.W.Edwards; 2/Lt. H.J.Edwards.
							Wounded:-	Capt.W.C.Cassels; Capt.H.G.E.Brown; 2/Lt.H.R. Felton; 2/Lt.A.F.Whorton; 2/Lt.J.A.Acworth.
1/8th Worcester Regt.	2	1	-	11	74	8	Killed:-	Capt.H.S.Benjamin; 2/Lt.C.J.Beacham.
							Wounded:-	2/Lt.H.G.Higman.
144 M.G.Company.	1	-	-	5	6	-	Killed:-	2/Lt.P.H.Morris.
144 T.M.Battery.	-	-	-	-	12	-		
1/4th Oxford & Bucks L.I.	-	-	-	-	6	1		
1/4th Royal Berks Regt.	-	-	-	4	12	-		
475 Field Coy,R.E.	-	-	-	1	-	-		
	13	16	1	175	534	85		

Casualties to noon 10th Oct, 1917.

Unit.	Officers			Other Ranks.		
	K	W	M	K	W	M
1/4th Oxford & Bucks L.I.	-	-	-	-	1	-
1/Bucks Battalion	-	-	-	3	14	-
1/4th Royal Berks Regt.	-	-	-	2	1	-
145 M.G.Company.	-	-	-	-	9	1
5th R.Sussex Regt.	-	-	-	-	3	-
2nd Field Ambulance.	-	-	-	1	3	-

Casualties to noon 11th Oct, 1917.

5th R.Sussex Regt.	-	1	-	-	-	-

2/Lt (A/Capt) T.W.Rose, M.C.

Casualties to noon 12th Oct.1917.

| | Officers | | | Other Ranks. | | |
Unit.	K	W	M	K	W	M
1/4th Oxford & Bucks L.I.	-	-	-	-	1	-
1/4th Royal Berks Regt.	-	-	-	2	4	-
145 M.G.Company.	-	-	-	1	7	2
1st Field Ambulance.	-	-	-	-	1	-

Casualties to noon 13th Oct.1917.

| 5th R.Sussex Regt. | - | - | - | 4 | 18 | - |

APPENDIX B

LIST OF HONOURS AND REWARDS AWARDED
TO OFFICERS, N.C.Os. and MEN OF THE 48TH DIVISION.
-oOo-   -oOo-   -oOo-   -oOo-

Month of October, 1917.

Regtl No.	Rank.	Name.	Unit.	Award.
200837.	Pte.	Millward, W.	1/7th Worc. R.	M.M.
7980.	"	Constable, S.	-do-	M.M.
--	Lt.(a/Capt).	H.A.Linfoot,M.C.,	7th Cheshire Regt. Attd. 1/6th R.War.R.	D.S.O.
--	2/Lt.(a/Capt).	J.A.Fletcher,M.C.	1/6th Glouc.R.	Bar to M.C.
--	2/Lt.	S.F.Sullivan.	-do-	M.C.
--	Capt.	A.H.Butcher.	1/7th Worc. R.	M.C.
--	"	T.C.F.Harris.	-do-	M.C.
--	"	W.N.Bushill.	1/7th R.War.R.	M.C.
--	2/Lt.(a/Capt).	E.Holt.	2nd Ox & Bucks L.I. Attd. 1/5th R.War.R.	M.C.
--	2/Lt.(a/Capt).	E.P.Q.Carter.	1/5th R.War.R.	M.C.
--	2/Lt.(T.Lieut)	C.E.Carrington.	-do-	M.C.
--	2/Lt.(a/Capt).	H.L.Westenholm.	-do-	M.C.
--	2/Lt.	W.C.MacFarlane.	1st Attd 1/7th R.War.R.	M.C.
--	"	E.J.Nicholls.	1/7th R.War.R.	M.C.
265385.	C.S.M.	G.H.Hayes.	-do-	M.C.
--	2/Lt.(a/Capt).	J.B.Musgrave.	4th Cheshire Regt. Attd. 1/6th R.War.R.	M.C.
--	T.Lt.	F.A.Shuffrey.	143rd M.G.Company.	M.C.
--	Capt.	J.B.Mitton.	1/1st S.M.Field Amb.	M.C.
200500.	Sgt.	O.Tomlin.	1/5th R.War.R.	D.C.M.
263951.	Pte.	W.Dodson.	1/7th R.War.R.	D.C.M.
243115.	Sgt.(a/C.S.M.)	J.R.Rubery.	1/6th R.War.R.	D.C.M.
202556.	Cpl.(L/Sgt.)	G.Collins.	1/4th Glouc.R.	D.C.M.
235168.	Pte.	W.Oldfield.	-do-	M.M.
202745.	"	T.Smith.	-do-	M.M.
M2/032583.	Cpl.	W.Clarke.	A.S.C.,M.T., Attd. 1/3rd S.M.Field Ambulance.	M.M.
240320.	Sgt.(a/CS.M.)	H.Everard.	1/6th R.War.R.	M.M.
--	2/Lt.	E.A.R.Josephs.	1/5th Glouc.R.	M.C.
--	T.2/Lt.	H.Miles.	2nd Attd.1/4th Ox & Bks L.I.	M.C.
--	2/Lt.	E.Press.	48th Signal Coy.R.E.	M.C.
--	Capt.	C.E.K.Herepath.	1/3rd S.M.Field Amb.	M.C.
240715.	C.S.M.	W.Middlecote.	1/5th Glouc. R.	D.C.M.
435443.	Pte.	G.Shakeshaft.	1/1st S.M.Field Amb.	M.M.
435169.	"	W.Raybould.	-do-	M.M.
240999.	Sgt.	J.J.Osbourne.	1/8th Worc. R.	M.M.
242564.	Pte.	E.J.Marchment.	-do-	M.M.
240110.	"	H.J.Styler.	-do-	M.M.
240291.	Pte.(a/Cpl)	H.Wood.	-do-	M.M.
240084.	"	A.E.Weston.	-do-	M.M.
26002.	"	A.W.Parry.	-do-	M.M.
201241.	" (L/Cpl)	H.Llewellyn.	1/4th Bn, Glouc.R.	M.M.
3204.	"	J.Chard.	-do-	M.M.
201150.	Sgt.	R.Lightfoot.	-do-	M.M.
202547.	Pte.	H.J.Whitnell.	-do-	M.M.
200063.	Sgt.	F.Marsh.	-do-	M.M.
200235.	Pte.(a/L/Cpl)	J.Burroughs.	-do-	M.M.
33193.	Pte.	C.Holland.	-do-	M.M.
12925.	"	H.Lewis.	1/7th Worc. R.	M.M.
203690.	"	G.Martle.	-do-	M.M.
200236.	Sgt.(a/C.S.M.)	M.Conway.	-do-	M.M.
201432.	Sgt.	A.J.Portman.	-do-	M.M.
10675.	"	S.E.Evans.	-do-	M.M.
266321.	Pte.	S.Brain.	1/6th Glouc.R.	M.M.
285192.	Cpl.	A.Green.	-do-	M.M.
265517.	"	A.C.Pickering.	-do-	M.M.
267478.	L/Cpl.	W.Tredwell.	-do-	M.M.
439131.	Cpl.	F.G.Lodge.	1/3rd S.M.Field Amb.	M.M.
439199.	Pte.	F.G.Clark.	-do-	M.M.
437359.	L/Cpl.	G.Pratt. R.A.M.C.(T)	1/2nd S.M.Field Amb.	M.M.
267467.	Sgt.	C.Wilcox.	1/6th Glouc.R.	M.M.
200280.	Cpl.	J.S.Catley.	-do-	M.M.

P.T.O.

Regtl No.	Rank.	Name.	Unit.	Award.
437062.	Pte.	S. Fearn. (R.A.M.C. (T.)	1/2nd S.M. Field Amb.	M.M.
437253.	"	W. Church.	-do-	M.M.
23943.	" (unp'd L/Cpl)	L. Selwyn.	145th M.G. Company.	M.M.
21116.	Cpl.	H.J. Geary.	-do-	M.M.
285063.	Pte.	S. Smith.	1/Bucks Bn.	M.M.
265637.	"	W. Cattell.	-do-	M.M.
265119.	" (L/Cpl)	A.G. Hollyoake.	-do-	M.M.
500226.	Sgt.	R.E. Russell.	No 3 Section, 48th Div. Sig. Coy. Attd. 144th Inf. Bde.,	Bar to M.M.
200180.	Sgt.	T. Dyson.	1/5th R.War.R.	M.M.
201683.	"	R. Falconer.	-do-	M.M.
200233.	"	L. Tyler.	-do-	M.M.
20624.	Pte.	J. Burrows.	-do-	M.M.
19568.	"	J.A. Maycock.	-do-	M.M.
200346.	"	W. Gaywood.	-do-	M.M.
203068.	" (a/L/Cpl)	S. Sutton.	-do-	M.M.
200496.	"	G. Deeley.	-do-	M.M.
240301.	Sgt.	F. Holloway.	1/6th R.War.R.	M.M.
200922.	Pte.	A. Harborne.	-do-	M.M.
260273.	"	J. Harfield.	-do-	M.M.
242858.	"	W.H. Mullett.	-do-	M.M.
28889.	"	W.C. Maskell.	-do-	M.M.
17929.	Cpl.	B. Reading.	-do-	M.M.
11101.	L/Cpl.	J. Knowles.	-do-	M.M.
9158.	"	R. Deeming.	-do-	M.M.
265951.	Pte.	J.J. Waite.	1/7th R.War.R.	M.M.
267127.	Sgt. (a/C.S.M.)	D. Field.	-do-	M.M.
265280.	L/Cpl.	J.C. Marston.	-do-	M.M.
266635.	Pte.	A. Smith.	-do-	M.M.
268240.	"	D. Aitken.	-do-	M.M.
26558.	"	F. Shaler.	-do-	M.M.
305513.	Sgt.	S.B. Patterson.	1/8th R.War.R.	M.M.
267838.	Pte.	S.J. Bayliss.	-do-	M.M.
305811.	Sgt.	R.M. Wood.	-do-	M.M.
24407.	Cpl (a/Sgt)	A.J. Charsley.	143rd M.G. Company.	M.M.
240062.	Dmr.	M.G. Jordan.	1/5th Glouc. R.	M.M.
21735.	Pte. (L/Cpl)	W.A. Sansom.	145th M.G. Company.	M.M.
--	2/Lt.	F.J. Byrne.	241st S.M. Bde. R.F.A.	M.C.
--	Capt.	R. Kennon.	1/3rd S.M. Field Amb.	M.C.
--	2/Lt.(a/Capt)	H.S. Powell.	1/6th R.War.R.	M.C.
830452.	Cpl.	G. Allen.	241st S.M. Bde. R.F.A.	D.C.M.
288402.	Pte.	D. McIlvenny.	A.S.C., M.T., Attd. 1/3rd S.M. Field Amb.	M.M.
118946.	"	C.F. Kent.	A.S.C., M.T., Attd. 1/2nd S.M. Field Amb.	M.M.
242914.	"	C.S. Gray.	1/6th R.War.R.	M.M.
242661.	L/Sgt.	A.W.A. Jeacock.	-do-	M.M.
306483.	Pte.	H. Peckham.	1/8th R.War.R.	M.M.
200336.	Sgt.	J.H. Brooks.	1/7th Worc. R.	D.C.M.
201565.	L/Cpl.	A. Breeze.	-do-	2nd Bar to M.M.

www.ingramcontent.com/pod-product-compliance
Lightning Source LLC
Chambersburg PA
CBHW080842010526
44114CB00017B/2356